Two week

Please

The culture of toleration in diverse societies

MANCHESTER
UNIVERSITY PRESS

The culture of toleration in diverse societies

Reasonable tolerance

edited by
Catriona McKinnon
Dario Castiglione

Manchester University Press
Manchester and New York
distributed exclusively in the USA by Palgrave

Copyright © Manchester University Press 2003

While copyright in the volume as a whole is vested in Manchester University Press, copyright in individual chapters belongs to their respective authors, and no chapter may be reproduced wholly or in part without the express permission in writing of both author and publisher.

Published by Manchester University Press
Oxford Road, Manchester M13 9NR, UK
and Room 400, 175 Fifth Avenue, New York, NY 10010, USA
www.manchesteruniversitypress.co.uk

Distributed exclusively in the USA by
Palgrave, 175 Fifth Avenue, New York,
NY 10010, USA

Distributed exclusively in Canada by
UBC Press, University of British Columbia, 2029 West Mall,
Vancouver, BC, Canada V6T 1Z2

British Library Cataloguing-in-Publication Data
A catalogue record for this book is available from the British Library

Library of Congress Cataloging-in-Publication Data applied for

ISBN 0 7190 6232 2 *hardback*

First published 2003

10 09 08 07 06 05 04 03   10 9 8 7 6 5 4 3 2 1

Typeset in Sabon
by SNP Best-set Typesetter Ltd., Hong Kong
Printed in Great Britain
by Biddles Ltd, Guildford and King's Lynn

Contents

Contributors

James Bohman
Danforth Professor of Philosophy at Saint Louis University. He is the author of *Public Deliberation: Pluralism, Complexity and Democracy* (MIT Press, 1996) and *New Philosophy of Social Science: Problems of Indeterminacy* (MIT Press, 1991). He has also recently edited books on *Deliberative Democracy* (MIT Press, 1997, with William Rehg) and *Perpetual Peace: Essays on Kant's Cosmopolitan Ideal* (MIT Press, 1997, with Matthias Lutz-Bachmann). He is currently writing a book on cosmopolitan democracy.

Dario Castiglione
Senior Lecturer in Political Theory at the University of Exeter. Recent publications include co-edited volumes on *The Constitution in Transformation: European and Theoretical Perspectives* (Blackwell, 1996); and *The History of Political Thought in National Context* (Cambridge University Press, 2001) and a Special Issue of *Res Publica* (2001) on *Toleration: Moral and Political*. He is currently completing a co-authored volume on Constitutionalism and a monograph on David Hume's Political Philosophy.

Rainer Forst
Assistant Professor of Philosophy at Goethe-University in Frankfurt/Main. He is the author of *Contexts of Justice. Political Philosophy beyond Liberalism and Communitarianism* (University of California Press, 2002; in German Suhrkamp, 1994). He is the editor of a collection of essays on toleration (*Toleranz*, Campus, 2000) and has just completed a historical and systematic study of the concept of toleration, *Toleranz im Konflikt* (Suhrkamp Verlag, forthcoming 2003).

Nancy Fraser
Henry A. and Louise Loeb Professor of Politics and Philosophy in the Graduate Faculty of the New School for Social Research, and co-editor of

Constellations. She is the author of *Unruly Practices: Power, Discourse, and Gender in Contemporary Social Theory* (Polity, 1989) and *Justice Interruptus: Critical Reflections on the 'Postsocialist' Condition* (Routledge, 1997); she is also the co-author of *Feminist Contentions* (Routledge, 1994) and *Redistribution or Recognition? A Political–Philosophical Exchange* (Verso, forthcoming 2003), and the co-editor of *Revaluing French Feminism* (Indiana University Press, 1992) and *Pragmatism, Critique, Judgment: Essays for Richard J. Bernstein* (MIT Press, 2003). Her current research is on globalisation.

David Heyd
Chaim Perelman Professor of Philosophy at The Hebrew University of Jerusalem. He is the author of *Supererogation* (Cambridge University Press, 1982) and *Genethics* (University of California Press, 1992), and editor of *Toleration: An Elusive Virtue* (Princeton University Press, 1996), as well as articles in ethics, political philosophy and bioethics.

Cécile Laborde
Lecturer in European Political Thought at King's College London. She is the author of *Pluralist Thought and the State in Britain and France 1900–1925* (Macmillan, 2000) and of a monograph in French on Muslim brotherhoods in Senegal and the editor of a Special Issue of the *European Journal of Political Theory* on 'Rawls in Europe' (2002). She has published a number of articles on contemporary political theories of patriotism, multiculturalism and citizenship. She is currently working on a book on republicanism in French and Anglo-American political philosophy.

Catriona McKinnon
Lecturer in Political Philosophy at the University of York. She has published papers on the role of self-respect in liberal justification, and on liberal constructivist approaches to justificatory values. She is the co-editor (with Iain Hampsher-Monk) of *The Demands of Citizenship* (Continuum Publishing, 2000), the author of *Liberalism and the Defence of Political Constructivism* (Palgrave, 2002) and edits the journal *Imprints: a journal of analytical socialism.*

Andrew Mason
Professor of Political Theory at the University of Southampton. He is the author of *Explaining Political Disagreement* (Cambridge University Press, 1993) and of *Community, Solidarity and Belonging* (Cambridge University Press, 2000) and editor of *Ideals of Equality* (Blackwell, 1998).

Matt Matravers
Lectures in political philosophy at the University of York. He is the author of papers on both distributive and retributive justice, the contributing editor

of *Punishment and Political Theory* (Hart Publishing, 1999), and, most recently, the author of *Justice and Punishment: The Rationale of Coercion* (Oxford University Press, 2000). He is currently working on a book on responsibility to be published by Polity Press.

Susan Mendus
Professor of Politics and Director of the Morrell Studies in Toleration programme at the University of York. She has published extensively on problems of toleration in modern and historical political philosophy. Her main publications comprise *Toleration and the Limits of Liberalism* (Macmillan, 1989), and, as editor and contributor, *After MacIntyre* (Polity, 1994) and *The Politics of Toleration* (Edinburgh University Press, 1999).

Jeremy Waldron
Maurice and Hilda Friedman Professor of Law at Columbia University. He has held posts in Oxford, Edinburgh, Berkeley and Princeton. He is the author and editor of numerous books and articles on law, philosophy, and political theory, including *The Right to Private Property* (Oxford University Press, 1988), *Liberal Rights: Collected Papers (1981–91)* (Cambridge University Press, 1993), and more recently *Law and Disagreement* (Oxford University Press, 1999) and *The Dignity of Legislation* (Cambridge University Press, 1999).

Stuart White
Tutorial Fellow in Politics at Jesus College, Oxford. He is interested in distributive justice and economic citizenship, and is currently working to complete a manuscript on this topic entitled *The Civic Minimum: An Essay on the Rights and Obligations of Economic Citizenship*.

Jonathan Wolff
Professor of Philosophy at University College London. Author of *Robert Nozick: Property, Justice and the Minimal State* (Polity, 1991), *An Introduction to Political Philosophy* (Oxford University Press, 1996) and *Why Read Marx Today?* (Oxford University Press, 2002). Currently working on issues concerning injustice and rectification.

Acknowledgements

This book originated in a project that the editors started while Catriona was at Exeter, consisting of a series of seminars and eventually in the Annual Conference of the UK Association for Legal and Social Philosophy on 'The Culture of Toleration' (University of Exeter, April 2000). Both the seminars and the proceedings of the conference were intellectually stimulating, while the discussions that followed the presentations were lively and tolerant. The papers from the conference were of a very high quality, and some of them have been published in other collections that we have edited; but the rationale of this volume developed independently of the conference itself, as we explain in the Introduction.

In the preparation of this volume we have incurred many debts. First, to the contributors themselves for their enthusiastic participation in the project; second, to the ALSP for the opportunity to organise the conference at Exeter; and finally to all participants in the conference itself for the stimulating discussions that sharpened our understanding of the debate on toleration.

We need further to acknowledge Jamie Gaskarth's help in the preparation of the final manuscript; the support of the British Academy in the organisation of the ALSP conference through a UK Conference Grant; and, separately, the support of the AHRB (Grant: RL/AN 6410/APN 10467) to Catriona McKinnon and the ESRC (Grant: L21352022) to Dario Castiglione.

Introduction: reasonable tolerance

Catriona McKinnon and Dario Castiglione

Theory and practice are often at odds. Yet there is something particularly strange in the way in which the received theory and the presumed practice of toleration in contemporary societies seem to go their separate ways. Theoretical statements on toleration posit at the same time its *necessity* in democratic societies, and its *impossibility* as a coherent ideal.[1] In her introduction to a comprehensive collection on tolerance and intolerance in modern life, Susan Mendus aptly makes the point that the commitment that liberal societies have to toleration 'may be more *difficult* and yet more *urgent* than is usually recognised'.[2] In contrast with the urgency insisted on by the theory, the practice can appear complacent: liberal democratic societies seem to have accepted the need for the recognition and accommodation of difference without registering its depth. So much so that 'practical' people often just dismiss such toleration as an excess of permissiveness. The success of 'zero tolerance' as a slogan for a less forgiving society bears witness to the diffusion of such a mood in public opinion.

This divergence between theory and practice is, however, more productive than it may at first appear. Arguably, much of the current literature on tolerance as an interpersonal attitude, and on toleration as a set of institutional arrangements for peaceful coexistence,[3] has fully internalised it. Indeed, the present state of the theoretical debate reflects the attempt to come to terms with the transformations that the ideal, the virtue, and, to a certain extent, the institutions of toleration have undergone, as we increasingly operate in a multicultural environment. The present collection is part of such an ongoing conversation, by which we try to make the theory of toleration more relevant to its practice, and strive to inform the practice with some of the principles and ideas of the theory.

In this introduction, we will briefly characterise the current debate, sketch both its main lines of development and some of its unresolved questions, and suggest, finally, how the chapters of this volume contribute to this debate.

As has already been mentioned, the renewed interest in issues of toleration come from the attempt to adapt its vocabulary to the challenges posed by the way in which 'difference' has become both more diffuse and more pervasive in our daily lives, through processes of individualisation, multi-culturalism, globalisation, and the multiplication of 'immigrant societies'.[4] As a rough and ready distinction, we suggest that, historically, the tolera-tion debate has entered its third phase. It first originated as a reasoned answer to the social and political conflicts that divided European societies along religious lines. Although the ascendancy of arguments for religious tolerance can be traced to considerations of prudence and political realism,[5] from a more principled perspective, toleration was supported along two main lines of reasoning. One was overtly sceptical and secularist, under-mining the truth-content of religious beliefs and their relevance for social and political coexistence; the other was more subtly latitudinarian, questioning the control that we have on our own beliefs, and the self-defeating nature of imposing outward conformity on intractable inner convictions.

The second phase of the toleration debate continued the process of making religious beliefs, and religion at large, a private rather than a public matter, by more firmly establishing the state as the neutral arbiter over its citizens' different ideas of the good life. The debate over liberal neutrality (a debate with the opponents of liberalism, but also within liberalism itself) superseded that about freedom of religion – of both worship and con-science. The relationships between the individual and the state, or the individual and public opinion, became central to the new conception of toleration, which rested on two important principles of what has been referred to as the 'modernist project': the assimilation of the individual in the democratic society, and the strict separation of public and private, with all forms of secondary associations placed firmly within the latter domain.[6] In spite of the many spirited defences of either liberal neutrality, or individ-ual autonomy, or the crucial distinction between self- and other-regarding actions, at the bottom of modern toleration seems to lie the prudential maxim of indifference to others: 'live and let live'; or perhaps the more guarded version: 'good fences make good neighbours'.

Slowly, but decidedly, the assimilationist drive that characterised the for-mation of nation-states across the modern world has been reversed because of pressures from both within and without. For better or for worse, the barriers of the private sphere have been weakened, if not entirely disman-tled, which opens up the operations of personal and private life to the uncomfortable scrutiny of the public eye, and subjects them to the criteria of justice. Moreover, pluralism has become, as Rawls claims, a 'fact' that moral and political philosophy cannot bypass when thinking about the terms of fair co-operation in society. These are the main features that char-acterise the third phase of discussions on toleration.

Within this new social and philosophical context, tolerance is still widely perceived, by philosophers as well as practically minded people, as a kind of response to difference that we cannot do without. The Final Report of the Advisory Group on Citizenship established by the British Government (the 'Crick Report'), for instance, places a heavy emphasis on tolerance in its learning outcomes (which schools have a statutory responsibility to deliver). The Report states that children ought to be disposed to the 'practice of toleration', and have the 'ability to tolerate other view points'.[7] But even in the absence of policy-based requirements that toleration be cultivated in citizens, it is reasonable to expect that political philosophers should reach some form of substantive agreement with respect to the nature, limits, and correct forms of expression of a concept as fundamental and important as toleration. Notwithstanding close scrutiny and the efforts of theorists on this front, agreement has proved impossible to achieve. If anything, toleration seems to have become a more contested ideal and a more elusive virtue, while its very formulation as a concept remains paradoxical: how can a person have reason to tolerate ideas, behaviour, and practices that, by definition, she has reason to believe to be wrong?

Although these aspects of the current debate on toleration are not entirely new, there is a feeling that, as a concept, toleration may have, so to speak, outreached its usefulness and may need radical re-thinking. We have raised this question in another context,[8] where we have argued that some of the more stringent analyses of toleration as a philosophical concept have somewhat distanced it from common usage, and have made the virtue of tolerance more demanding, while at the same time still questioning its internal coherence. However, there, as here, we wish to suggest that in spite of these difficulties, the recent debate has not been in vain. Indeed, it is our conviction that there may be something to be gained by re-thinking the concept of toleration in the light of ideas such as reasonableness and recognition which, although distinct, both point to a more positive and appreciative way of looking at others' experience and perspective. In the same way, democratic citizenship has been recast in a pluralist and inclusive form, with more attention being paid to valuing difference over assimilation, which keeps democratic citizenship open in principle to the aspirations and sensibilities of minorities and particular groups. However, we are not proposing an idyllic picture of the state of the debate. Both the difficulties and the urgency of the task of re-thinking toleration are all too evident, particularly after the disturbing events and the repercussions of the 11th of September. This volume contributes to the task by offering, in the first part, a number of sober reflections on how we may reformulate the idea of toleration in the light of the demands both of reason and of the recognition that others seek from us. The second, and perhaps more cautiously upbeat, part of the volume investigates the contexts within which our ideals and practices of toleration are continuously tested and transformed.

From a substantive point of view, one of the themes that runs through many of the chapters is the way in which reasonableness may be operationalised so to make the idea of toleration more internally coherent, while grounding tolerance as a principled practice. As we have already mentioned, in the past popular justifications of toleration relying on either some form of scepticism or prudential reasoning seemed sufficient to guarantee peaceful coexistence within the boundaries established by a combination of the international system, the nation state, and democratic politics. The problem with the merely prudential form of justification seems to be one of stability: on this view, toleration can be, at most, a *modus vivendi*. If the distribution of power changes such that peace could be maintained by one group forcibly imposing its views on the others, then what need have we for tolerance any more? If the most that can be said for tolerance is that, when power is roughly equal, it is the rational choice of those who would otherwise violently conflict, then arguments for tolerance look impotent in any context (of which our world is an example) in which power is not distributed roughly equally.

With respect to sceptical defences of toleration, the issue is more complex. Moral scepticism seems, on the one hand, incapable of establishing the limits of tolerance, thus allowing for a radical form of relativism regarding the actions that we are prepared to tolerate. But on the other hand, it cannot coherently sustain toleration itself, for the recommendation that one must be tolerant must itself be read as a relativistic statement, for consistency's sake. Epistemological scepticism, particularly of a moderate kind – viz., that there are truths, but that we are severely limited in our capacity to know them – appears more promising. However, it is subject to two combined objections. First, that as a philosophical doctrine it may be too controversial to be accepted widely, and second, that it may carry too little conviction to motivate in real life, for it appears to entail a counterintuitive conception of people's commitment to their own beliefs and values, suggesting that they hold their beliefs, and commit to their values, in a provisional way.

As a move away from merely prudential or deeply sceptical justifications of toleration, contemporary philosophers subscribing to some form of political liberalism have argued that the justification of political principles must proceed according to the ideal of public reason.[9] Broadly stated, this ideal is that any person who offers other people reasons for accepting or rejecting political proposals must take it that these reasons could be reasons for others. If the differences constitutive of pluralism cannot be expected to disappear even in ideal conditions, wherein each person exercises her reason correctly, then public reasons cannot simply map on to any one particular set of beliefs or values. If political justification in conditions of pluralism must conform to public reason, then each person must at least defend principles of toleration at the political level (and perhaps also cultivate tolerance as a personal virtue): anything less than toleration could be rejected by others in conditions of reasonable pluralism. In other words, on this story, people who reject toleration are unreasonable: they fail to propose political principles which, given the permanence of pluralism supported by the exercise of reason, all other people could accept.

Prima facie, the advantages of this approach to toleration over one justified by either a narrow *modus vivendi* or some form of *preliminary* scepticism are as follows.[10] If toleration is a requirement of reasonableness – and part of what it is to be reasonable is to accept that the free use of reason makes pluralism permanent – then, the forcible imposition of one particular set of beliefs or values cannot be justified by claiming that those who are coerced would come to accept these beliefs and values in ideal conditions, were they to exercise their reason correctly. A defence of toleration as a demand of reasonableness makes it impossible to justify intolerance in the name of the reason of those who are not tolerated; it makes crusades and inquisitions unjustifiable as obstetric exercises encouraging the proper use of reason on the part of those oppressed. The reasonableness-defence of toleration makes it a requirement of justice whatever the balance of power between those who share political problems. This defence also has advantages over some form of 'preliminary' scepticism. The thesis that pluralism is consistent with the proper exercise of reason by each person may seem, or so it is claimed, a less controversial philosophical doctrine than either moral or epistemological scepticism; for the requirement that, when offering justifications of political principles, each person accepts the 'burdens of reason' thesis, is less demanding than the adherence to either of the forms of scepticism outlined above.

There are, however, several possible objections to, and ways of developing the ideal of, reasonable tolerance as advocated by Rawls and by some other supporters of political liberalism. The contributions to the first part of the volume explore some of them. Jeremy Waldron, for instance, takes a less sanguine position on the way in which the application of the principle of reasonableness may solve real-life conflicts. By exploring the way in which the rules of social order and coexistence work in a liberal society, so as to guarantee that there are no direct conflicts between people pursuing different life styles (compossibility principle), and so that those very same rules do not prevent the pursuit of a life style with a reasonable degree of success (adequacy principle), Waldron concludes that in some real-life conflicts, it is unclear on whom the burden of reasonableness may fall. His is a kind of a-posteriori scepticism, which recognises that the principle of reasonableness may simply lead us to an impasse, whenever accommodation between different views and conceptions of the good is deeply problematic. The 'liberal algebra' of compossibility between liberties and their adequate protection (and/or promotion) is one that has no solution; but, Waldron sombrely adds, this is the case for any other kind of 'algebra' in conditions of pluralism, where people with different conceptions of the good come into social contact with each other and are, to a degree, sensitive to each other's pursuits.

A second kind of objection to the Rawlsian argument is that advanced by Matt Matravers and Sue Mendus, who regard Rawls's argument from the 'burdens of judgement' and Brian Barry's justification of impartiality by reference to a moderate epistemological scepticism as two ways of making toleration a requirement of reason that is limited in the sphere of practical political justification.[11] They argue that Barry's conception of reason imposes unacceptable existential costs on agents, and that Rawls's conception makes toleration a requirement of a *modus vivendi* only. Although less directly critical of the Rawlsian position, the other essays in the first part of this volume pursue the discussion of toleration and recognition along the more positive line suggested by Matravers and Mendus, by linking them more directly to a particular conception of justice. Rainer Forst identifies a 'respect' *conception* of toleration that, he argues, is required of those engaged in practical political justification and that addresses the paradoxes besetting the *concept* of toleration itself. This conception asks us to make it a requirement of justice – sustained by the criteria of reciprocity and generality, but also by a personal perception of the finitude of reason – that social and political arrangements should be such that the ethical identity of persons, as citizens, is the object of equal respect. Whether this takes us beyond the impasse outlined by Waldron, in which there is a direct conflict between ethical identities, is an interesting question. Nancy Fraser's own view of recognition, and of the dialectic between recognition and distribution in modern societies, offers a more pragmatic solution to the impasse, suggesting that respect of others is essential, but that this should be a consequence of the *moral* recognition of the 'parity of participation' to which everyone is entitled both as a member of society, and as a member of the particular group to which each person belongs. In her view, we should be more circumspect in dealing with the *ethical* dimension of identity politics, where pluralist solutions are not always available.

From within liberal theory, there is, however, another way of posing the question of toleration. As Catriona McKinnon suggests, the incommensurability of different ethical views is only part of the story of why the permanent fact of pluralism makes toleration a permanent requirement. Different conceptions of toleration can be justified with different accounts of the *character* of pluralism as opposed to its nature: questions about the character of pluralism are questions about the attitudes people can reasonably be expected to cultivate with respect to those who differ from them. As a mark of the changes in the ideal and practices of toleration that have gradually taken place in contemporary societies, both McKinnon and Forst, for example, note that there is a continuum of attitudes that are often referred to as 'tolerant', a theme that is also explored in other essays of this collection (notably in Wolff and Heyd; but also more indirectly in Waldron and Fraser). Such a continuum can be differently described, but it is well captured by Michael Walzer's distinction between five different attitudes to difference, all resulting in some form of acceptance: resignation, indifference, stoic endurance, openness, and full endorsement.[12] Resignation and indifference, though still very much used in common parlance, are often ruled out on philosophical grounds, for they lack the necessary moral tension that seems to be required by the idea of tolerance. Stoical resignation is perhaps the one that best captures the philosophical, and philosophically paradoxical, idea of toleration as accepting differences to which we deeply object. Openness and endorsement are also problematic for the same reason mentioned for resignation and indifference, but in reverse, in that the attitudes to difference they involve are not hostile. The important point within the present debate on toleration is that the demands of reasonableness, recognition, and democratic citizenship seem to require a move from a kind of stoic tolerance to a deeper engagement with difference captured by ideas of respect and sensitivity to others' identity and self-chosen aims and life styles.

The more open-minded attitude towards difference, which is a requisite of social coexistence in multicultural democratic societies, where no one has a privileged position from which to dispense toleration,[13] is the kind of attitude that ordinary language tends nowadays to identify with tolerance – what, in a non-technical sense, could be called a 'reasonable' response to difference. The second part of this volume is an attempt to explore the internal coherence of such a transformation when applied to different contexts. James Bohman, for instance, argues that openness to others in discourse, and their treatment as free and equal, is part of a kind of reflexive toleration that pertains to public communication in the deliberative context. In such a context, individuals recognise each other as part of the same democratic community, and they do so both by taking each other's reasons seriously, but also, and even more crucially, by taking each other's perspectives fully on board. From a different perspective, Andrew Mason's discussion of 'cities' and 'communities' develops a parallel argument on the importance of coming into contact with others. His focus is on the different images, and the related values and attitudes, engendered respectively by cosmopolitan city life and narrow communitarian engagements. In fact, his view is that this opposition is usually overdrawn. He claims that the ideas of city and community can be made to work in complementary ways in an account of reasonable tolerance.

A similar tension between the virtues of sameness and difference is explored in Jonathan Wolff's contribution. Here, toleration is seen in relation to the ethos of a society, a group, or an organisation, and is treated as a dynamic process. In this sense, tolerance is part of the process through which a certain state of affairs and ethos are changed or adapted. Toleration involves overcoming certain fixed ideas or rigidities by accepting the innovative value that difference may bring at different levels of values, principles or practices. The same dynamic element is central to Cécile Laborde's conceptual and historical analysis of the way in which the practice and principles of toleration have operated in the complex political debate that, in France, developed around the notorious affair of the headscarves. Her analysis emphasises the important ideological role that the idea of *laïcité* played in that discussion, unveiling the complex cluster of meanings and values that this is intended to mobilise, but also the transformative role that such discussions have on the definition of our very ideals and concepts. So, in practical situations, appeals to toleration may only acquire a meaning when this is placed in a more complex discursive and institutional context.

The importance of considering toleration within a context in which a plurality of values may operate, so that the exercise of tolerance may come into external conflict with the application of other principles – something that is separate from its 'internal' paradoxes – is brought to the fore by both Stuart White's and David Heyd's contributions. In the separate contexts of work and education with which they deal, equality of opportunity and moral instruction, respectively, seem to come into conflict with the second-order virtue of tolerance, since this, even when does not require from us things objectionable in themselves, undermines the operations of the other principles. Nevertheless, both White and Heyd stress that tolerance remains an important element within our universe of values, and that in such cases its proper application may have to follow certain background rules, which reflects the different interests and aims that the different principles are meant to either protect or promote.

In conclusion, most of the contributors to this volume would seem to agree that, though perhaps imperfect and 'transitory' in character, or even as second-best options, both the virtue of tolerance and the institutions of toleration remain necessary ingredients for democratic societies to be able to accommodate reasonable difference reasonably.

Notes

1 Cf. B. Williams, 'Tolerating the intolerable', in S. Mendus (ed.), *The Politics of Toleration: Tolerance and Intolerance in Modern Life* (Edinburgh: Edinburgh University Press, 1999), pp. 65–75; and more generally many of the contributions in D. Heyd (ed.), *Toleration: An Elusive Virtue* (Princeton, NJ: Princeton University Press, 1996).

2 S. Mendus, 'My brother's keeper: The politics of intolerance', in Mendus, *The Politics of Toleration*, pp. 1–12.

3 This is a useful distinction, but one that it is difficult to maintain in common language, where the two syntagmas are used interchangeably. Although we wish to keep to the conceptual distinction, we are not strictly adhering to the use of tolerance and toleration with these exclusive meanings; nor are the contributors of this volume. For the distinction, cf. M. Walzer, *On Toleration* (New Haven, CT and London: Yale University Press, 1997), p. xi, and pp. 8–13.

4 Michael Walzer talks of 'immigrant societies' as a regime of toleration reflecting the way in which the population constituting those countries belong to separate cultural and ethnic groups, which may have settled at different times in the history of that particular land: *On Toleration*, pp. 30–5.

5 Cf. C. Hill, 'Toleration in seventeenth-century England: Theory and practice', in Mendus, *The Politics of Toleration*, pp. 27–44.

6 Part of this story is told by Cécile Laborde's contribution to this volume, though she mainly addresses the French debate. Michael Walzer refers to democratic

assimilation as one of the aspects of the 'modernist project', while he points to group self-determination within the international context as the other aspect. Both are pointers to the importance of the nation-state as the central element of the modernist project: *On Toleration*, pp. 83–7.

7 'Citizenship for 16–19 year olds in education and training', *Report of the Advisory Group to the Secretary of State for Education and Employment* (Further Education Funding Council Publications, 1998), Appendix A.

8 Cf. D. Castiglione and C. McKinnon, 'Introduction: Beyond toleration?', in idem. (eds), *Toleration: Moral and Political*, Special Issue of *Res Publica. A Journal of Legal and Social Philosophy*, 7:3 (2001) 223–30.

9 Cf. J. Rawls, *Political Liberalism* (Columbia, NY: Columbia University Press, 1993), Lecture 2, §§1–2, pp. 48–58.

10 We say *preliminary*, to distinguish these two kinds of sceptical approaches (moral and epistemological) from those that come to a sceptical conclusion not on the basis of an analysis of the grounds for toleration, but after having examined the reasons for toleration in their substantive operation. This distinction will become clear below, in discussing Waldron's position. The distinction between 'antecedent' and 'consequent' scepticism is not new: David Hume suggests it in *An Enquiry concerning Human Understanding*, ed. T. L. Beauchamp (Oxford: Oxford University Press, 1999), Section 12, Part I, §§ 3 and 5, pp. 199–200, although his use is different, and differently motivated, from the one here suggested.

11 B. Barry, *Justice as Impartiality* (Oxford: Oxford University Press, 1995), pp. 168–73.

12 Walzer, *On Toleration*, pp. 10–12.

13 Glen Newey, 'Is democratic toleration a rubber duck?', in Castiglione and McKinnon (eds), *Toleration: Moral and Political*, 315–36, at pp. 324–30.

Part I
Re-thinking toleration

1

Toleration and reasonableness

Jeremy Waldron

Traffic

In the streets of a large city, people drive their cars for different reasons and to different destinations. Because the roads are crowded and because these different journeys cut across each other, with people going different ways through various intersections, there is a potential problem. If two vehicles pass through the same intersection at the same time, there may be a collision, and if there is, one or both of the drivers may fail to reach their destinations. (Indeed, one or both of them may be hurt, maimed or killed and their vehicles damaged, perhaps beyond repair.)

The point of traffic rules is, first and foremost, to prevent such collisions, and ensure that the roads are safe for drivers and their vehicles. But that is not their only point. If the whole point were 'safety-first', it could be accommodated by requiring all drivers to proceed at 5 mph and to stop and get out at each intersection in order to ascertain that it is safe to proceed. But then, few people would get to the destinations they want to reach at anything like the time they want to reach them. Fortunately, the aim of a good set of traffic rules is also to ensure that everyone can proceed to their destinations as expeditiously as possible, under the condition that proceeding to these destinations must not make it impossible for others to proceed expeditiously to theirs. In other words, the streets and the rules governing their use attempt to accommodate everyone's purpose in using them. The rules say: 'No matter where you want to go or why, we will allow you to proceed to your destination. Each of you just has to accept the few restrictions that are necessary to extend this right to each and every other driver.'

So we impose a speed limit, and we ask people to obey stop lights. We have rules about the right of way at uncontrolled intersections. We enforce following distances and overtaking restrictions. Probably nobody gets to her destination as quickly as she would if she had the streets to herself. Probably no one has exactly the sort of trip he would prefer. But the restrictions we think are reasonable. There is no one for whom they destroy the *point* of driving. The rules simply modify the way each person pursues her purposes on the streets so as to make her use of them compatible with their use by everyone else.

Liberal algebra

It is not my aim in this chapter to talk about traffic laws. But I believe they provide a useful analogy for thinking about a difficulty – which, I fear, is an irresolvable one – facing modern liberal theories of toleration.

Liberals envisage a whole society, not just a network of streets, in which aims of all sorts can be pursued. As they negotiate their way through life, people aim at different values and pursue different goods. These pursuits pose a problem of social order, which consists in the possibility (likelihood, inevitability) that the activities inspired by various people's aims will come into conflict with one another. Conflicts arise, as they did in the traffic analogy, when the activity of one agent cuts across or collides with the activity of another, in such a way that the actions in question cannot both take place. The legal rules of a liberal order may be viewed, like traffic rules, as a way of dealing with that possibility of conflict. For example, it is the job of property law to address the possibility of conflict between different persons' attempts to make use of the same material resources. They do this, crudely, by indicating for every resource who is allowed to make which use of that resource and when. But it is not just property: there are rules governing the time and manner in which parades and demonstrations can be mounted; and there are restrictions on the exercise of political liberty designed to preclude the possibility of collision between one person's angrily brandished fist and another's arrogantly positioned nose. All these arrangements are supposed to be governed by the liberal ideal of securing order in a way that is fair to the aims and activities of all.

This aspiration of modern liberalism is Kantian in inspiration: Act externally in such a way that the free use of your will is compatible with the freedom of everyone according to a universal law.[1] The idea is that although different people have very different conceptions of value and happiness, a set of constraints can be formulated that, if accepted, would allow each person's pursuit of his own ends to coexist – without conflict – with the pursuit of ends by each and all of the others. Although, in order to avoid conflict, each person has to accept some restrictions, the idea is that no one will be required to labour under such extensive or burdensome restrictions as to make the pursuit of his chosen ends impossible.

Formally speaking, the liberal claim may be described as the task of specifying a set of constraints on conduct (call it set C), satisfying two conditions: (1) no two actions permitted by C conflict with one another; and (2) for each individual who is subject to C, the range of actions permitted by C is adequate for the pursuit of his ends. I shall call these the requirements of *compossibility*[2] and adequacy. Together they amount to something like algebraic specifications for the formal structure of a liberal society. Although there is no guarantee that the simultaneous equations of this liberal algebra admit of a solution, liberals remain optimistic. Their optimism is not in a utopian spirit, but in the belief that a practicable set of constraints can be formulated and realised under the familiar circumstances of modernity, taking people as they are, and laws – in only a mildly reformist spirit – as they might be.

Compossibility and adequacy together

To say that two actions conflict, for the purposes of the compossibility requirement, is to say that the performance of one of them interferes with the performance of the other (and perhaps vice versa). Direct physical incompatibility – like two people struggling to use the same tool at the same time – is the clearest type of conflict.

Conflict is not the same as opposition (or disapproval). It means more than that two actions are inspired by rival ideals, or that the agents are opposed, each to the other's action, or that one of them wishes the conduct of the other would not occur. I may oppose or disapprove of someone's conduct without my disapproval (or my own contrary pursuits) conflicting with or impacting adversely upon them. This familiar distinction is of course crucial to our understanding of liberal toleration: as a liberal, I tolerate something even though I disapprove of it; that is, I subscribe to a social structure that makes room even for activities to which I am utterly opposed.

There are, however, intriguing cases in between, one of which I want to put on the table at this stage. Think back to the framework of my traffic analogy. My friends and I are holding a funeral procession for some dear departed colleague. But the procession is continually broken up by bikers weaving noisily in and out of the cortège, to the extent that it seems to us that our procession has been ruined. How should we analyse this case?

Perhaps an argument could be made that the actions (by us) required for the successful pursuit of our funereal end actually conflict with the actions of the bikers. On this analysis, a set of constraints, C, that permitted both the bikers' actions and the mourners' actions would fail the test of compossibility. But that argument may not work: there may not literally be any physical incompatibility – for it may be part of the bikers' aim to weave skilfully in and out of the procession in a way that does not cause any of the funeral vehicles to slow down or any of the mourners to break step.

Even so, there does seems to be a deeper incompatibility. If C permits bikers or skateboarders to behave in a way that ruins the procession, then maybe we have to say that C fails the test of adequacy. For although it may be true that all the actions or behaviours that the mourners actually need to perform are permitted by C, still acceptance of and submission to C means that the mourners' ends are bound to be frustrated by actions of the bikers also permitted by C.

By itself, compossibility is a relation between actions, not directly a relation between ends. Ends come into the picture when we consider adequacy: or rather, the relation between ends – the idea of a Kantian 'kingdom of ends'[3] – comes from the combination of compossibility and adequacy, not from compossibility alone. To focus on adequacy as well as compossibility is to indicate our desire for a liberal, not just a Hobbesian, peace. Whether the liberal order respects and makes room for each of us is not just a matter of whether it protects us from collisions. It is a matter of how much room is left for our freedom. And that in turn is not just a question of how many actions are permitted to each of us (whether that rises above a certain minimum or whatever). It is a question of how the permitted minimum stands in relation to the ends we take it upon ourselves to pursue.

Now consider again our example of the bikers and the mourners. The complaint of the mourners is not a complaint that actions they want or need to perform are prohibited. Their complaint is that their actions are frustrated by permissions granted to others. This indicates two possible ways of formulating the condition of adequacy. We may formulate it as:

2a For each individual P who is subject to C, the range of actions permitted to (be performed by) P by C is adequate for the pursuit of P's ends,

or as:

2b For each individual P who is subject to C, the range of actions permitted to anyone by C is such that action within C is adequate for the pursuit of P's ends.

According to (2b), the permissibility of the bikers' actions under C would mean that C fails the test of adequacy so far as the mourners' ends are concerned. But this result would not follow under (2a).

Which of the two should we adopt? I think we have no choice but to adopt the second version, (2b). The importance of complementing compossibility with adequacy is that a liberal theory ought to be concerned about whether each individual has enough freedom for him to flourish as a person with ends of his own to pursue. We are not just interested in reducing conflict; we are trying to reconcile something that is important and adequate in each person's case with something that is important and adequate in the case of each of the others. If we were to reject (2b), and plump for (2a) only, our concern for adequacy would be in danger of appearing implausibly one-dimensional. Although pretending to be concerned with whether a person has room to pursue his own ends, our concern would run out once we were assured that certain actions – in the sense of bodily movements – were available to him. But the pursuit of one's ends is a more complicated matter than that. It depends not just on action – in the sense of bodily movement – in the abstract, but on action under a description, and the description may well involve a reference to circumstances that include the actions of others.[4]

Maximisation and equality

Apart from the issue between (2a) and (2b), how strong is this requirement of adequacy? The proposition that C must be adequate for the pursuit of P's ends does not entail that P is assured of success in pursuing whatever aims she has set herself. That is her responsibility, or it may be a matter of good or bad fortune, or it may be a matter of competition with others; but at any rate, success is not what the liberal order purports to offer individuals. Adequacy has to do with the efforts one might undertake in pursuit of one's ends: the idea is that a set of constraints fails the test of adequacy if it denies her what one might call a fair shot at pursuing her ends. In many situations, what counts as a fair shot cannot be defined except by reference to the overall structure, and that introduces a potential for circularity, which is reasonably well understood.[5] But, in other cases we understand the contrast between pursuit and success reasonably well. A set of constraints is not reasonable if it prevents me from ever demonstrating my political convictions in public; but it is not unreasonable simply by virtue of failing to guarantee that I win over any adherents. A set of constraints is not reasonable if it prevents me from doing anything that my religion prescribes in the way of worship; by the same token, it is not made reasonable by the mere fact that my religion itself makes provision for its own attenuated practice under conditions of oppression and persecution. That provision is to be understood as a response by religion to something that the liberal ideal forbids, not as a relaxation of the demands that the accommodation of this religion imposes.

However we define it, the constraint of adequacy is weaker than two other constraints with which might have defined the liberal ideal. One is maximisation (in the case of each individual). Kant, for example, talks about a constitution allowing 'the *greatest possible human freedom* according to laws, by which *the liberty of every individual can co-exist with the liberty of every other*.'[6] Some of John Rawls's early formulations indicated something similar: individuals are to have a right 'to *the most extensive* basic liberty compatible with a similar liberty for others.'[7] The idea of maximisation is easy enough to apply in cases where simple Pareto-improvements of liberty are possible: where at least one person's liberty can be enhanced without diminishing that of anyone else. But it is a much more difficult conception to apply when we face trade-offs and the interpersonal comparisons that they involve.

The other somewhat stronger constraint would be a constraint, not just of adequacy but of equality. The Rawlsian formulation just quoted referred not only to compossibility and maximisation but also to the idea of 'a *similar* liberty for others'.[8] In *Political Liberalism*, the equality constraint is more prominent: 'Each person has an *equal* claim to a fully adequate scheme of *equal* basic rights and liberties, which scheme is compatible with *the same* scheme for all.'[9]

Equality here may be understood in two ways. It might mean that the liberties must be the same for everyone: if P has a right to do X, then everyone in the society must have a right to do X. Alternatively, it might mean that, even if the liberties are different, their net effect must be such as to enable the persons who enjoy them to advance their respective aims to an equal extent.

The second interpretation takes us back to – and perhaps compounds the problem about – the relation between adequacy and success. Now we have to calculate the relation between ends and activities, not just in terms of adequate pursuit, but in terms of constraints on conduct that secure for each agent the same degree of success in pursuit of his end as is secured for others in pursuit of theirs. We sometimes pretend that we can do these calculations. We ask whether some sect or activity is having to bear an unfair proportion of the restraint required on all sides for an orderly social life, although I am not sure whether we can figure all that out. At any rate, adequacy by itself is sufficient to pose the difficulty that I want to address, so – in the present context – there is no need to consider any idea of equality that goes beyond that.

What about the first interpretation of equality? Does a liberal order assume that the set of liberties made available to one person for the pursuit of his conception of the good will be the same as the set of liberties made available to each other person? The assumption that they will be the same is appealing, for it coincides with slogans about 'the rule of law' and 'equal rights'.

But I think there are good reasons to question it. In the real world, we have to come to terms with the fact that people pursue not only different aims, but aims with different and disparate shapes. Consider the variety of religious conceptions. Some people will belong to small, intensely sectarian groups; some will belong to Churches that are organised on a cosmopolitan scale (such as Islam or Roman Catholicism). For some the essence of religious practice may be community action; for others it may be a cloistered monastic ideal. Some may belong to Churches (like Episcopalianism) that retain some of the official character they had before they were disestablished; some may practice cults like spiritualism that are frowned on in official circles. Some people will be tormented by religious doubt; others will live contented lives of secular atheism; still others will be crusading atheists. Since people's aims are so utterly disparate in their character and content, it is likely that the activities that count as the pursuit of those aims will be different also, and if so, it is likely that the liberties and protections that the parties need or require will differ accordingly.

For example, someone who belongs to an organised Church may think it important to have a right to freedom of worship, whereas a contented secular atheist may say that he has no use for such a right. By this I mean that if the atheist is asked whether freedom of worship is an important liberty for every person, he may quite reasonably answer 'No'. No doubt, we could abstract from the term 'worship' and find some very vague description (freedom of conscience, perhaps, conjoined with freedom of assembly) that he would recognise as a right that everyone needed. But I think such abstraction would very quickly end up with our saying simply that everyone had a right to pursue his own aims, and that is not being denied. What is in question is whether that universal right entails equal or uniform rights at a more concrete level.[10]

A difficult case

Let me now develop an example that, I think, poses a fearful difficulty for this sort of Kantian algebraic liberalism that I have been trying to characterise.

In the modern world, most societies for which liberal arrangements are thought to be practicable contain many persons who satisfy each of the following descriptions. P is an entrepreneurial pornographer: he enjoys pornography, he enjoys catering to others' tastes for pornography, and he rather relishes the shock that his pornographic wares occasion in unwilling passers-by. Q is a devout Muslim: he abhors pornography, but is constantly distracted by P's display of it. Q's concern about pornography is not just a concern for himself – he also despairs of being able to bring up his children as pious Muslims in a social environment polluted by P. P, on the other hand, is fond of saying to his own children things like 'It's a lurid and exciting world out there, my boys. Enjoy!' R is a secular humanist, who has no children and no interest in anyone else's children. He manages to pursue his own aims and hobbies in a way that is impervious to public displays of pornography. He is not one of P's customers, but he is not particularly distracted by P's behaviour; nor for that matter is there any incompatibility between his conduct and ideals and those of Q.

Arguably, it is not possible to find a set of constraints satisfying conditions (1) and (2), above, that can accommodate the ends of P and Q and R. P and R could certainly live together. And Q and R could live together, provided R didn't try to enter Q's mosque in a state of undress, etc. But P and Q cannot live together in a liberal arrangement (with or without R). P's pursuit of his way of life makes Q's way of life impossible; and the conditions for Q's pursuit of his way of life make P's way of life impossible.

The example is schematic but by no means unrealistic. Something like this happens in multicultural settings all the time. Readers will have no difficulty in recognising this as the crux of the difficulty in the Salman Rushdie affair. With slight alterations, we can equate P with Rushdie, and Q with those hundreds of thousands, perhaps millions, of Muslims, in Britain who were deeply offended by the publication of Rushdie's book, *The Satanic Verses*. So this is the sort of difficult case I want to talk about.

The peremptory response

How difficult is this case? It is often said that this is to be expected, since the liberal principle of toleration was never supposed to be a principle of unrestricted range. Look at Locke on atheism, or even, in his early work, on Roman Catholicism.[11] No one can tolerate everything. Some things are necessarily excluded from the scope of toleration. If someone loves murder, or torture, a liberal society cannot guarantee him a niche that is adequate for his purposes. Suppose I get my kicks from enslaving other people: I am an Aristotelian slave-hunter; I go out looking for what I regard as 'natural slaves' to capture, as other people hunt deer or wild boar. Patently this conception of the good cannot be accommodated within the liberal scheme I have outlined. Room cannot be made for me to pursue this end except at the expense of completely frustrating some other people's pursuit of their ends (viz., those who might fall victim to my slave-hunting).

Because cases like these are extreme and distasteful, it is tempting to present the dismissal of the aims of sadists, torturers, slave-hunters, rapists, murderers etc., from the realm of ends to which the liberal claim is said to apply, as obvious and more or less peremptory. But such a response is unsatisfactory.

It is unsatisfactory, first, because it doesn't help us with more problematic cases – cases like the one I have developed. In the example of the pornographer and the Muslim, we concluded that P and Q cannot live together in a liberal arrangement any more than our imagined slave-hunter and his victims could live together. But, even if the incompatibility between P and Q is like the incompatibility between the slave-hunter and his victim, it is not clear who, in the case of P and Q, is like the slave-hunter and who is like the victim. Is P like the slave-hunter because he insists on flaunting his pornographic wares in a way that makes Muslim life impossible for Q? Or is P like the victim because his exhibitionism is crowded out by Q's imperious insistence on a certain sort of pious environment? If a liberal society cannot accommodate P and Q together, then which of them should it throw out? P or Q or both? And what is the principle on which that is to be decided?

Second, the strategy of peremptorily excluding certain ends as unreasonable or clearly unacceptable, etc. from the ambit of toleration underestimates the ambition associated with the liberal model itself. Liberalism makes a very strong claim: namely, that it is the liberal algebra itself that provides the reasons for excluding these ends. The point of liberal algebra is to explain the wrongness (and hence the legitimate excludability) of things like murder, rape, assault, fraud, and non-consensual sadism. The prohibition of such actions is supposed to be explained and justified in virtue of their being comprised in any set of constraints C that satisfies adequacy and compossibility. That explanatory point is simply defeated if it turns out that the success of the liberal claim relies on our presupposing that of course such ends and actions can be excluded.

Rawlsian 'reasonableness'

Modern liberals in the Kantian and Rawlsian tradition wildly overestimate their ability to think through these cases. They are led to do so by their possession of technical jargon, philosophical terminology that they use to characterise – but cannot use to justify – the idea of an unacceptable action, or an aim that may legitimately be excluded from the Kantian kingdom of ends.[12]

Consider the terminology of reasonableness – the contrast between the reasonable and the rational – put about by John Rawls and his followers. Persons are reasonable, says Rawls, when the conceptions of the good for which they demand accommodation are adopted and put forward in a way that is sensitive to the need for a fair scheme of cooperation. The liberal commitment to allowing individuals to pursue their aims is complemented by an insistence that individuals be reasonable in choosing what aims to pursue. Each person must take into account that he lives in a society with others, each of whom in turn has a life to lead by his own lights. Each must take account of this situation in conceiving his ethical and religious aims and obligations. Though individuals view themselves as 'self-originating sources of claims' in the sense that the pursuit of the good as they conceive it carries weight in its own right without being derived from any antecedent social conception, still they must not think of themselves as 'tied to the pursuit of the particular final ends they have at any given time, but rather as capable of revising and changing these ends on reasonable . . . grounds.'[13] People must be prepared to tailor and discipline their conceptions of the good so they fit together into a just and practicable social structure. As Rawls puts it:

> The principles of right, and so of justice, put limits on what satisfactions have value; they impose restrictions on what are reasonable conceptions of one's good. In drawing up plans and in deciding on aspirations men are to take these constraints into account. We can express this by saying that in justice as fairness the concept of the right is prior to that of the good.[14]

In the present context, the concept of the right is the concept of a regime regulated by compossibility and adequacy. Individuals are entitled to choose only those ends that they have reason to believe may be accommodated within a regime governed by these constraints. They may not simply cling to their given religious or ethical convictions without regard to their implications for the compossible practice of other people's aims and pursuits.

Fair enough. But how does it cut in our difficult case? Given that P and Q cannot together satisfy the constraints that interest us, which of them is to be regarded as unreasonable? Is it P or Q who has chosen a conception of the good that is incompatible with liberal assumptions?

The difficulty becomes even more acute if we imagine that P was once a fanatical pornographer to the point of rampant exhibitionism and voyeurism, in a way that used to offend people like R, but that he underwent expensive therapy and re-education so that his residual pornographic ideals could fit reasonably into a liberal society. Unfortunately, he had not counted on having to accommodate himself to Q's sensitivities as well as R's, and he is inclined to draw the line at this point, insisting that he has already given up as much as he can reasonably be expected to give up. And something similar may be true of Q. Perhaps he used to believe that he could not pursue the pious life of Islam and bring up his children as good Muslims in a society desecrated by the mere presence of unbelievers like R. But he painfully changed his outlook, so that he could live at peace in England with neighbours like R. But now the problem of P has come up. Is it reasonable to expect Q to accommodate himself further to this sort of blasphemous presence? (More reasonable, I mean, than to expect P to pull in his horns to accommodate the sensitivities of Q?)

Perhaps we can appeal to some other aspect of Rawlsian reasonableness to help us here. For it is well-known that 'unreasonable' has two meanings in Rawls's later work. On the one hand, as we have just seen, it refers to a person's acceptance of the subjection of the good to the right: his willingness to tailor his ends so that they can be practised on fair terms with the practice of the ends of others, similarly disciplined. On the other hand, 'unreasonable' is used by Rawls to refer to a conception of the good whose divergence from other conceptions is not intelligible in light of what he calls 'the burdens of judgment'. This is a quasi-epistemic conception, comprising the various hazards, vicissitudes and perspectives involved in the conscientious exercise of people's powers of reason and judgement in the circumstances of modern human life.[15] I don't want to go into this in any detail – it is quite familiar to Rawls aficionados, and quite important. What I want to stress is that although Rawls casts the net of this quasi-epistemic sense of the reasonable quite wide – leaving open the possibility that reasonable people will come up with quite different conceptions of the good,[16] and stressing that 'many of our most important judgments are made under conditions where it is not to be expected that conscientious persons with full powers of reason, even after free discussion, will arrive at the same conclusion'[17] – although he concedes all that, Rawls does think that a society will be justified in controlling and excluding aims that are unreasonable in this epistemic sense, 'so that they do not undermine the unity and justice of the society'.[18]

It is not hard to see why he would want to do this. But it is hard to see why he would want to say it. For a view may be mad but harmless, or a whole society may comprise stupid but perfectly compossible beliefs. The real danger for Rawlsian theory is the converse: views that are reasonable in the sense of not crazy, but whose reasonableness is problematic in the sense of their orientation to compossibility with others. I have argued elsewhere that these definitions of 'unreasonable' can come apart.[19] Militant Islam provides an example of a comprehensive conception whose claims are not at all unreasonable in the quasi-epistemic sense, but may seem nevertheless unreasonable in the sense of openness to accommodation with other conceptions.

At any rate, I do not think unreasonableness in the epistemic sense – in the burdens of judgement sense – provides any basis for distinguishing between the conceptions of P and Q. An alternative strategy, within the fabric of late Rawlsianism, may be to ask whether Q's – the Muslim's – sensitivities can be stated in publicly accessible terms? If they cannot, then maybe they have no claim to be respected in a liberal society, for Q cannot state his complaint against P, and against the system that permits P, in publicly accessible terms.[20] On this approach, the trouble with Q's insistence on a certain sort of moral environment, free from pornography and blasphemy, is that it depends on premises that are internal to his religious faith, and that might seem perhaps arbitrary from an external point of view.

This does show, I think, some of the difficulties involved in defining adequacy. If our constraint were success as opposed to adequacy, presumably the success criterion would have to be understood on the terms posed by each conception of the good. It is of no use to say that one's pursuit of one's own aims is successful, if it does not seem successful by one's own lights. And the same must surely apply to adequacy – even accepting a distinction between adequacy and any guarantee of success. I don't think there is any way of saying that a set of permissions is adequate for the practice of a religion except by paying attention to how that set of restrictions seems from the internal point of view of the religion. To abandon any interest in that would be, in effect, to abandon any real concern for adequacy. An externally stated adequacy condition – which was quite at odds with internal conceptions – would be arbitrary and unmotivated. So there is a delicate line to walk here. We want reasons affecting the constraint set to be stated publicly. But by subjecting the constraint set to a criterion of adequacy, we accept that it is important to comprehend how it seems from the point of view of each of the conceptions that it purports to accommodate. So I think we have to say something like this. Even if this particular aspect of Q's faith cannot itself be comprehended publicly – and often it can – still, we can publicly comprehend Q's good-faith insistence that not being allowed to practise it undermines his conception of the good. (By analogy, one does not need to grasp the mysteries of transubstantiation in order to understand the difficulties that any general prohibition on the consumption of wine would pose for the Catholic practice of the Mass.)

The original position

A similar result may be reached by considering the thought-experiment that dominated Rawls's earlier work. Consider the predicament of someone in the original position who thinks it possible he turn out to be a person like Q. Of course, people in the original position do not know which aims they will want to pursue. No one thinks of himself as a Muslim, say, while he is in this choice situation. But the parties have general knowledge, and they know that aims of this sort are commonly pursued. Each must therefore take into account the possibility that he will end up holding an aim of this sort. With this possibility in mind, how should he bargain or deliberate? Now Rawls's argument for religious liberty goes as follows:

> [I]t seems evident that the parties must choose principles that secure the integrity of their religious and moral freedom. They do not know, of course, what their religious or moral convictions are, or what is the particular content of their moral or religious obligations as they interpret them. . . . Now it seems that equal liberty of conscience is the only principle that the persons in the original position can acknowledge. They cannot take chances with their liberty by permitting the dominant religious or moral doctrine to persecute or suppress others if it wishes. Even granting (what may be questioned) that it is more probable than not that one will turn out to belong to the majority (if a majority exists), to gamble in this way would be to show that one did not take one's religious or moral convictions seriously, or highly value the liberty to examine one's beliefs.[21]

However, if one thinks it possible that one will turn out to be Q, then one might think it possible that an acknowledgment of equal religious liberty for certain others – say a cult of pornographic Satanism by P – will be inimical to the practice of one's faith. On the other hand, each person in the original position will also think it possible that he adheres to the outlook of P or to some similar conception that sits ill with the sensitivities of a person like Q. Contemplating this possibility, the guy in the original position will be reluctant to sign up for any principle of sensitivity that limits his freedom in this regard.

So the person in the original position is in a bind. He wants to leave room for the possibility that he may hold sensitive religious convictions, and he wants to leave room for the possibility that he may hold a conception whose practice sits ill with those sensitivities. What is he to do? He cannot gamble with his ability to discharge whatever religious obligations he turns out to hold, by plumping either for a principle that favours a given sensitive aim or for a principle that favours pornographic aims. He faces a dilemma. The actual incompossibility of aims of these various types is represented in the intractability of this decision problem for each person behind the Rawlsian veil of ignorance.

The generalisation

Here is a general formulation of the difficulty. We take a set of individual ends $\{e_1, e_2, \ldots e_n\}$ for which no set of constraints can be designed that satisfies the requirements of adequacy and compossibility, and we consider that the exclusion of just one particular end – say, e_n – would remove the difficulty, leaving us with a set of ends – $\{e_1, e_2, \ldots e_m\}$ – that can be ordered by liberal principles. This, then, is seen as a fact about e_n which warrants its exclusion not on any intrinsic or qualitative ground (its wickedness or offensiveness as an end), but simply on the ground of its formal incompatibility with other ends in the set, in relation to the systemic requirements of a liberal order. On this basis, we say that activities in pursuit of e_n may legitimately be prohibited in a liberal society, and that e_n itself may be proscribed as an end, in the sense that people must recognise a responsibility to come up with something other than e_n as their account of what makes their respective individual lives worth living.

The difficulty is fairly obvious. If the problematic set of ends we began with suffers from incompossibility, this is presumably on account of some conflict between activities in pursuit of e_n and activities in pursuit of some other end – say, e_m. It is not the intrinsic quality of e_n that warrants its exclusion but only its affront to compossibility. So why is that not a ground for excluding e_m rather than e_n from the set of acceptable ends? Why should the blasphemer's ends be excluded rather than the particularly sensitive aims of the pious? After all, there is a sense in which each places burdens on the other. Or why should restrictions be placed on the person whose way of life requires an environment free of pornography rather than on the person whose life style involves the flaunting of pornographic images? The purely formalistic liberal strategy seems incapable of answering these questions.

Types of aim

Perhaps we can distinguish among types of end, and rule certain types out because of their inherent incompatibility with liberalism.

There are some aims that people pursue that are simply aims for themselves, aims whose successful pursuit by them does not require the involvement or participation of anyone else. Without prejudice to the content of these purposes, I shall call them protestant aims. The spirit of a protestant aim is captured in John Locke's characterisations of religious practice:

> seeing that one man does not violate the right of another by his erroneous opinions and undue manner of worship, nor is his perdition any prejudice to another man's affairs, therefore, the care of each man's salvation belongs only to himself. [. . .] Every man in that has the supreme and absolute authority of judging for himself. And the reason is because nobody else is concerned in it, nor can receive any prejudice from his conduct therein.[22]

Protestant aims may be contrasted with communal aims. It is the mark of a communal aim that it cannot be successfully pursued by anyone unless all or most of the members of a specified community are also involved in its pursuit. An example is the aspiration to work and worship in the life of an established Church, such as the Church of England (if not in its present form, then in at least some of its earlier manifestations). A person with this aim may enjoy the mingling of ecclesiastical and local politics in the life of the parish; he may revel in the fact that his bishop is also a leg-islator in the House of Lords; he may welcome the use of state funds for church buildings; and he may take pride in the special role his Church plays in the official ceremonial life of the nation. None of these attitudes can be sustained unless all other British subjects play a part in the activities of his Church, whether they like it or not: they must be affected by parish gov-ernment, bound by a legislature that includes bishops in the second chamber, required to pay taxes for the support of the Church and to endure the Anglican liturgies in ceremonies of coronation, the opening of Parliament, etc. Methodists, Roman Catholics and atheists in the popula-tion might welcome the disestablishment of the Church of England and the separation of Church and State. But for many Anglican parishioners, that will undermine much of what they cherish in their faith. An independent Episcopalian Church, of the kind found in the United States, faithful to Anglican liturgies but purged of its official status, may not answer to their aspirations at all. Other examples of communal aims along these lines, include forms of religious establishment like the institution of *Sharia* (Islamic law) in a Muslim society.

Now, perhaps we can insist that liberalism need not tolerate or accom-modate communal aims, inasmuch as such aims are directly in conflict with liberalism's own aspiration to set out the structure of a free society. Such an approach would focus on the difference between conceptions of the good life that are adopted and followed purely as individual aims, and concep-tions of the good that purport to govern a whole society. Suppose for a moment that we are dealing with a conflict in society between a particular protestant aim, Y, and a full-blown communal aim, Z. Suppose too, that Z is a communal aim that claims the whole population of the society, includ-ing the adherents of Y, as the relevant community to which it is to be applied. Then one reason for objecting to Z – one reason for singling out Z as the aim to be excluded for the sake of compossibility – is that Z is in effect a competitor to the liberal ideal of compossibility itself. Z is a com-peting principle of social organisation. If this is so, then obviously adher-ents of liberal compossibility must reject Z, since they are not in a position to tolerate competition at this level.[23]

The trouble with this line of argument is that it works only for the clear-est cases of aims that purport to compete with compossibility. Standing between protestant and communal aims are aims that I shall describe as 'sensitive'. Our earlier case of the funeral procession, at the beginning of the chapter, provides a good example. If the mourners require everyone to participate in the procession, their aim is a communal one. Usually, however, they require only some forbearance or mark of respect: their complaint against the bikers is not that the bikers are failing to join the procession. Their complaint is that the bikers are failing to modify their pursuit of their own (perhaps perfectly legitimate) aims, in a way that would be sensitive to the conduct of the funeral.

A very well-known example of such demand for sensitivity is that of millions of Muslims in the West, responding to the publication of Salman Rushdie's book *The Satanic Verses*. Many who condemned the book emphasised that while they do not require others to become Muslims or abide by *Sharia*, there are limits on their own ability to practise their faith under conditions of insult and blasphemy.[24] The followers of Islam take their faith to be sensitive to the behaviour of others in society, inasmuch as its proper practice requires them to exact a certain respect on the part of others or at least the avoidance of offensive displays of disrespect.

It is, of course, not only Islam that is sensitive in this way. There are similar Christian concerns about blasphemy. Launching a private prosecution of *Gay News* for blasphemous libel in 1977, Mary Whitehouse explained, 'I simply had to protect Our Lord.'[25] Some Muslims feel that Christian denominations have lost their substance, because they have ceased to be so sensitive:

> Many writers often condescendingly imply that Muslims should become as tolerant as modern Christians. After all, the Christian faith has not been undermined. But the truth is, of course, too obviously the other way. The continual blasphemies against the Christian faith have totally undermined it. Any faith which compromises its internal temper of militant wrath is destined for the dustbin of history, for it can no longer preserve its faithful heritage in the face of corrosive influences. The fact that post-Enlightenment Christians tolerate blasphemy is a matter for shame, not for pride.[26]

Some have even argued that all religious convictions should be understood to be sensitive in this way, so that a claim can be made on behalf of any believer to the forbearance of others so far as his own faith is concerned.[27]

The point I want to make is that the solution we considered a moment ago – the solution that purports to rule out any aim (such as an illiberal communal aim) that directly competes with liberalism – will not work for merely sensitive conceptions of the good such as modern Islam. The Islamic faith held by Q in our example is not a competitor with liberalism. On the contrary, as I said before, we can imagine that Q has modified his faith precisely so that it can fit into certain forms of liberal society.

Someone may reply that perhaps the sensitivity of Islam is the shadow cast by its historic pretensions to compete with the liberal vision. Those pretensions are concealed at the moment, but it is no secret that many Muslims do aspire to the realisation of illiberal systems of Islamic law.

However, there is no guarantee that this is true of every sensitive conception, no guarantee that it is true of sensitivity in general.

In any case, we are simply not in a position to say that the only aims entitled to respect in a liberal order are those that have no connection, logical or genealogical, with full-blown views about the good society. Thoughtful people do not form their conceptions of the good life in isolation from any thought of what a good society would be. For most people, views about the consideration and assistance they owe to others form an important part of their personal ethic, and it would be utterly artificial to suppose that those views were in turn unrelated to wider ideas about what we might owe each other in society. It might be tidier, from the liberal point of view, if people's conceptions of the good life were defined strictly as individual aims, rather than as fragments of theories about how best to organise a human society. It might be tidier if individual aims were unrelated to any thinking about the problems and possibilities posed by large numbers of humans living together. But it is utterly unrealistic. Such a requirement would exclude not only all communal aims, and most sensitive aims, but most protestant aims as well.

Who is causing the problem?

We are not even entitled to say that sensitive aims are the cause of incompossibility. A set of aims that includes some that are sensitive is not necessarily incompossible. A sensitive aim may coexist with a number of others, provided that their practice does not encroach on the sensitivities specified. For example, the following set of religious aims:

S: {Islam, pious Christianity privately practised, pious Judaism privately practised}

seems a perfectly compossible set. It is true that the inclusion of a sensitive aim, X, in any set of other aims does indicate a potential for incompossibility. For one of the other aims *may* involve practices that offend the sensitivities of the proponents of X. For an aim to be sensitive is for its proponents to be concerned as part of the pursuit of their own aim about the aims that others pursue and the activities that others perform. So there is always a danger that X will sit ill with some other aim in a given set. It is not necessary for incompossibility that there be protestant aims in the set. A given sensitive aim may be incompatible with other sensitive aims if the practices of the latter do not accord with the sensibilities of those who practise the former. The sensitive forms of Islamic faith that I have mentioned may sit well with certain protestant forms of Christian piety, but sit ill with the militant proselytising of an evangelical Christian faith.

I should emphasise finally that, although the presence of a sensitive (or a communal or a competitive) aim seems necessary for intrinsic incompossibility, we should not say that such aims are the cause of incompossibility.

The cause of incompossibility, where it occurs, is the combination of X with some other aim that sits ill with it. The presence of both is necessary; taking either one away would resolve the incompossibility.

In a situation of incompossibility, each party to the conflict can insist that she is choosing her convictions from a set of compossible aims. Consider again the conflict between Salman Rushdie and the followers of Islam. Rushdie will say that he is choosing his aim (the freewheeling secular exploration of a cosmopolitan inheritance) from a set that includes a number of aims that others pursue in modern society. He will say that he is perfectly willing to live and let live, so far as those other aims are concerned. He may, for example, oppose the shallow values of Hollywood, but he does not propose to ban or picket any films. He may oppose traditional Christian values as well, but he is perfectly prepared to live in peace with their proponents, adjusting the pursuit of his own ideals accordingly. True, the set from which he chooses does not include all possible aims. Most prominently, it does not include the sensitive aims of Islam (which *The Satanic Verses* offended). But the Rawlsian formula recognises this: some aims must be excluded in the name of reasonableness if compossibility is to be secured.

The trouble is: his Islamic opponents can make exactly the same sort of claim. They too have chosen their (sensitive) aim from a compossible set (like S, mentioned earlier), a set that includes many of the other aims pursued in modern society. They do not agree, for example, with Christians about the nature of Jesus, or with the Jews about the extent and scope of God's revelation, but they have shown themselves willing to live in peace and mutual toleration with a number of Christian and Jewish denominations. As much as the set from which Rushdie chooses his aims, theirs is not all-inclusive. Specifically, it excludes aims that involve as part of their pursuit a willingness to blaspheme the name of the founder of their religion. They exclude that in the name of reasonableness: they cannot see why Rushdie and others should regard themselves as entitled to pursue such an aim, given that there are two million Muslims living with them in Britain.

So there is an impasse. Rushdie is being reasonable and he is choosing from a compossible set – one, however, that excludes the sensitive aims of modern Islam. The followers of Islam are being reasonable and choosing from a compossible set – but one that excludes what they regard as blasphemy. In each case, the feature of the excluded aim that leads to its exclusion is precisely a feature that is central to the practices of the proponent of that aim. Rushdie cannot live the life he wants to lead unless he can treat his religious heritage as playfully as he did in *The Satanic Verses*. His opponents cannot live the life they want to lead unless they can vindicate the name of the Prophet. Who is to give way? Neither the idea of compossibility, nor the Rawlsian idea of reasonableness or the constraints of right, indicates an answer.

To put it another way, several Kantian kingdoms of ends are imaginable. In one, people like Salman Rushdie write their novels as they please, and others practise their religions as they please, but the domain of religion is restricted to those that do not translate mere offence into pressure for a legal requirement that others refrain from blasphemy. In another kingdom of ends, a sensitive religion like Islam is practised and other individual ends (including alternative religious faiths) are tolerated, but Rushdie-style blasphemy is excluded by a broad framework of respect for Islamic faith and perhaps for any other faith that demands it. From the point of view of compossibility, there is nothing to choose between these worlds. People like Rushdie are going to feel intolerably constrained in the second kingdom of ends; but then those who burned his book in Bradford evidently felt intolerably constrained in the first place.

Asymmetry?

The hunch that there must be a solution to this problem rests, I think, on the view that there is an asymmetry to conflicts such as the one we have been discussing. Someone may say, 'The Islamic militants are trying to kill Rushdie whereas he is not trying to kill them.' But leave aside the particular issue of the *fatwa*, which is, in a sense, a response to the conflict rather than the basis of it. Consider the view of those more moderate Muslims who are not trying to assassinate anyone but who still think that in a just society the publication of books like *The Satanic Verses* would not be allowed.[28] Then the alleged asymmetry presumably goes like this: 'All Rushdie is doing is offending their sensitivities, whereas they are proposing to limit his liberty.' Is this difference, between what they propose to do to him (restrict publication) and what he proposes to do to them (insult their faith), sufficient to determine the issue in favour of one party or the other?

Again, the answer is 'No'. Recall the earlier discussion of equality and difference, and our rejection of any simple notion of equality as a constraint on our algebra. I suggested there that if people's aims and activities are quite different in their character and content, then it is likely that the liberties and protections that they respectively require in order to pursue their aims will differ accordingly. What Rushdie needs, for example, is freedom of speech, freedom to publish (and be damned?), and protection from the wrath of those he expects to offend. What his Islamic opponents need is something different: protection from blasphemous insult. But though the needs are different, they are on a par so far as the theory of compossibility is concerned. For, in abstract terms, each requirement is what is necessary for the pursuit of the aim in question. From this abstract point of view, there is no asymmetry. What Rushdie demands encroaches on the pursuit of Islamic aims, and what the Muslims demand encroaches on the pursuit of Rushdie's aims. Each is demanding something that would make life intolerable for the other. Thus, nothing is gained in the argument by pointing out that the rights the Muslims demand are rights that Rushdie, for example, would be happy to repudiate. They may claim the right to be protected from blasphemy or from demonstrations of disrespect for their cherished beliefs. If the line of argument I am exploring here is correct, it is no reply to this claim that secular atheists are willing to disown any such protection. For example, the fact that Salman Rushdie does not need to be protected from ridicule in order to be able to pursue his own good does not show that others do not need such protection in order to be able to pursue theirs. Different aims may require different liberties and different protection.

Can we say perhaps that his demand (for freedom) is not intentionally or intrinsically opposed to the pursuit of their aim, while their demand (for protection from such blasphemy) is intrinsically and intentionally opposed to the pursuit of his aim? After all, there is nothing intrinsically anti-Islam in a demand for freedom of speech, whereas there is something intrinsically anti-infidel in a demand for respect for the Prophet. This will not do either. Both positions can be described abstractly without reference to the other: his is a demand for freedom, theirs is a demand for respect. On the other hand, even the abstract specification in each case makes reference to the idea of an other: respect is always accorded by someone, freedom is always freedom from someone's constraint. Anyway, under certain descriptions, Rushdie's claim is inherently inimical to theirs, for what he claims is exactly the right to make fun of a heritage that is theirs as well as his. On their account (which we must take seriously) it is part and parcel of Islam 'to vindicate the reputation of God and his spokesman against the militant calumnies of evil';[29] freedom to blaspheme is freedom to assault Islam. In any case, it is not at all clear why the intentionality of the conflict should make a difference. Extrinsic conflict (such as conflict arising out of scarcity) is as much a source of incompossibility as intrinsic, and we should still have to deal with that impasse even if a given demand on scarce resources made no reference at all to any other demand.

Aggressive liberalism

Perhaps in the end what liberals have to do is simply to bite the bullet and insist – in an explicitly partisan way – that the only aims whose inclusion can be countenanced in a compossible order are aims that are positively imbued with the idea of such an order. Compossibility, they might insist, is not only a liberal idea, but an idea for liberals, that is, an idea for those who have formed their life plan in the specifically protestant spirit characteristic of modern individualism. I have my doubts about this aggressive liberalism, though I have advocated it elsewhere (as a solution to certain difficulties afflicting liberal neutrality) in the following terms:

> It is true that the liberal has a decidedly individualistic account of what constitutes a conception of the good life. . . . But so what? The liberal has not arbi-

trarily plucked her account of what it is to have a conception of the good life out of the air. She has settled on that view . . . because of the fundamental principles and values that underlie her position. She thinks that the shaping of individual lives by the individuals who are living them is a good thing; and she fears for the results if that process is distorted or usurped by externally applied coercion, even the coercion of *Gemeinschaft*. On the basis of these concerns and these fears, she identifies moral views of this individualistic sort as those between which legislative neutrality is required.[30]

After all, the very idea of compossibility emerged in modern (Kantian) thought around a specific conception of individualistic autonomy and fulfilment, and aggressive liberals may want to insist that the solicitude of compossibility be confined to individual lives that are governed by that conception. Underlying the commitment to compossibility, it is this conception of the self that is cherished. Apart from that conception, the Kantian kingdom of ends, or the formal idea of compossibility, is not worth pursuing as an ideal.

But I now think this aggressive liberalism is unsatisfactory as a solution to the problem we are addressing. The main difficulty is that by restricting the field of aims among which compossibility is sought, this approach artificially restricts the range of real problems to which compossibility can provide the basis for a solution. Compossibility turns out to be a recipe not for live-and-let-live in the real world, but for mutual admiration among liberal individualists in an artificial world, exclusively populated by them and their imitators. Opponents of liberalism would be entitled to say that if the rules of the game have changed in that way, then they should be able to make idealistic assumptions as well, and assume whatever is necessary to present communitarian conceptions in a rosy light.

It has always been one of the advantages of the liberal approach to political theory that it prides itself on dealing with the real world of men and women as they actually are.[31] Its claims about pluralism and the need for toleration have been based on the actual dissent about value that can be expected to emerge when men and women engage in thought about their lives and their relations with others under less than perfect conditions. What Rawls has called in his recent writings 'the burdens of reason' are important here. They are the real-life circumstances that make it more or less inevitable that, with the best will in the world, people will come up with different religious, philosophical and moral convictions.[32] But exactly this realism precludes any aggressive assumption that we are addressing a society in which only protestant aims need to be considered or taken seriously.

The aggressive liberal might protest – and this is the last response I will consider – that at least some communal or sensitive conceptions may be accommodated in the order he envisages, provided they are represented in a suitably individualistic form. The aggressive liberal might, for example, treat each communitarian as though his vision of society were a private hobby-horse, and each militant follower of Islam as though his aspiration to *Sharia* were just another innocuous protestant sect. But he would with-hold support and respect for those visions to the extent that their propo-nents went beyond these individualist 'caricatures'.

Again, in the end that is a travesty of a solution. If the Rushdie affair has taught us anything, it has shown that people will not put up with having their ideas 'respected' in this truncated sense. Such an approach, tidying up recalcitrant conceptions so that they fit neatly into the Kantian kingdom of ends, may satisfy a theorist's urge for order, but will do nothing to address the real problem of social order that, as we saw at the beginning, evoked the idea of compossibility in the first place. It seems more honest to admit defeat in the long search for a solution to the algebra of compossibility, than to adopt the artificial expedient of treating the proponents of com-munal or militantly sensitive religions as though they were liberals.

Impasse

I have argued myself to a standstill on this. I have no rabbit to pull out of the hat. It seems to me that, in a world where many people's ethics and reli-gions are sensitive to the activities and attitudes of others, there is no deter-minate solution to the problem of compossibility.

This conclusion is bleak and uncomfortable. It means that we can no longer confront issues like the case of Salman Rushdie with the conviction that there is a perfectly good solution of live-and-let-live, if only people would restrain themselves sufficiently to adopt it. There is no such accom-modating solution. It means that we can no longer organize liberal aspira-tions around the formula of the kingdom of ends. The algebra intimated in Rawls's principle of an adequate liberty for each, compatible with a similar liberty for all, is insoluble. Other conceptions, other formulations for lib-eralism must be found.

It is worth noting, finally, that although the difficulty is primarily one for liberal political philosophy, there is precious little comfort for the oppo-nents of liberalism in the conclusions we have reached. For when they are finished saying 'I told you so', they too must confront a world in which there is no solution like 'live-and-let-live', no principles for accommodat-ing the reality of the adherents of different kinds of values living side-by-side. That reality is likely to be troubling even to those who advocate the social institution of some particular conception of the good (on either com-munitarian or perfectionist grounds).

For perfectionists and communitarians, as much as their liberal oppo-nents, must be prepared to engage with the real world. They must engage with a world in which, as a matter of fact, a number of rival conceptions of the good and the pious are at war with one another. They may lament the ethical and religious pluralism of modern society, and urge the merits of their own favoured conception, but anyone can do that. Rawls is right: for the foreseeable future, this is the world we must live with. In other words, the problem of incompossibility between conceptions of the good is at least a practical problem for everyone in modern society, not just for liberals or for those who celebrate pluralism. The opponents of liberalism – the perfectionists or the communitarians – may offer the institutionalisation of a single conception of the good as their first-best solution's to the dilemmas of modern society. But since there is no chance whatsoever of that solution's being adopted, they must tell us something about their second-best. At that level, seeking the compossibility of such conceptions as there happen to be in society seems to be the counsel not just of liberal political philosophy, but of ordinary common sense. To the extent that this is so, the conclusions of the argument I have expounded in this chapter should be taken as a disturbing and discomforting challenge to us all, not just as a way of embarrassing liberalism.

Notes

This chapter is based on the Austin Lecture that I gave as part of the ALSP Conference on 'The Culture of Toleration' held in Exeter in April 2000.

1 See I. Kant, *Groundwork of the Metaphysic of Morals*, edited by H. J. Paton (London: Routledge, 1991), Chapter 2, pp. 71–106.

2 I adopt this term from H. Steiner, 'The structure of a set of compossible rights', *Journal of Philosophy*, 74 (1977), pp. 767–75. See also H. Steiner, *An Essay on Rights* (Oxford: Blackwell, 1984), pp. 86–101.

3 Kant defines a kingdom as 'a systematic union of different rational beings under common laws', and a kingdom of ends as 'a whole of all ends in systematic conjunction (a whole both of rational beings as ends in themselves and also of the personal ends which each may set before himself)', *Groundwork*, p. 95.

   Initially, the kingdom of ends is presented in Kant's philosophy as an interpretation of morality. In moral life it provides a test for our individual decision-making: 'A rational being must always regard himself as making laws in a kingdom of ends. [. . .] Thus morality consists in the relation of all action to the making of laws whereby alone a kingdom of ends is possible' (*Groundwork*, p. 96). However, as Kant moves from moral to political philosophy, the idea of a kingdom of ends remains important. The legislator should keep the kingdom of ends in mind, not merely as an ideal of personal morality, but as a model for the legal and constitutional system he is establishing. So, it is not really the case that the idea of a kingdom of ends is drawn from Kant's moral philosophy and adapted for us in his political philosophy. It really works the other way round: the model of an ideal political order serves as a concept whose deployment in intentionality is the mark of a morally good will. Thus, its use as a model for a legal system does not presuppose any requirement that citizens' actions be motivated in any particular way (e.g. by the kingdom of ends as an idea). We begin with the idea of a set of constraints reconciling the external freedom of each person with the external freedom of everyone else (under conditions of plurality of ends); that is the basis for normative thought about politics and law. It is only when we take that idea and consider its use as a possible touchstone for individual motivation that we move into the realm of morality.

4 I do think though that the difference between (2a) and (2b) is very interesting, though I cannot say that I have entirely settled my thoughts on this subject, or that I have even been able to state them entirely clearly.
5 See R. Dworkin, 'What is equality? I Equality of welfare', *Philosophy and Public Affairs*, 10:3 (1981) 185–246.
6 I. Kant, *Critique of Pure Reason*, trans. J. M. D. Meiklejohn (London: Dent & Sons, 1934), Transcendental Logic II, Dialectic, I, i: 'Of Ideas in General', p. 220.
7 J. Rawls, *Theory of Justice* (Oxford: Oxford University Press, 1971), p. 60, emphasis added.
8 *Ibid.*, emphasis added.
9 J. Rawls, *Political Liberalism* (New York: Columbia University Press, 1993), p. 5, emphasis added. In *Justice as Fairness: A Restatement* (Cambridge, MA: Belknap Press of Harvard University Press, 2001), p. 111, Rawls indicates that compossibility is a matter of mutual adjustment among the liberties of different persons: 'these liberties are bound to conflict with one another; hence the institutional rules specifying them must be adjusted so that each liberty fits into a coherent scheme of liberties. . . . Nor is it required that in the finally adjusted scheme, each basic liberty is equally provided for (whatever that would mean.) Rather, however these liberties are adjusted, that final scheme is to be secured equally for all citizens.'
10 The consequences of rejecting this interpretation of equality are interesting. In a simple two-person case, the rights claimed by P, as necessary for the pursuit of his aims, may be different from the rights claimed by Q, as necessary for the pursuit of hers. Of course, the rights claimed by P will be correlative to duties imposed on Q and vice versa. But although P's rights are correlative to Q's duties, and P's duties correlative to Q's rights, P cannot simply take the set of rights he has and the set of duties he has and, replacing proper names with variables, regard them as correlative. He is therefore no longer able to work out what duties he has simply by considering what would be correlative to the rights that he claims. He must really pay attention to the situation and the needs of the other person, Q, because these may differ significantly from anything he can extrapolate from his own case, or any understanding of what he would demand if we were standing in their shoes.

Notice how this provides a sensible way through many of the difficulties associated with the idea of difference. Consider, for example, the provision that must be made in the workplace and employment law for pregnancy. It may be a mistake to try and bring this provision under some general rubric that is applicable equally to men as well as women, some rubric about special provision for illness, for example, or disability. It may be more sensible to say simply that the situation of all or some women is different from the situation of all men in this crucial respect – that women may become and/or may want to become pregnant, and that therefore what women need in order to pursue a plan of life may simply differ from what men need. Since our commitment is just to the universal proposition that everyone is to have whatever is necessary for the pursuit of his or her own good, it will not be surprising if the rights of women turn out to differ in detail from the rights of men. Accordingly, it will not be possible for a man to work out in detail what he owes a woman in the way of respect, assistance or forbearance, simply by extrapolating from the respect, assistance, and forbearance that he takes himself to be entitled to.

11 The popular idea that the toleration of Catholicism is rejected in John Locke's *A Letter Concerning Toleration* (ed. J. H. Tully, London: Hackett, 1983) is of course quite wrong. Cf. J. Waldron, *Locke, God and Equality: Christian Foundations of Locke's Political Thought* (Cambridge: Cambridge University Press, 2002).

12 For Thomas Hobbes, the technical term was 'compleasance'. Though Hobbes was not a conventional liberal, he believed – as much as any conventional liberal – that there are limits on the individual ends that can be accommodated in a peaceful society. He suggested (in what he called the Fifth Law of Nature) that everyone has a duty to adapt his ends to make accommodation possible: 'A fifth Law of Nature, is COMPLEASANCE; that is to say, That every man strive to accommodate himself to the rest. For the understanding whereof, we may consider, that there is in mens aptnesse to Society, a diversity of Nature, rising from their diversity of Affections; not unlike to that we see in stones brought together for building of an Edifice. . . . [T]hat stone which by the asperity, and irregularity of Figure, takes more room from others, than it selfe fills; and for the hardnesse cannot be easily made plain, and thereby hindereth the building, is by the builders cast away as unprofitable, and troublesome.'

'So also', Hobbes continued, 'a man that by asperity of Nature, will strive to retain those things which to himself are superfluous, and to others necessary; and for the stubbornness of his Passions, cannot be corrected, is to be left, or cast out of Society, as cumbersome thereunto' (*Leviathan*, ed. R. Tuck, Cambridge: Cambridge University Press, 1996, p. 106). That's all very well – a fine image, and dandy terminology – but how does it work in our tough case? Is it the Muslim who, by the asperity of his nature, strives to establish an environment that he doesn't really need, at the expense of a freedom that is necessary for the pornographer? Or is it the pornographer who is the stumbling-block, insisting on a freedom that spoils the wall for others? Even the building-block image doesn't really help. If I have three stones with which to finish the wall, and it is the case, first, that A and B will fit in, so long as the rather more angular C is excluded, and, secondly, that B and C will fit in, so long as a spheroid A is excluded, which is to be thrown away: A or C? Whose irregularity, asperity, and stubbornness is the problem here?

13 J. Rawls, 'Kantian constructivism', *Journal of Philosophy*, 77:9 (1980) 515–72, at p. 543, and pp. 521–2.

14 Rawls, *Theory of Justice*, p. 31. See also *Political Liberalism*, p. 174.

15 Rawls, *Political Liberalism*, p. 56.

16 *Ibid.*, p. 58 'Different conceptions of the world can reasonably be elaborated from different standpoints and diversity arises in part from our distinct perspectives. It is unrealistic . . . to suppose that all our differences are rooted solely in ignorance and perversity, or else in the rivalries for power, status, or economic gain'.

17 *Ibid.*

18 Rawls, *Political Liberalism*, p. xvii.

19 See J. Waldron, 'Justice revisited' (A Review of Rawls, *Political Liberalism*), *The Times Literary Supplement*, 18 June 1993, pp. 5–6.

20 This response is suggested by Rawls's remarks about Aquinas on heresy in Rawls, *Theory of Justice*, pp. 215–16.

21 Rawls, *Theory of Justice*, pp. 206–7.

22 Locke, *A Letter Concerning Toleration*, pp. 42–3.

23 Something like this has been used by Ronald Dworkin to argue against the counting of 'external preferences' (such as the Nazi preference that no weight be given to the preferences of non-Aryans) in a utilitarian calculus: 'Utilitarianism must claim . . . truth for itself, and therefore must claim the falsity of any theory that contradicts it. It must itself occupy, that is, all the logical space that its content requires. . . . A neutral utilitarian cannot say that there is no reason in political morality for rejecting or dishonouring [the Nazi's] preference, for not dismissing it as simply wrong, for not striving to fulfill it with all the dedication that officials devote to fulfilling any other sort of preference. For utilitarianism itself supplies such a reason: its most fundamental tenet is that people's preferences should be weighed on an equal basis in the same scales, that the Nazi theory of justice is profoundly wrong. . . . Political preferences, like the Nazi's preference, are on the same level, purport to occupy the same space as the utilitarian theory itself. Therefore, though the utilitarian theory must be neutral between personal preferences like the preferences for push-pin and poetry, as a matter of the theory of justice, it cannot be neutral between itself and Nazism', R. Dworkin, 'Rights as Trumps', in J. Waldron (ed.), *Theories of Rights* (Oxford: Oxford University Press, 1984), pp. 153–67, at pp. 155–7. If we substitute 'liberal compossibility' for 'utilitarianism' and 'communal conception, Z' for 'Nazism' in this passage, we can see it as a version of the present line of argument.

24 Dr Mughram Ali Al-Ghamdi, Chairman of the UK Committee on Islamic Affairs, has asserted: 'No individual with the slightest grain of self-respect can accept being insulted and it is a more serious matter when a whole world community is subject to outrageous abuse of its inviolable sanctities', as cited in L. Appignanesi and S. Maitland (eds), *The Rushdie File* (London: Fourth Estate, 1989), p. 113.

25 Cited in P. Jones, 'Respecting beliefs and rebuking Rushdie', *British Journal of Political Science*, 20 (1990) 415–37, at p. 419. I am obliged to Professor Peter Jones for the references in footnotes 49–52.

26 S. Akhtar, in *The Guardian*, 27 February 1989, quoted in Jones, 'Respecting beliefs', p. 417.

27 Jones, 'Respecting beliefs'.

28 I have in mind here the request by Abdul Hussain Choudhury that the English law of blasphemy be extended to cover instances of this kind: see *R v Chief Metropolitan Stipendiary Magistrate, ex parte Choudhury* (1991) 1 All ER 306.

29 S. Akhtar, *Be Careful with Mohammed!* (London: Bellew, 1989), p. 103.

30 J. Waldron, 'Legislation and moral neutrality', in R. Goodin and A. Reeve (eds), *Liberal Neutrality* (London: Routledge, 1989), pp. 61–83, at p. 80.

31 See also the discussion in J. Waldron, 'Theoretical foundations of liberalism', *Philosophical Quarterly*, 37 (1987) 127–50.

32 Rawls, *Justice as Fairness*, pp. 35–7.

2

The reasonableness of pluralism

Matt Matravers and Susan Mendus

Introduction

In 'The Idea of an Overlapping Consensus', John Rawls remarks that the aims of political philosophy depend upon the society it addresses, and that modern, democratic societies are characterised by 'the fact of pluralism': they are societies in which different people have different and conflicting comprehensive conceptions of the good, different and conflicting beliefs about the right way to live morally speaking.[1] Moreover, and troublingly, these differences are not explicable simply by reference to stupidity, in-attention or faulty reasoning.[2] On the contrary, in many cases they are the predictable outcome of the operation of reason, which, Rawls claims, stands under 'burdens'. These burdens render pluralism *reasonable*, unavoidable and not in any way regrettable. Rawls specifies the burdens of judgement as follows:

   a. The evidence – empirical and scientific – bearing on the case is conflicting and complex, and thus hard to assess and evaluate.

   b. Even when we agree fully about the kinds of considerations that are relevant, we may disagree about their weight, and so arrive at different judgements.

   c. To some extent all our concepts, not only moral and political concepts, are vague and subject to hard cases; and this indeterminacy means that we must rely on judgement and interpretation [. . .] within some range [. . .] where reasonable persons may differ.

   d. To some extent [. . .] the way we assess evidence and weigh moral and par-ticular values is shaped by our total experience, our whole course of life up to now; and our total experiences must always differ.

   e. Often there are different kinds of normative considerations of different force on both sides of an issue and it is difficult to make an overall assessment.

   f. Any system of social institutions is limited in the values it can admit so that some selection must be made from the full range of moral and political values that might be realized [. . .] Many [of these] hard decisions may seem to have no clear answer.[3]

Rawls goes on to claim that the fact that reason stands under these burdens both tells us why pluralism is to be expected and explains why it is not lamentable. He writes: 'to think of the fact of pluralism as a disaster is like thinking of the outcome of the operation of reason under conditions of freedom as a disaster'.[4]

So if the aim of political philosophy depends on the society it addresses, the aim of political philosophy in modern democratic societies, characterised by the fact of reasonable pluralism, will be to find ways in which people might live together harmoniously despite the persistence of reasonable disagreement about the highest good or the best way to lead one's life. One such way, endorsed by Rawls and those 'liberal impartialists' who have followed him, is to hold that since pluralism about conceptions of the good is reasonable, it is unjust or illegitimate for one group of people to insist on the superiority of their conception of the good and to use that as a reason either to impose their conception of the good on another group of people, or to repress any conflicting conception of the good. This might be called the 'injustice of imposition'.

The injustice of imposition is often held to follow from the reasonableness of pluralism; but the conclusion that it is unjust, or illegitimate, to impose a conception of the good on those who do not hold it (or, alternatively, that it is unjust to repress a conception of the good simply because one does not share it) cannot be drawn simply from the reasonableness of pluralism itself. That judgement operates under burdens, and that reason is indeterminate in matters of the good, does not tell us what we ought, or ought not, to do. What is needed is some further claim, such as a commitment to equal respect. So the argument is something like the following: people are owed equal respect, and that fact, when taken together with the fact that reason is indeterminate, delivers the conclusion that we ought not to impose a conception of the good on those who do not hold it (and, of course, are not unreasonable in refusing to hold it). It may be that, especially in Rawls's recent work, this moral component is to be understood as built into the idea of 'reasonableness' in reasonable pluralism, in which case the argument will not need to proceed in two distinct steps. Nevertheless, even on this interpretation it is possible to discern two aspects of reasonableness, one epistemological, the other moral.

Our aim in this chapter is to examine two arguments that purport to underpin the move from the reasonableness of pluralism to the injustice of imposition. On the one hand, there are those (including, for the most part, Rawls) who hold that, since pluralism about conceptions of the good is reasonable, we must not, in attempting to settle questions of justice, invoke the truth of any conception of the good. This is the method of avoidance (or of epistemological restraint). On the other hand, there are those (including Brian Barry) who endorse the conclusion that what follows from the reasonableness of pluralism is the injustice of imposition, but argue that this must be underpinned not by the method of avoidance, but by scepticism.

We begin with Barry's sceptical argument (in the next two sections). In the first of them we argue that in presenting the case for scepticism and against epistemological restraint, Barry misrepresents epistemological restraint. Moreover, we claim that underpinning the injustice of imposition with scepticism exacts substantial existential costs given the connections that there are between conceptions of human flourishing and views on the status of conceptions of human flourishing. In the following section we argue that scepticism cannot, in any case, deliver an unequivocal grounding for the injustice of imposition unless a clear distinction can be drawn between types of beliefs. Such a distinction is, we claim, implausible. We then return to the method of avoidance and ask whether it can legitimise the move from pluralism to the injustice of imposition. Our conclusion is that it cannot: where arguments from scepticism succeed only by undermining the permanence of pluralism, arguments from avoidance succeed only by undermining the priority of justice. Both scepticism and avoidance are epistemological arguments, and the move from the reasonableness of pluralism to the injustice of imposition requires a moral, not an epistemological, foundation.

Scepticism and the reasonableness of pluralism

What follows from the fact of pluralism at the epistemological level? Brian Barry claims that what follows is scepticism, understood as doubt rather than denial.[5] Since we cannot persuade others of the truth of our own conception of the good, we must hold that conception with some doubt, and doubt is all that is necessary in order to generate (moderate) scepticism.

Rawls, however, resists this conclusion because he believes that political liberalism ought, so far as possible, to stand back from questions of the highest good and from metaphysical and philosophical questions generally. In a society characterised by reasonable pluralism, there will not only be conflicting conceptions of the highest good, or the right way to lead one's life, there will also be conflicting metaphysical and epistemological views underpinning those different conceptions. Therefore, in arriving at principles of justice, no conception of the good should be advanced as true, nor should any metaphysical or epistemological claim be assumed. For Rawls, then, political liberalism is severely political. It is not simply political as distinct from moral; it is also political as distinct from metaphysical, epistemological, or more generally philosophical. On his account it is not simply the case that people have conflicting conceptions of the good. It is also the case that they have conflicting views about the status of those conceptions of the good, and therefore a truly 'impartialist liberalism' must remain agnostic both about comprehensive conceptions and about the metaphysical or epistemological underpinnings of those conceptions. Barry dissents. He draws a distinction between what is comprehensive and what is controversial, and argues that while 'impartialist liberalism' both can and must distance itself from a commitment to any comprehensive conception of the good, it is futile for it to attempt to distance itself from saying anything controversial. 'Scepticism', Barry writes,

> is not a view of human flourishing. It is an epistemological doctrine about the status of conceptions of what constitutes human flourishing. Scepticism is, of course, a controversial view and some people would deny it. But there is no way of avoiding the affirmation of a position that is not universally accepted if one is to get anywhere at all. My claim is that the case for scepticism cannot reasonably be rejected.[6]

As was noted above, Barry's argument is that scepticism cannot reasonably be rejected precisely because of reasonable pluralism. Modern democratic societies are ones in which reasonable people fail to persuade each other about which conception of the good is the correct one, and this failure is sufficient to generate moderate scepticism even in the most intransigent case, the case of personal religious revelation:

> Suppose that God were (as it seemed to me) to grant me a vision in which certain truths were revealed. A partisan of epistemological restraint would suggest that I might be absolutely convinced of the veridical nature of this revelation while nevertheless admitting that others could reasonably reject my evidence. But is this really plausible? If I concede that I have no way of convincing others, should that not also lead to a dent in my own certainty?[7]

For Barry, then, everything hinges on the extent to which the agent's inner convictions can legitimately withstand his or her failure to persuade others. His claim is that the method of epistemological restraint is one that supposes that people might legitimately continue to hold their beliefs with certainty even though they are unable to persuade others of the truth of those beliefs. And this, Barry claims, is an implausible supposition. Even in the strongest case, my inability to persuade others should dent my own certainty, and that dent is sufficient to force a move from avoidance to scepticism. However, that move is not a disaster, since scepticism is not itself a view of human flourishing but only an epistemological claim about the status of conceptions of human flourishing.

Two points merit consideration here: the first is that Barry's argument misrepresents the aim of the method of avoidance, which is precisely to detach questions of inner conviction from the success or failure of persuasive strategies. Barry supposes that we cannot justify imposing on others because, and only because, we cannot be certain ourselves. But the method of avoidance aims to render questions of certainty irrelevant to the legitimation of political power. Thus, Rawls need not maintain that it is legitimate to carry on believing with conviction even when we cannot persuade others. He need only insist that, even if we do retain conviction, that does not in itself legitimise imposition.

The second, and connected, point is that the argument from scepticism, as advanced by Barry, rests crucially upon the appropriate existential condition of the agent in the modern world. According to Barry, it is *because* we are not entitled to certainty in the face of our inability to persuade others that we must move to moderate scepticism as the foundation of liberal neutrality. However, this claim undermines Barry's own distinction between views of human flourishing and epistemological doctrines about the status of views of human flourishing. To see this, consider the following passage from Charles Taylor's 'Sources of the self'. Taylor claims that in the modern world we are in:

> a fundamentally different existential predicament from that which dominated most previous cultures and still defines the lives of other people today. That alternative predicament is one in which an unchallengeable framework makes imperious demands which we fear being unable to meet. We face the prospect of irretrievable condemnation or exile, or of being marked down in obloquy forever, of being sent to damnation irrevocably [. . .] the form of danger here is utterly different from that which threatens the modern seeker, which is something close to the opposite: the world loses altogether its spiritual contour, nothing is worth doing, the fear is of a terrifying emptiness, a kind of vertigo, or even a fracturing of our world and body space.[8]

On Taylor's account, one very important factor contributing to what he calls our different 'existential predicament' is that we can no longer hold our own beliefs unquestioningly: the plurality of different conceptions of the good (in Taylor's terms, different 'frameworks') has a tendency to leave us in a state of doubt even about our most deeply held religious and moral convictions, for we are constantly made aware of the fact that our framework is but one among many others.

However, and as is clear from Taylor's remarks, it is this condition of doubt or uncertainty which is itself our problem. In modern societies, characterised by the fact of pluralism, the manner in which we can properly hold our beliefs has been seriously undermined by comparison with a world in which they functioned as unquestionable frameworks. And our different existential predicament is, for him, largely a consequence of the different epistemological status of our conceptions of the good. It is the very fact that we can no longer hold our views unquestioningly that itself contributes in large part to the sense of vertigo that Taylor describes.

To put the point more generally, Taylor's analysis suggests that the plurality of competing conceptions of the good generates uncertainty, and that a conception of the good that is held with a degree of uncertainty is, in important respects, a different conception of the good from one that is held with assurance. It is not merely *what* we believe that contributes to and constitutes our ability to flourish; it is also *the way in which* we are entitled to believe it. If this is right, then while scepticism might not be a 'view of human flourishing', it is nevertheless something that may contribute to or detract from our ability to flourish. The religious believer who can hold a belief in God unquestioningly is in a significantly different condition from the religious believer who can hold that belief only provisionally: the declaration 'I know that my Redeemer liveth!' has a different status from the declaration 'I believe that my Redeemer liveth, but since I am unable to persuade others I must entertain doubt.' Thus, Barry's distinction between conceptions of the good and views about the epistemological status of conceptions of the good is unstable and, in consequence, so is the distinction between what is comprehensive and what is controversial. Scepticism is not itself a comprehensive conception of the good; but it is a view that has consequences for comprehensive conceptions of the good.

Barry's appeal to a form of scepticism that is grounded in the degree of certainty that the agent is entitled to feel about his or her beliefs is therefore one that yokes together the 'existential' condition of the agent and the justification of liberal impartiality. His argument for scepticism depends upon the claim that if the agent cannot persuade others of his views, then he must hold them only provisionally, and it is the inappropriateness of continuing to hold one's beliefs with certainty despite one's inability to persuade others that motivates Barry's appeal to scepticism and that in turn underpins the move from the reasonableness of pluralism to the injustice of imposition. It is, however, precisely the importance of separating existential condition from justification that motivates Rawls's project. *Pace* Barry, Rawls's reluctance to ground political liberalism in moderate scepticism is not simply a forlorn hope that he can avoid saying anything controversial. It is also a desire to justify political arrangements without undermining any comprehensive beliefs and, as Taylor's analysis indicates, the argument from moderate scepticism cannot perform this trick because it depends crucially on the claim that if I cannot persuade others of the truth of my comprehensive belief, I must hold that belief only provisionally. To accept this is to accept that the justificatory project of scepticism has extensive existential costs. It protects the injustice of imposition only by sacrificing the commitment to the reasonableness of pluralism.

Scepticism and the injustice of imposition

Our concern in this chapter is with the transition from the reasonableness of pluralism to the injustice of imposition. In the last section, we suggested that it would be unwise for the 'impartialist' to underpin this move with a commitment to scepticism, and that the reason it would be unwise is because scepticism as an epistemological doctrine is not easily separable from comprehensive conceptions of the good or conceptions of human flourishing. The desire of the 'impartialist' to stand back from comprehensive doctrines will be undermined by the endorsement of scepticism. In this section we question whether scepticism is capable of delivering the injustice of imposition.

One case that seems to support the argument is that in which orthodox Catholics wish to organise society around their religious beliefs. The objection to such a proposal is that their desire is a desire to impose a conception of the good on others who do not share it. Since reason is indeterminate in these cases (pluralism is reasonable) and since, moreover, people are owed equal respect, it would be unjust to allow the orthodox Catholics to have their wish. Here, then, is a case in which the reasonableness of pluralism, when combined with a commitment to equality of respect, delivers the injustice of imposition.

Two considerations are pertinent here: first, and as we have seen already, the reasonableness of pluralism is held, by Barry at least, to follow from the fact that we lack certainty *vis-à-vis* our conceptions of the good. And we lack certainty (or should lack certainty) simply because we often lack the resources to persuade others of what we believe. So the reasonableness of pluralism is vindicated by lack of certainty. The second consideration concerns the scope of the indeterminacy of reason. Is this a doctrine that holds quite generally, or is it to be confined to conceptions of the good?

Take the first point first: the reasonableness of pluralism is supported by the fact that we cannot always persuade others of our beliefs, and the claim is that, since we cannot persuade others, we must lack certainty ourselves. However, this argument has its limitations. Very many questions concerning the use of public power can only be resolved with recourse to empirical claims about the world, and in many cases we will be *uncertain* about these claims. Consider the case of the sustainable use of resources. Any proposal for the use of political power to restrict current consumption in order to provide a just distribution of the Earth's resources over generations must confront the problem that we lack certainty about the consequences of current levels of consumption. We cannot know with certainty what the consequences of continuing to consume at current rates will be, and yet we do not deem that lack of certainty to be disabling in arriving at decisions about public policy. In brief, then, the indeterminacy of reason is differently understood in the different cases. Where conceptions of the good are involved, the claim is that any uncertainty, however small, is sufficient to legitimise the injustice of imposition; but where factual or scientific matters are concerned, the case appears to be different, and the standard of reason invoked is simply that one be 'certain enough' or that one follow, in Barry's phrase, 'the consensus of the scientific community'.[9]

One obvious response here is to note that liberal impartiality is meant to apply only to the procedures (often, constitutional procedures) by which public policy is decided. It is not necessarily meant to apply to the policies themselves. Thus, as long as the procedures by which environmental policies are arrived at can be justified without reference to a privileged conception of the good, the absence of certainty over the consequences of current consumption need not stymie policy making. This is the move made by Barry, who glosses the procedural requirements of neutrality as follows: 'decisions should be open to public debate, capable of being defended by rational arguments, and so on'.[10]

In citing 'rational arguments' and 'the consensus of the scientific community', Barry appears to be relying on a common-sense claim that the indeterminacy of reason (the reasonableness of pluralism) is confined to conceptions of the good, and this brings us on to the second question raised above: what is the scope of the doctrine of the indeterminacy of reason? If it is to be scepticism that grounds the injustice of imposition in cases of conceptions of the good, but that allows public policy to proceed where there is doubt about the facts of the matter, then it must be held that the indeterminacy of reason reigns over conceptions of the good, but does not apply to those beliefs about the world (and to rational argument in relation to that world) that are needed for decisions to be arrived at in areas such as intergenerational justice. However, in order to defend that contention, we need to be able to make a clear distinction between conceptions of the good on the one hand, and beliefs about the way the world is (scientific or factual beliefs) on the other.

The idea that there is such a distinction is flatly denied by some for whom science is on a par with ethics and aesthetics. 'Pragmatism', Richard Rorty writes,

> does not erect Science as an idol to fill the place once held by God. It views science as one genre of literature – or, put the other way around, literature and the arts as inquiries on the same footing as scientific enquiries [. . .] Physics is a way of trying to cope with various bits of the universe; ethics is a matter of trying to cope with other bits.[11]

So, for Rorty and those like him, the idea that science or rules of rational enquiry can be neutral is a mistake. There is no distinction between conceptions of the good and beliefs about the way the world is.

Rorty's stance is controversial, and it is open to the 'liberal impartialist' to disassociate herself from it. However, what might be taken to be the opposing view of the nature and status of science is no more supportive of the distinction that is needed to sustain the sceptical grounding of the injustice of imposition. Consider the argument that science is different; that it provides us with testable predictions (and unless it does so, it is not science); that (in relevant circumstances) we have reason to act in accordance with those beliefs that have withstood testing and the threat of being falsified. Such a view may be able to differentiate between conceptions of the good and 'scientific' beliefs. After all, the idea is to distinguish between the falsifiable predictions of science and other propositions (and, in so doing, to draw attention to closed systems). However, this view does not distinguish between these different kinds of claims in a way that allows the 'liberal impartialist' to call upon science as neutral.

The difficulty is that in adopting what we might call a 'positivist' conception of science, and in using the consensus of the scientific community as a touchstone for scientific results, the 'impartialist' threatens to undermine many conceptions of the good that include, or are underpinned by, different beliefs about the way the world is and about how we come to know how it is. The positivist conception of science will provide clear guidance on what is to count as 'evidence', as 'rational enquiry', and so on – guidance about which we cannot be certain, but the status of which can, on the positivist model, be distinguished from non-science, or pseudo-science. However, the declarations of this science may be challenged by, for example, Christian fundamentalists who regard the Bible stories of Noah's ark and of the destruction of Sodom and Gomorrah as providing evidence relevant to current decisions and the claims of future generations. In short, the positivist model provides the distinction between beliefs about the good and beliefs about the world, and it provides us with confidence in some beliefs of the latter kind; but it does so at a cost to impartiality.

The root of the problem lies with the interdependence of conceptions of the good and conceptions of how the world is. As Hilary Putnam notes in his discussion of Bernard Williams's views of truth in science and in ethics:

> Consider, for example, the question as to whether we can condemn the Aztec way of life, or, more specifically, the human sacrifice that the Aztecs engaged in. On Williams' view, the Aztec belief that there were supernatural beings who would be angry with the Aztecs if they did not perform the sacrifices was, as a matter of scientific fact, wrong. This belief we *can* evaluate. It is simply false. . . . But we cannot say that the Aztec way of life was wrong. Yet the feature of the Aztecs' way of life that troubles us (the human sacrifice) and their belief about the world that conflicts with science were interdependent. If we can say that the Aztec belief about the Gods was false, why can we not say that the practice to which it led was wrong?[12]

The issue, as is highlighted by this quotation, is that a Rortyan conception of science will not distinguish the status of 'scientific' and 'ethical' claims; but then it will also not provide the 'impartialist' with enough material to construct the decision procedures necessary for making public policy in contested areas. The positivist conception, by contrast, does distinguish between the two types of claims, but it delivers too much. It delivers the materials, but only by denying that they are contested.

Taken together, these arguments suggest that the indeterminacy of reason understood as delivering moderate scepticism plays different roles in different contexts. Specifically, lack of certainty is deemed sufficient to deliver the injustice of imposition in cases that concern conceptions of the good, but not in cases that concern facts about the way the world is. This is the force of the sustainability case. However, it is not clear that beliefs about the way the world is can be so sharply differentiated from beliefs about the good. This is the force of the examples of the fundamentalist Christian and the Aztec, and of the discussion of conceptions of science. The idea that there is *impartial* space in deliberating over procedures for a conception of 'rational argument' or for considering facts about the world is implausible. Any such space will be as infected with controversy and uncertainty as are disputes about the nature of the good.

Our concern is with the transition from the reasonableness of pluralism to the injustice of imposition. We have argued that the attempt to underpin this transition, and to justify the injustice of imposition, with moderate scepticism faces three obstacles. First, there is an interconnection between conceptions of the good and the epistemological status of conceptions of the good. This interconnection destabilises the distinction between the controversial and the comprehensive. The controversial claim of moderate scepticism undermines some conceptions of the good. Second, the proponents of scepticism must attribute very different standards of certainty in respect of beliefs about conceptions of the good and beliefs about the way the world is, yet the justification of there being such different standards is moot. Third, people's views about the way the world is will characteristically be influenced by their conceptions of the good. There is a two-way relationship between beliefs about the way the world is and conceptions of the good. In falling back on a particular picture of how the world is, the 'impartialist' must accept either that this is to fall back on just one view amongst many, or insist that it is the best view (of those currently available). In both cases the price paid for acquiring the injustice of imposition (if it can be acquired at all) is borne by the respect for pluralism.

Epistemology and the reasonableness of pluralism

We began by noting, with Rawls, that the aims of political philosophy depend upon the society it addresses, and that, in modern societies characterised by reasonable pluralism, one very important aim of political philosophy is to show how people may live together in conditions of justice and stability while subscribing to different, and conflicting, comprehensive conceptions of the good. We have further argued that, if scepticism delivers the injustice of imposition, it does so only by sacrificing respect for the significance and permanence of pluralism. In this section our question is, 'Can the method of avoidance fare any better?' Our argument is that it cannot because the conception of belief that it deploys, and that it needs in order to respect the significance and permanence of reasonable pluralism, is one that cannot, at the same time, show the injustice of imposition.

As we have seen, Rawls believes that pluralism is permanent because it is the outcome of the operation of reason under conditions of freedom. Additionally, he believes that pluralism is significant because, in the modern world, 'belief matters'. He writes:

> When moral philosophy began, say with Socrates, ancient religion was a civic religion of public social practice, of civic festivals and public celebrations. Moreover, this civic religious culture was not based on a sacred work like the Bible, or the Koran, or the Vedas of Hinduism. The Greeks celebrated Homer and the Homeric poems were a basic part of their education, but the Iliad and the Odyssey were never sacred texts. As long as one participated in the expected way and recognized the proprieties, the details of what one believed

were not of great importance. It was a matter of doing the done thing and being a trustworthy member of society, always ready to carry out one's civic duties as a good citizen – to serve on juries or to row in the fleet in war – when called upon to do so. It was not a religion of salvation in the Christian sense and there was no class of priests who dispensed the necessary means of grace; indeed the ideas of immortality and eternal salvation did not have a central place in classical culture.[13]

However, he goes on to argue that this early understanding has changed in two highly significant ways: first, the medieval period saw the rise of 'salvationist' conceptions of religion; second, the Reformation period witnessed the fragmentation of religion into distinct sects, each of which had its own view of the route to salvation. What we find, therefore, in the post-Reformation period is a dramatically altered conception of the significance of religious belief, which comes to be, no longer a matter of indifference, but a matter of supreme importance on which depends one's prospects of attaining life everlasting. Moreover, Rawls argues that the significance accorded to belief in this period has survived into the modern age and has become a central feature of modernity. So, if the aims of political philosophy depend on the society it addresses, then modern political philosophy is faced with the task of demonstrating the injustice of imposition in a world in which (reasonable) pluralism is permanent and in which belief matters.

It is against this background that Rawls now advocates the method of avoidance (epistemological restraint). It is because pluralism is permanent and because belief matters that a truly 'impartialist liberalism' must remain agnostic both about comprehensive conceptions and about their epistemological or metaphysical underpinnings. But if belief matters, in what sense exactly does it matter, and what kind of defence of 'impartialist liberalism' can be generated from the contention that belief matters?

One way of answering this question may be found by turning to the philosophy of John Locke. In *Political Liberalism*, Rawls refers approvingly to Locke's defence of toleration, and it is not difficult to see the parallels between that defence and Rawls's own endorsement of epistemological restraint: both writers eschew a defence of toleration grounded in scepticism; both insist on the significance of individual belief; both insist that the state must remain agnostic about questions of truth and falsity. Crucially, for our purposes, however, Locke's defence of toleration contains within it an argument for the significance of belief. It gives us a sense in which 'belief matters'. Locke writes: 'No man can, if he would, conform his faith to the dictates of another. All the life and power of true religion consists in the inward and full persuasion of the mind; and faith is not faith without believing.'[14] So, in the religious context, belief matters because the faith that is required for salvation is a faith that depends crucially upon the individual's recognising and acknowledging something for himself.

Moreover, the importance of believing for oneself (of the 'inward and full persuasion of the mind') is not restricted to the religious context, but is a specific case of Locke's more general epistemology as given in the *Essay on Human Understanding*, where he writes:

> For I think we may as rationally hope to see with other Men's Eyes, as to know by other Mens Understandings. So much we ourselves consider and comprehend of Truth and Reason, so much we possess of Real and True Knowledge. The floating of other Mens Opinions in our brains makes us not a jot more knowing, though they happen to be true. What in them was Science, in us is but Opiniatrety, whilst we give up our assent to reverend Names and do not, as they did, employ our own Reason to understand those Truths, which gave them reputation . . . In the Sciences, everyone has so much, as he really knows and comprehends: what he believes only and takes upon trust, are but shreads . . . Such borrowed Wealth, like Fairy-Money, though it were Gold in the hand from which he received it, will be but Leaves and Dust when it comes to use.[15]

So, our question is 'Why does belief matter?' and Locke's answer is that, in the religious context, it matters because it is only sincere and inner belief that is pleasing to God, and the state lacks the means to coerce such belief. Hence the futility of persecution designed to save the soul of the heretic. However, and for Locke, the religious case is not unique, for in all other contexts, too, it is important that we come to see things for ourselves and not rely on the opinion of others, or take things on trust.

As a piece of epistemology, Locke's story is highly implausible, for it is surely the case that, especially in science, we do take things on trust, and indeed we often (perhaps usually) have no choice but to do so. Beliefs about the way the world works, its construction and composition, rest on complex scientific considerations, and in the modern world there can be few, if any, who are in a position to 'find out for themselves' before taking penicillin for example, or sending the car to the garage. These are areas where we cannot sensibly expect to be able to do anything other than take things on trust. Additionally, it might be thought that, even in the area of the moral, we sometimes both can and should take things on trust. Annette Baier's recent work in moral philosophy mounts a very powerful case for the indispensability of trust in moral contexts,[16] and, as we have seen, Hilary Putnam has gone yet further, urging that the very distinction between what we accept as scientific fact and what we believe to be morally right is less clear than is often supposed. So, as an epistemological claim, Locke's theory is suspect in three distinct ways: it is not a theory that can plausibly be defended in the area of science; it is contentious even in the area of the moral; and in any case the moral and the scientific are intertwined.

However, we will not dwell on these objections, important though they are, for our main aim is not to cast doubt on Locke's claim that belief matters, but rather to establish whether there is an interpretation of it that shows how the reasonableness of pluralism can lead to the injustice of imposition. It is, after all, in this context that Rawls insists that the modern world is one in which 'belief matters', and what we therefore need is not a set of objections to that claim but, if possible, a plausible interpretation of it. To this end, we will examine the defence of toleration that follows from Locke's concept of belief. Famously, Locke claims that coercion works by operating on a person's will. That is to say, in coercing someone we attempt to influence their decision-making via threats or inducements. However, he goes on to insist that belief is not subject to the will. That is to say, I cannot alter my beliefs simply by deciding to change them, or willing that they change. It then follows that all attempts to coerce religious conformity are strictly irrational, since they involve deploying means utterly inappropriate for the desired end. They are an attempt to change belief by changing the will; but belief is not subject to the will. Waldron puts the matter this way:

> Laws, Locke says, are of no force without penalties and the whole point of penalties is to bring pressure to bear on people's decision-making by altering the pay-offs for various courses of action so that willing one particular course of action (the act required or prohibited by law) becomes more or less attractive to the agent than it would otherwise be. But this sort of pressurizing is crazy in cases of action which men are incapable of performing no matter how attractive the pay-off or unattractive the consequences. Sincerely believing a proposition that one takes to be false is an action in this category . . . the imposition of belief, then, by civil law has been shown to be an absurdity.[17]

Again, we are not here concerned with whether or not Locke's position is a plausible one. There are certainly reasons for doubting that it is, and some of those reasons are given by Waldron in the article quoted from above. What does concern us, rather, is the *kind* of defence of toleration that Locke's theory, if true, would support. And here there are reasons for thinking that it cannot deliver a principled defence, but only, and at most, a *modus vivendi*.

This general point is noted by a number of commentators, but comes in different guises. Thus, Waldron notes that, by insisting on the irrationality of persecution, Locke ignores entirely the question of whether and why persecution is morally wrong. He writes: 'what one misses above all in Locke's argument is a sense that there is anything morally wrong with intolerance, or a sense of any deep concern for the victims of persecution or the moral insult that is involved in the attempt to manipulate their faith'.[18] Similarly, Paul Kelly concludes his discussion of Locke with the reflection that: 'In the "Two Tracts" Locke suggested that toleration would invite anarchy and disorder, in the "Essay" and "Letter" he argued that toleration of practices consistent with civil order was most likely to contribute to peace and stability. In each case what differs is the perception of the threat posed to the social order, and the policy most likely to remedy it. There is no attempt to advance a principled argument for toleration as a necessary component of the good society.'[19] And again, Russell Hardin claims that 'Locke did not

assert fairness as a prior or trumping principle against any particular religious value. Rather, he argued for accommodation as a practical antecedent
to achieving any religious value. It is the practical consideration of opposing forces that makes agreement to less than one's full theory of the good
reasonable.'[20]

What all this suggests is that Locke's defence of toleration, based as it is
in an epistemological premise, cannot deliver a moral conclusion. At best,
it will explain why persecution may be irrational, ineffective, or a waste of
time; but it will be impotent to explain its moral wrongness or injustice.
The injunction to refrain from persecution, not because it is wrong, but
because it is irrational, looks very much like a *modus vivendi* account, and
the more so if we concede to Waldron the further claim that, even if coercion cannot operate directly on belief, it can easily operate on the epistemic
apparatus surrounding belief:

> suppose the religious authorities know that there are certain books that would
> be sufficient, if read, to shake the faith of an otherwise orthodox population.
> Then, although again people's beliefs cannot be controlled directly by coercive
> means, those who wield political power can put it to work indirectly to rein-
> force belief by banning everyone on pain of death from reading or obtaining
> copies of these heretical tomes. Such means may well be efficacious, even
> though they are intolerant and oppressive, and Locke, who is concerned only
> with the rationality of persecution, provides no argument against them.[21]

Recall that the motivation for this discussion of Locke is to try to find
an interpretation of the claim that 'belief matters' that will sustain the fact
of pluralism while simultaneously showing the injustice of imposition. And
the charge that successive commentators level against Locke is that his
account is impotent to do the latter. As an account of why belief matters it
is suspect; but even if its understanding of belief were correct, it still would
not deliver the right kind of defence of toleration, because it cannot show
why imposing one's views on those who do not concur with them is morally
objectionable. It can only, and at most, show why such imposition is ineffective, imprudent, or irrational.

If correct, then this conclusion has important implications for the general
(Rawlsian) project of attempting to defend impartial theories of justice via
epistemological abstinence, for what is suggested here is that to the extent
that epistemological abstinence is indeed an *epistemological* position, it
cannot sustain a defence of toleration as a requirement of justice. This is
the burden of all the comments referred to above. Epistemology shows us
only, and at most, why a particular policy of persecution might be ineffective or irrational; it cannot show us why it might be morally wrong. So, in
the modern context, if we interpret the claim that 'belief matters' as a
Lockean claim about the epistemic conditions of belief, then we have no
more than a *modus vivendi* defence of toleration.

Conclusion

Our aim in this chapter has been to ask how the injustice of imposition might follow from the reasonableness of pluralism, and we have considered several epistemological arguments designed to effect the transition. The argument from scepticism has been rejected both because it exacts heavy existential costs and because it requires belief to play different roles in different contexts – something that it cannot do given the difficulty inherent in distinguishing between facts on the one hand, and conceptions of the good on the other. Epistemological restraint is also problematic because it rests upon a conception of belief, and an understanding of how belief matters, that can deliver only a *modus vivendi* defence of toleration. The argument from epistemological restraint cannot tell us why imposition is unjust as distinct from imprudent. If these arguments are persuasive, then they suggest that the move from the permanence of pluralism to the injustice of imposition is one that requires, not an epistemological, but a moral foundation. To say this is, of course, to say nothing about the nature of that moral argument; it is only to suggest that, without some moral argument or other, 'impartialist liberalism' cannot adequately address the problem of modernity, which is to show that, in a world characterised by pluralism, imposition is not merely inefficacious, but unjust.[22]

Notes

This chapter originated in conversations at the University of Michigan, Ann Arbor, where we gave separate papers to a seminar on religious toleration. We are grateful to Stephen Darwall and Edwin Curley for the invitation to that seminar. Earlier versions of our joint efforts resulted in a paper at the University of Hull and the University of Southampton. Our thanks to the participants on those occasions, and to Catriona McKinnon for very helpful written comments.
 1 J. Rawls, *Collected Papers*, ed. S. Freeman (Cambridge, MA: Harvard University Press, 1999), pp. 421–48.
 2 J. Rawls, *Political Liberalism* (Columbia, NY: Columbia University Press, 1993), pp. 55–8.
 3 *Ibid.*, pp. 56–7.
 4 *Ibid.*, p. xxiv.
 5 B. Barry, *Justice as Impartiality* (Oxford: Oxford University Press, 1995).
 6 *Ibid.*, p. 174.
 7 *Ibid.*, p. 179.
 8 C. Taylor, *Sources of the Self: The Making of the Modern Identity* (Cambridge: Cambridge University Press, 1989), p. 18.
 9 Barry, *Justice as Impartiality*, p. 161n.
10 *Ibid.*, p. 161.
11 R. Rorty, *Consequences of Pragmatism* (Brighton: Harvester Press, 1982), p. xliii.
12 H. Putnam, *Renewing Philosophy* (Cambridge, MA: Harvard University Press, 1992), p. 106.

13 Rawls, *Political Liberalism*, p. xxi.
14 J. Horton and S. Mendus (eds), *John Locke: A Letter Concerning Toleration in Focus* (London: Routledge, 1991), p. 18.
15 J. Locke, *An Essay Concerning Human Understanding*, ed. P. Nidditch (Oxford: Oxford University Press, 1975), I. iv. 23.
16 A. Baier, *Moral Prejudices: Essays on Ethics* (Cambridge, MA: Harvard University Press, 1994), pp. 95–202.
17 J. Waldron, 'Locke: Toleration and the rationality of persecution', in Horton and Mendus (eds), *John Locke*, pp. 98–124, at p. 104.
18 *Ibid.*, p. 120.
19 P. Kelly, 'John Locke: Authority, conscience and religious toleration', in Horton and Mendus (eds), *John Locke*, pp. 125–46, at p. 144.
20 P. Kelly, *Impartiality, Neutrality and Justice* (Edinburgh: Edinburgh University Press, 1998), p. 149.
21 Waldron, 'Locke: Toleration and the rationality of persecution', pp. 116–17.
22 Our separate, and rather different, attempts to provide such a moral foundation may be found in M. Matravers, *Justice and Punishment: The Rationale of Coercion* (Oxford: Oxford University Press, 2000) and S. Mendus, *Impartiality in Moral and Political Philosophy* (Oxford: Oxford University Press, 2002).

3
Toleration and the character of pluralism

Catriona McKinnon

This chapter addresses two influential ways of thinking about which political principles we ought to adopt. The first way of thinking starts with expectations about how persons ought to relate to one another in political discourse. Political principles are justified by reference to these expectations. The second way of thinking starts with certain values around which, it is claimed, people ought to structure their lives. Political principles are then justified by reference to these values. These approaches to political justification are in competition, and arguments for political principles of toleration and beyond can be made on either approach.

In the work of John Rawls we find an example of the first, 'constructivist', approach. Constructivist values are taken to be appropriate in political justification because people exercising their practical reason to solve shared problems of justice would be committed to these values. Constructivist justificatory values are the values of people who aim at peaceful co-existence and profitable cooperation in political society. Different accounts of what counts as peaceful co-existence and, especially, profitable cooperation yield different constructivist values.[1] I shall offer an interpretation of Rawls whereby political principles of toleration and beyond are justified in virtue of the legitimate expectation that citizens themselves move beyond toleration in their political discourse by engaging with one another in public reason.

In the work of Joseph Raz we find an advocate of the second, 'perfectionist', approach. Perfectionist justificatory values are to be found in a true moral theory, or true faith, and are claimed to be appropriate as justificatory values in virtue of their place in a true moral theory, or true faith. Raz argues for multiculturalist political principles that transcend toleration by appeal to the perfectionist value of personal autonomy. On this approach, we start with values embedded in a true moral theory and justify political principles by reference to these values, independent of the expectations we have of those to whom the principles are justified.

My argument will be that one way of pinpointing what is at issue between perfectionist and constructivist political justifications is to examine assumptions about the *character* of pluralism that inform each approach. These assumptions relate to the interpersonal attitudes we can expect of people facing shared problems of justice in conditions of pluralism. I shall argue that these assumptions are not implicit in – and cannot be derived from – assumptions about the *nature* of pluralism, but must instead be argued for separately. If, as Raz thinks, the most we can expect of persons in pluralism is toleration, then the justification of political principles beyond toleration – for example, his multiculturalist principles – cannot be constructed from expectations about the interpersonal attitudes people will adopt in pluralism. This makes sense of Raz's perfectionist appeal to a true moral theory to support justificatory values beyond political toleration. Raz drives a wedge between what we can expect of persons and what we can justify as a matter of political principle with certain claims about the inevitability and appropriateness of conflict and hostility between people facing political problems, whereas these assumptions are absent from Rawls's constructivism. If Raz's claims are true then Rawls's approach is undermined, because the expectations of persons upon which it relies are unrealistic or inappropriate. If the most that can be expected of citizens is toleration then the logic of an appeal to perfectionist values to justify political principles beyond toleration is clarified and the perfectionist approach to political justification becomes more attractive.

Let me clear the ground for this argument by making some brief remarks, in the next section, on the relationship between toleration *qua* personal attitude and toleration *qua* political principle.

Toleration: political and personal

Toleration can be conceived as a personal attitude or as a political principle. All defences of toleration as a personal attitude or as a political principle consist of arguments to show that toleration is the appropriate response to people who differ from us, and whom we dislike or of whom we disapprove.

The object of toleration in the personal and political spheres is a disliked or disapproved of person. Persons to be tolerated can differ from us in terms of their values, practices, beliefs, ends, forms of community and association, dispositions, tastes, or preferences. By placing the personal and political concepts of toleration on spectrums of possible responses to disliked and disapproved of people we can clarify what toleration demands. On each scale, toleration marks a substantial shift of principle or attitude; each stage subsequent to toleration should be thought of as transcending the previous stage. Each stage represents a more positive set of responses to disliked and disapproved of differences than the preceding stage.

Toleration as a political principle

Repression

Perhaps the historically most common political response to disliked and disapproved of people has been the attempt to crush them, repress them, or drive them out. Principles of repression are sometimes accompanied by a denial that the disliked and disapproved of person differs, deep down, from the repressor. But repression born of the denial of difference repudiates its own basis, as repression would be unnecessary if it were true that difference did not exist. However, not all political repression need contradict its own basis. Repressive states can admit the existence of disliked and disapproved of people and attempt to justify their repression of these people by asserting the superiority of a world in which these people cease to differ from their repressors, and the acceptability of the use of state coercion to bring about this state of affairs.

Official discouragement

Political agents who agree that a world free of disliked or disapproved of people is a better world, but who shrink from repression and the coercion required to create this world, might adopt a policy of official discouragement. Here the attempt is to impede access to ways of life incorporating the disliked or disapproved of differences without repressing people who already practise these ways of life. We can see the distinction between repression and official discouragement by considering certain policies towards homosexuality. The UK legislation overturned by the 1959 Wolfenden Report was repressive: in making homosexual sex between men a crime this legislation aimed at preventing the practice of this kind of sex between existing gay men with the coercive power of the law. But there are ways of being intolerant of homosexual people without attempting to repress them, as evinced in Section 28 of the Local Government Bill in the UK.[2] Section 28 does not explicitly attempt to repress homosexual activity between gay people but aims instead to restrict the flow of information about homosexuality, and thereby indirectly to discourage young and closeted people from reflecting on their sexual preferences.

Toleration

Toleration of disliked or disapproved of people requires refraining from repression and official discouragement of the practices constitutive of these differences. Because interference can take the form of direct coercion, as in the case of repression, or insidious distortion, as in the case of discouragement, a political principle of toleration demands refraining from both. Principles of toleration are adopted by states when they refuse to interfere with peoples' pursuit of life styles associated with the disliked or disapproved of differences by means of force or propaganda. But a tolerant society need not be one in which people who differ from the majority in disliked or disapproved of ways are invited to participate in the major political and social institutions of that society. The political principle of toleration is negative: it demands restraint with respect to the use of state power as it affects people who lead lives disliked or disapproved of by the majority, or by those with the most political power. Of course, no thinker recommends that the scope of political toleration be unlimited. Dislike and disapproval are often responses to aspects of persons causing genuine harm to others, or to society. To accommodate these cases many thinkers use a 'harm principle' to set the limits of toleration; where they disagree is on what constitutes harm.

Political inclusion

Toleration only demands action when abstention has not been observed, so as to put right the wrongs of official discouragement or repression. But political responses to disliked and disapproved of people can go beyond toleration. In addition to refraining from using political means to interfere with citizens' pursuit of disliked and disapproved of lifestyles, the state can also attempt to include these people in its major political, social and economic institutions. This principle can be used to justify equal opportunities legislation, including policies of positive discrimination and quota systems. It can also underpin certain policies in education such as citizenship education, which asks that children be made to cultivate a range of skills necessary for good citizenship and a healthy degree of participation and interest in the political life of their society. Most non-libertarian political philosophers endorse some principles of political inclusion.

Official promotion

A final possibility is that the state actively promotes the differences that prompt dislike and disapproval in the institutions of civil society. Policies designed to preserve minority languages, to protect opportunity for religious worship and traditional dress through restrictions on employment legislation and schooling requirements, and to enable same-sex and religion-based polygamous marriages can all be justified by reference to principles of official promotion. Official promotion is a strong principle variously defended as demanded by equal opportunity for self-respect, a concern for the conditions of personal autonomy, equal concern and respect, and recognition of relationship between individual freedom and an agent's social context, and other liberal and communitarian ideals.

Personal toleration

Repression

As at the political level, a common response to disliked and disapproved of people at the personal level is an attempt to repress them. Repression is often motivated by hatred of others, disgust at their way of life, or simple indifference towards them. However, repression is also sometimes practised in the name of the salvation, character, or well-being of the repressed person. As at the political level, repression at the personal level is sometimes accompanied by the claim that the repressed person is actually no different at heart from the repressor, and is contradictory in the same way.

Toleration

The personal attitude of toleration demands a principled refusal to interfere with disliked or disapproved of people so as to change the aspects of the person that prompt dislike or disapproval.[3] The personal attitude of toleration demands the principled avoidance of the use of force against persons to eradicate their disliked or disapproved of differences. It also prohibits the use of propaganda at the personal level. As well as refraining from physical coercion as a way of changing the disliked or disapproved aspects of a person, the tolerant person does not engage in verbal bullying of people whom she dislikes and of whom she disapproves. This is not to say that the tolerant person does not attempt to persuade the person whom she tolerates of the error of her ways. But there is an important difference (often hard to discern) between persuasion and harassment. Anti-abortionists who picket abortion clinics may conceive of themselves as attempting to persuade women entering the clinics of the error of their ways; but arguably they are actually harassing these women. Although personal toleration is compatible with attempts at persuasion, such engagement is not demanded by personal toleration. People can exhibit the virtue of toleration by simply minding their own business. As at the political level, no thinker argues that toleration at the personal level is appropriate with respect to all disliked and disapproved of people. Some disliked and disapproved of people are intolerable.

Engagement

Moving beyond toleration, the next level of response to disliked and disapproved of people is an attempt to engage with them as disliked and disapproved of people (i.e. without denial of their differences). The attitude of engagement demands that a person attempt to understand the values, practices, beliefs, ends, forms of community and association, dispositions, tastes, or preferences of people whom she dislikes and of whom she disapproves, either by attempting to engage them in some kind of discussion about their differences, or by imaginatively reconstructing their point of view. Engagement requires empathy and an attempt at interpretation of the other person's situation so as to understand the meaning of the symbols, practices, exchanges, and language that constitute that situation. But a person's engagement with another does not require that she come to a complete understanding of the person whom she dislikes and of whom she disapproves, let alone that she overcome her dislike or disapproval.

Engagement simply requires that a person genuinely attempt to understand the disliked and disapproved of other in terms of her beliefs, motivations, the relationship between her beliefs and motivations, her history, her biography, her self-image, and her values.

As with toleration, it is not the case that engagement is always appropriate. The limits of engagement might be set with the harm principle associated with toleration (remembering that engagement transcends toleration) in conjunction with some 'comprehensibility' principle. The comprehensibility principle would establish the extent to which persons can, or ought to, engage with disliked and disapproved of others by specifying the points at which another's beliefs or behaviour become incomprehensible. Some insane people might be beyond the limits of engagement in virtue of their cognitive disorder; some very evil people might exceed these limits in virtue of the monstrous nature of their values and preferences.

Appreciation
The final level of personal response to difference asks that people overcome their dislike of one another even in the face of their disapproval of one another. Friendship, family relations, and relations of love can all involve attitudes of appreciation. Appreciation does not demand that a person deny her differences with others. Such denials are damaging; when one person subsumes her identity in the identity of another it is a sign of an unhealthy relationship, not devoted love.

With these rough scales of response to difference in place, we can isolate three key questions of political justification:

1 What sorts of political principles are justified in conditions of permanent pluralism?
2 What sorts of personal attitudes can we legitimately expect people to adopt in response to one another in conditions of permanent pluralism?
3 How, if at all, do the attitudes specified in (2) affect the justification of principles specified in (1)?

With respect to (1), no political philosopher on the contemporary scene defends political principles of repression. Some thinkers defend political principles of official discouragement, but such defences are rare. Most contemporary political philosophers defend some principles of toleration, and all non-libertarian liberal thinkers defend some principles beyond toleration. The principles specified in answer to (1) will in some part provide an answer to (2): people ought to adopt those attitudes demanded by the political principles of (1). With respect to question (3), one way of seeing how the attitudes specified in answer to (2) must affect the principles specified in answer to (1) is through examination of the argument for political toleration from pluralism. This argument purports to justify political principles of toleration without reference to personal attitudes of toleration, and by reference only to the *incommensurable nature* of the differences that contribute to pluralism. In criticism of this argument I shall show that some assumptions about citizens' personal attitudes must be made before political toleration can be claimed to be appropriate. Revealing these assumptions shows that reflections on the nature of pluralism are a red herring with respect to arguments for political toleration: in making such arguments, we must focus instead on the character of pluralism.

Toleration and the nature of pluralism

Pluralism is a view about the nature of the differences between people to which personal attitudes and political principles of toleration respond. Pluralists argue that many differences between values, ends and options are incommensurable in two important senses. First, many different values, practices, ends, or forms of association are not realisable within the life of a single person or a single community (the thesis of practical incompatibility). And second, it makes no sense, or is inappropriate, to compare many different values, practices, ends or forms of association in terms of their value (the thesis of evaluative incomparability).[4] For Raz, the 'mark of incommensurability' is a failure of transitivity with respect to the value of certain options (ends, values, practices, etc.).[5]

> Two valuable options are incommensurable if (1) neither is better than the other, and (2) there is (or could be) another option that is better than one but is not better than the other.[6]

Taking two options, A and B, the failure of transitivity in (1) shows that A and B *per se* cannot compared in terms of their value, and the failure of transitivity in (2) shows that there is no master-value C that enables comparison of A and B in terms of their value. Raz's account of evaluative incomparability improves on Isaiah Berlin's famous account. Berlin took the denial of evaluative incomparability to entail the assertion of a master-value making possible evaluative comparisons. But Raz makes it clear that options are incommensurable both when they cannot be ranked by reference to a master-value, and when they simply cannot be ranked.[7] The denial of evaluative incomparability does not entail the assertion of a master-value.

The argument from pluralism for political principles of toleration is as follows:

1 Given incommensurability conflict between those with different ends and values is a permanent feature of the world.
2 Given incommensurability it is illegitimate to impose certain values and ends on people by restricting their negative liberty in such a way as to force or encourage the adoption of other preferred values and ends.[8]
3 Therefore, repression and official discouragement are illegitimate. Political principles of toleration are the least to which we ought to be committed.

The argument is that if differences between people are inevitable and incommensurable then political principles of toleration will always be necessary to ensure that those with power do not use coercive force or propaganda to attempt illegitimately to eradicate those who differ from them. Political principles of toleration are necessary for preserving peace, stability and justice between people divided by incommensurable differences.[9] This argument for toleration only succeeds given a commitment to individual freedom as negative in Berlin's sense.[10] As my interest here is in the liberal tradition, and all liberals place some value on negative liberty, I will not address this commitment (although we might ask what the truth of the thesis of evaluative incomparability would add to the normative injunction in (2)). Instead, I want to focus on a more serious flaw in the argument.

Political toleration is a response to disliked and disapproved of differences. However, the argument from pluralism does not establish that incommensurable differences will prompt dislike or disapproval. The two theses of incommensurability appearing as premises in the argument from pluralism assert the existence of ineradicable and evaluatively incomparable differences: they address the *nature* of pluralism. What they do not establish is the *character* of the disagreements between those separated by incommensurable differences. It could be the case that the two theses of incommensurability are true and yet political toleration is unnecessary: those separated by incommensurable differences might not dislike and disapprove of one another. Or it could be the case that the two theses of incommensurability are false and political toleration is necessary: those separated by commensurable differences might dislike and disapprove of one another. Given that the two theses of incommensurability do not establish that those separated by incommensurable differences will dislike and disapprove of one another, the argument for toleration from pluralism is a red herring. To understand the need for toleration, and the prospects for transcending it, requires an account of the character of pluralism. The focus of this account will be what personal attitudes towards disliked and disapproved of others can reasonably be expected of people. All arguments for political principles of toleration and beyond must operate with some assumptions about the character of pluralism. Examination of these assumptions as they appear in the work of Rawls and Raz explains their different approaches to the justification of political principles.

The character of pluralism: the Rawlsian picture

On Rawls's view, the values of political justification are derived from the exercise of persons' practical reason as it addresses principles securing the conditions for peaceful and profitable cooperation in political society. According to Rawls, people so conceived will address one another in public reason when attempting to solve their political problems. Rawls's conception of justice is justified to the extent that these expectations are legitimate.

The only resources Rawls has for political justification are these expectations; Rawls denies that he need invoke any values beyond these expectations in order to justify his political principles. For citizens to address one
another in public reason demands that they move beyond the personal
attitude of toleration to attitudes of engagement.

For Rawls, a stable and just society is one in which there is an overlapping consensus among reasonable citizens on a conception of justice. Given
the fact that pluralism is permanent, this conception of justice cannot
be justified by reference to any one comprehensive moral, religious, or
philosophical doctrine. Citizens who differ on questions of doctrine can
nevertheless reach an overlapping consensus on a conception of justice by
debating political questions in public reason. When citizens address one
another in public reason they present their proposals to one another in
terms that they reasonably expect one another to understand and accept,
and are disposed to act on proposals agreed in public reason, given the
assurance that all other citizens will also act on these principles: 'The point
of the ideal of public reason is that citizens are to conduct their fundamental
discussions within the framework of what each regards as a political conception of justice based on values that others can reasonably be expected
to endorse, and each is, in good faith, prepared to defend that conception
so understood.'[11]

When citizens achieve the ideal of public reason they 'think of themselves
as if they were legislators' in order to consider which principles and
policies they would adopt using public reason.[12] If they find a discrepancy
between the principles and policies they would adopt in public reason, and
the principles and policies adopted by their actual political representatives,
then they have a duty to use democratic means to change the way in which
their representatives legislate.

Rawls's public reason demands a personal attitude of engagement
because it is realised in a process of deliberation between citizens. For a
person to determine how to present her political proposals in public reason,
where these proposals are informed by her religious, moral and philosophical beliefs, requires that she attempt to understand the religious, moral and
philosophical beliefs informing the political proposals of others. Until she
engages with others in this way she cannot engage in public reason. Admit-
tedly, the degree of personal engagement demanded by Rawls's ideal of
public reason is limited to the political sphere. But given that citizens' political proposals are informed by their non-political values and beliefs, public
reason can demand a substantial degree of engagement with others on
non-political issues.[13] 'When citizens deliberate, they exchange views and
debate their supporting reasons concerning public political questions. They
suppose that their political opinions may be revised by discussion with other
citizens: and therefore these opinions are not simply a fixed outcome of
their existing private or nonpolitical interests.'[14]

Rawls's description of how overlapping consensus might arise reveals a dynamic conception of relations between citizens in political community. In discussion of the sixteenth-century wars of religion he claims that the resolution of these wars with principles of religious toleration was not a result of an overlapping consensus on these principles, but rather the result of a certain balance of power (and some exhaustion) establishing a *modus vivendi*.[15] Rawls argues that it is possible to move from such a *modus vivendi*, via a constitutional consensus, to an overlapping consensus, and that moving through these stages of consensus stimulates important changes in citizens' attitudes to one another.[16]

In a *modus vivendi*, citizens exhausted by war acquiesce to certain political principles of toleration. Recognising that these principles secure the important good of political stability for themselves and those they care for, citizens reach a constitutional consensus by coming to agree on liberal political principles guaranteeing certain basic political rights necessary for safeguarding democratic electoral procedures. Consensus on such a constitution requires the limited use of public reason: citizens affirm the constitution as a good for themselves and their fellow citizens, disregarding the balance of power between them.

The move from constitutional to overlapping consensus involves a broadening of the scope of the consensus and a deepening of the relations between the conception of justice and citizens' conceptions of the good.[17] Once stable constitutional consensus is established, citizens make their political claims through the democratic procedures established by the constitution. Within the framework of minimal political rights necessary for a stable democracy, citizens discuss wider and more controversial questions of political inclusion and official encouragement. These involve a discussion of the distribution of rights to freedom of thought, expression and association *per se*, questions of distributive justice, the distribution of power and opportunity in society, and access to the social bases of self-respect. Citizens addressing one another in public reason on these questions of political inclusion and official encouragement must engage with one another on a level deeper than that required by stable constitutional consensus, because the questions of justice they discuss intersect with their comprehensive doctrines to a much greater degree than constitutional essentials. For example, in a diverse society there is likely to be far more disagreement over the appropriate patterns of economic redistribution than over the principle of universal suffrage. Overlapping consensus emerges when citizens agree on principles of justice to govern, not just the distribution of political rights attaching to democratic procedures, but also matters relating to the basic structure of society: its main political, social, and economic institutions.[18] Citizens moving towards overlapping consensus on political principles beyond toleration must adopt personal attitudes of engagement that demand more than toleration.[19]

To sum up, the fact that Rawls's central justificatory tool – public reason – requires engagement on the part of citizens separated by differences shows that Rawls conceives of the ideal character of pluralism as non-hostile. Hostility involves a turning away from or rejection of another person: those separated by differences prompting hostility cannot engage in public reason. Debate in Rawls's public reason is only possible between those who differ – often to the extent of disliking and disapproving of one another – yet who are willing to make attempts at interpretation and understanding. The success of Rawlsian political justification relies on the claim that citizens ought to adopt attitudes of engagement. If it can be shown that citizens are incapable of adopting these attitudes, or ought not to adopt them, then the justification of liberal principles must proceed according to a different model.

The character of pluralism: the Razian picture

Raz's argument for political principles beyond toleration invokes the value of personal autonomy rather than the expectation that individuals themselves move beyond the personal attitude of toleration. On Raz's view, an appeal to perfectionist values in political justification is necessary because the *competitive character* of pluralism makes any expectations that people move beyond the personal attitude of toleration illegitimate. If this is true then our expectations of persons ought not to inform our justification of political principles beyond toleration, and Rawlsian constructivism in political justification is called into question.

> Competitive pluralism not only admits the validity of distinct and incompatible moral virtues, but also of virtues which tend, given human nature, to encourage intolerance of other virtues. That is, competitive pluralism admits the value of virtues possession of which normally leads to a tendency not to suffer certain limitations in other people which are themselves inevitable if those people possess certain other, equally valid, virtues.[20]

The two theses of incommensurability asserted by Raz establish the inevitability of differences between persons in possession of different sets of virtues, and that evaluative comparisons between the options to which these virtues attach is often inappropriate. The claim that Raz adds to these theses with his characterisation of pluralism as competitive is that these conflicts will be accompanied by certain 'appropriate emotional or attitudinal concomitants or components' that make personal attitudes of engagement inappropriate.[21] This is a claim about the *character*, rather than the nature, of pluralism.

> Conflict is endemic . . . pluralists can step back from their personal commitments and appreciate in the abstract the value of other ways of life and their attendant virtues. But this acknowledgement coexists with, and cannot replace, the feelings of rejection and dismissiveness towards what one knows is in itself

valuable. Tension is an inevitable concomitant of accepting the truth of value pluralism.[22]

Raz thinks that in conditions of competitive pluralism the most we can legitimately ask of people whose ineradicable conflict with one another reaches beyond their values, beliefs, practices etc. to their moral emotions is the personal attitude of toleration. Given that the moral emotions attaching to conflicts between incommensurables are, according to Raz, entirely appropriate and not to be revised once an all-things-considered judgement about the conflict has been made by the agent, we cannot expect more of people than that they refrain from acting on these emotions.

Raz claims: 'I am not simply wrong in inclining to be intolerant of another person's meanness or vulgarity. These rightly trigger intolerant responses. A person who does not react to them in this way is lacking in moral sensibility. Yet it is a response which should be curbed.'[23]

It is important to note that by characterising pluralism as competitive Raz is not simply making the claim that engagement has limits. All thinkers can agree on this point. By registering the sorts of differences that Raz thinks breed appropriate hostility it becomes clear that he conceives of pluralism as competitive both at the edges and at the centre. Ordinary vices like vulgarity, cultural differences, and even professional differences are Raz's examples of characteristics for which 'attitudunal concomitants' of hostility are appropriate.[24] Hostility in Raz's competitive pluralism is not simply reserved – as it should be – for very bad people. Hostility permeates relations between those with different cultures, religions, professions, and weaknesses.

If toleration is the most we can ask of people as a personal attitude in conditions of competitive pluralism, can political principles beyond toleration be justified? Not on a model of political justification whereby principles are constructed from our reasonable expectations of citizens. But once the justification of political principles is detached from what we can legitimately expect of citizens, political principles beyond toleration become justifiable even when we can expect nothing but toleration from citizens.

Raz's argument for political principles of official encouragement – his multiculturalism – does not rely on the expectation that individuals as citizens ought to cultivate attitudes of engagement.[25] Raz's argument for multiculturalism is consistent with the possibility that no person adopts an attitude of engagement towards those whom she dislikes and of whom she disapproves. Rather than offering multiculturalist principles as the object of an overlapping consensus between citizens discussing political questions in public reason, Raz argues for these principles by reference to the value of protecting the conditions of personal autonomy for all, which he takes to be a political value independent of expectations about how citizens ought to regard this value.[26] Raz conceives of personal autonomy as achievable only in conditions in which a person has a certain minimum of mental faculties, a variety of adequate options from which to choose goals that will contribute to her well-being, and a degree of freedom from coercion. A principle of toleration (the 'harm principle') ensures freedom from coercion, and multiculturalist principles protect a variety of meaningful cultural options.

Raz's characterisation of pluralism as inevitably, appropriately and deeply competitive makes the expectation that citizens move beyond the personal attitude of toleration in their political discourse illegitimate. This characterisation of pluralism forces liberals to adopt forms of political justification that trace connections between moral values and political principles independent of the question of what sorts of attitudes we can expect from citizens.

If Rawls is right about the character of pluralism then it is not clear why we should invoke perfectionist values in justification of political principles beyond toleration. If Raz is right about the character of pluralism then we cannot avoid invoking perfectionist values in justification of political principles beyond toleration. To decide between these two approaches we need to know who is right about the character of pluralism. I shall not attempt to establish this here. Instead, I shall lay out some considerations that each side might invoke in defence of its characterisation of pluralism.

The prospects for engagement

There are two broad ways of understanding Raz's claims about the competitive nature of pluralism. One relates to human nature, and the other relates to the appropriateness of competition in pluralism independent of facts about human nature.

The first way of understanding the claim about the competitiveness of pluralism is as a claim about human nature: human psychology makes engagement between those who dislike and disapprove of one another, if not impossible, then rare and difficult. If human nature makes certain attitudes inevitable even in the best of conditions then the justification of political principles must not demand that these attitudes are overcome. Human nature means that dislike and disapproval breed repulsion, dismissal, and avoidance, all of which militate against engagement. Raz seems to make this claim in stating that '[c]ompetitive pluralism not only admits the validity of distinct and incompatible moral virtues, but also of virtues which tend, given human nature, to encourage intolerance of other virtues.'[27]

This account of the competitive character of pluralism relies on a brute claim about human nature: human psychology makes engagement between those who dislike and disapprove of one another rare and difficult. This sweeping claim will be difficult to defend. But Raz's political perfectionism can be supported by a far more modest claim about the impossibility, or rarity and extreme difficulty, of engagement with disliked or disapproved of others *in the political realm* in order to discuss questions of justice. If this claim is true then any form of political justification reliant on the expectation that citizens will engage in public reason to discuss political questions is threatened.

Such engagement in the political sphere probably is rare and difficult; but the fact that something is difficult does not mean that it is not required or appropriate. Furthermore, it is not clear that the best explanation for this fact is that human nature prevents such engagement at the political level. As Cohen and Rawls point out, liberal political institutions and procedures educate citizens to democratic citizenship.[28] If human nature is not opposed to engagement *per se*, they argue, then moving from *modus vivendi* through constitutional consensus to overlapping consensus brings about changes in citizens enabling them to engage with one another in public reason. The requirement that citizens engage in public reason is most pressing when a democratic political culture has evolved against the background of an overlapping consensus. Although we have not yet experienced a political community that approximates to this ideal, the expectation that citizens engage in public reason can remain central to political justification in virtue of the claim that, by so engaging, people create political institutions that better enable them to engage, and that a political community organised around these institutions is more peaceful and profitable than one without these institutions. On this view, we might argue that the reason why it is rare to find citizens engaging in public reason is not that human nature as it is realised in political life militates against this; rather – being charitable – we might claim that many states have simply failed to move beyond *modus vivendi*, or have failed to achieve the right constitutional consensus, in which case the conditions in which it becomes easier for people to engage in public reason are missing. As these failures are corrected the expectation that citizens address one another in public reason becomes more insistent, although on this picture the expectation is always legitimate. An alternative, uncharitable, explanation of this failure might be that people are just too lazy and weak-willed to do what is required of them *qua* citizens.

The second way of reading Raz on competitive pluralism is as making a purely normative claim: the attitudes that thwart engagement are appropriate or desirable independent of any facts about human nature that make these attitudes inevitable. It is hard to envisage an argument for the appropriateness of attitudes that thwart engagement in the absence of claims about how human nature opposes engagement. Such an argument would have to establish that it is appropriate that, for example, soldiers hate students, that corporate raiders sneer at conservationists, and that priests damn prostitutes. Apart from the fact that these are not typical – perhaps not even common – attitudes of the first type of person to the second type, it is not clear in what sense these attitudes could be claimed to be appropriate. Are they morally desirable? Are they necessary virtues of participation in the life to which they attach?[29] Are they cognitively appropriate to ensure some sort of coherence in a person's mental life? Each of these readings of the pure normative claim would be difficult to support, but they all have the same counter-intuitive implication. Soldiers who like students, corporate raiders who praise conservationists, and priests who bless prostitutes fail to have attitudes that they ought to have. Defending this implication on any reading of the pure normative interpretation will be a tall order.

Conclusion

In conclusion, I have argued that strategies of justification with respect to political principles of toleration and beyond are shaped by conceptions of the character of pluralism, as opposed to conceptions of its nature. This means that assessment of these competing strategies must focus on claims about what can reasonably be expected of persons in conditions of pluralism. Until we have a way of settling this question, the jury must remain out with respect to the question of whether political principles should be justified by reference to a true moral theory, or instead by reference to the imperatives of practical reason as it is exercised by people facing problems of justice in conditions of pluralism.

Notes

This chapter is based on a paper I presented at the Universities of Reading, Exeter, Manchester, and York. I would like to thank the audiences at each of these events for their comments.

 1 For a defence of a form of Constructivism that takes self-respect and its social conditions as a core justificatory value, see my *Liberalism and the Defence of Political Constructivism* (Basingstoke: Palgrave, 2002).
 2 Section 28 began as a Private Member's Bill in 1986, and was eventually passed on 20 February 1988 as part of the Local Government Bill. Section 28 states that: (1) A local authority shall not – (a) intentionally promote homosexuality or publish material with the intention of promoting homosexuality; (b) promote the teaching in any maintained school of the acceptability of homosexuality as a pretended family relationship.
 3 The qualification that restraint must be principled to count as toleration separates toleration from indifference.
 4 See I. Berlin, 'The pursuit of the ideal', in *The Crooked Timber of Humanity* (London: Fontana Press, 1990); 'The decline of utopian ideas in the west', *ibid.*; 'Two concepts of liberty', in *Four Essays on Liberty* (Oxford: Oxford University Press, 1969). See also J. Raz, *The Morality of Freedom* (Oxford: Clarendon Press, 1986) and 'Incommensurability and agency', in R. Chang (ed.), *Incommensurability, Incomparability and Practical Reason* (Cambridge, MA: Harvard University Press, 1997); C. Taylor, 'Leading a life', *ibid.*; B. Williams, 'Conflicts of values', in *Moral Luck: Philosophical Papers 1973–1980* (Cambridge: Cambridge University Press, 1981).
 5 Raz writes only of options being incommensurable, but as options involve practices, forms of association, values and beliefs, his account of incommensurabil-

ity can be extended to cover this range of differences to which personal and political toleration responds.

6 J. Raz, *The Morality of Freedom*, p. 325.

7 On Berlin's conflation of commensurability and value monism see J. Griffin, 'Incommensurability: what's the problem?', in R. Chang (ed.), *Incommensurability, Incomparability and Practical Reason*, p. 36; and J. Griffin, *Well-Being: Its Meaning, Measurement and Moral Importance* (Oxford: Clarendon Press, 1986), pp. 89–92.

8 See Berlin, 'Two concepts of liberty'.

9 For analysis of Berlin's version of this argument see G. Crowder, 'Pluralism and Liberalism', *Political Studies*, 42:2 (1994) 293–303. See also I. Berlin and B. Williams, 'Pluralism and Liberalism: A Reply', *Political Studies*, 42:2 (1994) 306–9.

10 See Berlin, 'Two Concepts of Liberty'.

11 J. Rawls, *Political Liberalism* (New York: Columbia University Press, 1993), p. 226.

12 J. Rawls, 'The idea of public reason revisited', in S. Freeman (ed.), *John Rawls: Collected Papers* (Cambridge, MA: Harvard University Press, 1999), p. 577.

13 See B. Herman, 'Pluralism and the community of moral judgement', in D. Heyd (ed.), *Toleration: An Elusive Virtue* (Princeton, NJ: Princeton University Press, 1996), pp. 81–105.

14 Rawls, 'The idea of public reason revisited', p. 580. It is important to be clear that my claims about engagement in public reason do not rest on a conflation of what Rawls calls 'reasoning from conjecture'. A person engaging in this form of reasoning with another attempts to reason from what she conjectures to be the other person's beliefs, values, etc., to a particular conclusion: she can then present this chain of reasoning to the other person as a reason for her to accept this conclusion. See Rawls, 'The Idea of Public Reason Revisited', p. 594. My claim here is rather that for a person to present her own proposals in public reason requires that she attempt to understand the different views of others whom she addresses.

15 Rawls, *Political Liberalism*, p. 148. That Locke's *Letter Concerning Toleration* does not consist of arguments made in public reason lends support to Rawls's claim.

16 J. Cohen, 'A more democratic liberalism', *Michigan Law Review*, 92 (1994) 1503–46.

17 Rawls, *Political Liberalism*, pp. 164–8.

18 Rawls, *ibid.*, pp. 158–68.

19 Rawls describes the forms of engagement needed for what he calls a 'reasonable moral psychology' in terms of a willingness to propose and abide by fair principles of justice, the maintenance of trust and confidence given sustained and successful social cooperation, and the willingness to participate in social arrangements so as to support them: *Political Liberalism*, p. 86.

20 Raz, *The Morality of Freedom*, p. 404.

21 *Ibid.*, p. 405.

22 Raz, 'Multiculturalism: a liberal perspective', in *Ethics in the Public Domain* (Oxford: Clarendon Press, 1994), p. 165.

23 Raz, *The Morality of Freedom*, p. 404.

24 See Raz, 'Multiculturalism: a liberal perspective'.

25 *Ibid.*
26 'The autonomous person is a (part) author of his own life. The ideal of personal autonomy is the vision of people controlling, to some degree, their own destiny, fashioning it through successive decisions throughout their lives': Raz, *The Morality of Freedom*, p. 369.
27 Raz, *The Morality of Freedom*, p. 404.
28 Cohen, 'A more democratic liberalism'; Rawls, *Political Liberalism*, p. 71.
29 This interpretation is suggested by the following extract from J. Raz, 'Free Expression and Personal Identification', *Ethics in the Public Domain*: 'A Christian can approve of the way of life of the Muslim, and vice versa . . . But not without reservations. There are aspects of the other's practices, attitudes, and beliefs that each of them must take exception to, must disagree with. Disagreement, condemnation, and even hostility to certain aspects of rival ways of life is an essential element of each way of life' (pp. 150–1). See also A. MacIntyre, 'Toleration and the Goods of Conflict', in S. Mendus (ed.), *The Politics of Toleration* (Edinburgh: Edinburgh University Press, 1999).

4

Toleration, justice and reason

Rainer Forst

In contemporary debates about the idea and the problems of a multicultural society the concept of toleration plays a major but by no means clear and uncontested role. For some, it is a desirable state of mutual respect or esteem, while for others it is at best a pragmatic and at worst a repressive relation between persons or groups./

In the following, I want to suggest an understanding of toleration that both explains and avoids these ambiguities. First, I distinguish between a general concept and various more specific conceptions of toleration.[1] This brief discussion shows that the concept of toleration is marked by two paradoxes that a conception of toleration should be able to resolve. On that basis, four paradigmatic conceptions of toleration are outlined, but I argue in favour of one of them, the 'respect conception', on normative grounds, while subsequently I draw out its epistemological implications. The central thesis that I put forward is that toleration is a *virtue of justice* and a *demand of reason*. The conclusion takes up again the two paradoxes mentioned at the beginning and how they are solved by the conception I propose.

The concept of toleration and its paradoxes

The general concept of toleration should be explained by six characteristics, which I shall briefly outline below.

(1) First, there is always a particular 'context of toleration'. This refers, on the one hand, to the relation between the tolerator and the tolerated: for instance, between parents and children, between friends, between members of a religious community, between citizens, and even between 'strangers', who share none of these more specific contexts. Depending on these contexts, the reasons for toleration and for its limits can differ. On the other hand, the question arises as to whether the subjects of toleration are individuals or groups or 'the state', as well as whether the objects of toleration are practices, single acts, or beliefs, to name just a few possibilities.

(2) It is essential to the concept of toleration that the tolerated beliefs or practices are judged to be wrong or bad; following Preston King, this can be called the 'objection component'.[2] If this component is absent, there is either indifference or affirmation – two attitudes that are incompatible with toleration. The objection must be normatively substantive, but is not necessarily restricted to 'moral' reasons; for, when discussing the concept of toleration generally, it would be inappropriate to exclude other forms of normative critique, such as, for instance, aesthetic critique.[3]

(3) Besides the 'objection-component', toleration requires a positive 'acceptance component' (also King's term), which does not cancel out the negative judgement but gives certain positive reasons which trump the negative ones in the relevant context. The said practices or beliefs, then, are considered to be wrong, but not intolerably wrong. In the case in which both the objection and the acceptance reasons are called 'moral', this leads to the much discussed paradox as to how it can be morally right or even a moral duty to tolerate what is morally wrong or bad.[4] In order to resolve this paradox, a conception of toleration is required that explains the meaning of 'moral' – and of 'right' versus 'wrong' and 'bad' – in a differentiated way.

(4) The concept of toleration entails the idea of certain 'limits of toleration'. They lie at the point where reasons for rejection become stronger than the acceptance reasons (something that still leaves open the question of the appropriate means of intervention). It is important to see that the reasons for rejection need not be identical with the reasons for objection;[5] they can be independent or (what is more likely) internally connected to the reasons of acceptance, which specify certain conditions and limits for that acceptance. It furthermore needs to be stressed that there are two limits involved here. The first one lies between the normative realm of the practices and beliefs one agrees with, and the realm of the tolerable practices and beliefs that one finds wrong but still can accept in a certain way. The second limit lies between this latter realm and the realm of the intolerable, which is strictly rejected (the limit of toleration properly speaking).

Another paradox emerges here, which is that toleration necessarily implies intolerance towards those who are seen as intolerable and, quite often, as intolerant as defined by those limits. The concept of tolerance makes no sense without certain limits, though as soon as these are substantively defined, tolerance seems to turn into nothing but intolerance. There is thus no 'true' tolerance.[6] To avoid this paradox, a conception of toleration must be able to show how far its limits can be drawn in a mutually justifiable and non-arbitrary way.

(5) The exercise of toleration cannot result from compulsion, since the tolerating subjects would then be under an impossibility of voicing their objections and acting accordingly. If this were the case, they would merely 'endure' or 'suffer' certain practices or beliefs against which they are powerless. To conclude from this, however, that the tolerating party must be in

a socially dominant position, having the power to interfere with the practices in question, is not justified. A minority that does not have this kind of power may still be tolerant and convinced that in the case in which it had such power it would not use it to the disadvantage of others.[7]

(6) Finally, toleration as a practice and tolerance as an attitude must be distinguished. A legal-political practice within a state that guarantees certain liberties to minorities can be called tolerant, as can also the personal attitude of accepting certain practices one finds objectionable. The former, though, can exist without the latter, for example where a state grants certain rights to minorities even though the majority of its citizens may disagree with such a policy, whilst the government acts on purely strategic motives. An analysis of toleration that is focused on the political-structural level of the peaceful coexistence of different cultural groups[8] thus leaves open the crucial question as to what kind of attitude or virtue of tolerance citizens of a state can expect from one another.

Four conceptions of toleration

The following discussion of conceptions of toleration is not to be understood as a reconstruction of a linear historical development, nor should these conceptions be regarded as 'regimes of toleration' located in different historical and social circumstances. Rather, they represent different understandings of what toleration consists in, understandings that can be simultaneously present in a society, so that conflicts about the meaning of toleration may be understood as conflicts between these conceptions.[9]

The first one I call the *permission conception*. Here, toleration is a relation between an authority or a majority and a dissenting, 'different' minority (or various minorities). Toleration then means that the authority (or majority) gives qualified permission to the members of the minority to live according to their beliefs on the condition that the minority accepts the dominant position of the authority (or majority). As long as the expression of their difference is limited – that is, is an *exercitium privatum*, as it was traditionally called – and as long as the groups do not claim equal public and political status, they can be tolerated on both pragmatic and principled grounds. On pragmatic grounds, because this form of toleration is regarded as the least costly of all possible alternatives and does not disturb civil peace and order as the dominant party defines it (but rather contributes to it). On principled grounds, because one thinks it is morally wrong (and in any case fruitless) to force people to give up certain deep-seated beliefs or practices.

The permission conception is one that we find in many historical documents and precedents illustrating a politics of toleration (such as the Edict of Nantes in 1598 or the Toleration Act 1689) and that – to a considerable extent – still informs our understanding of the term. Here toleration means that the authority or majority, which has the power to interfere with the practices of a minority, nevertheless 'tolerates' them, while the minority accepts its dependent position. The situation or the 'terms of toleration' are non-reciprocal: one party allows another certain things on conditions that the first one specifies. Toleration appears in the sense of a *permissio negativa mali*: not interfering with something that is wrong but not 'intolerably' harmful. It is this conception that Goethe had in mind when he said: 'Tolerance should be a temporary attitude only: it must lead to recognition. To tolerate means to insult.'[10]

The second conception, which can be called the *co-existence conception*, is similar to the permission conception in regarding toleration as the best means to end or avoid conflict. Here also toleration is not understood as a value in itself or as a moral duty: it is primarily justified in a pragmatic-instrumental way. Where the two conceptions differ, however, is in the constellation of power between the parties. With respect to the co-existence conception, its circumstances are not those in which an authority or majority stands over a minority, but rather one of groups, roughly equal in power, who see that for the sake of social peace and their own interests toleration is the best of all possible alternatives (a historical example is the Peace Treaty of Augsburg 1555). These groups prefer peaceful co-existence to conflict and agree to a reciprocal compromise, to a certain *modus vivendi*. The relation of tolerance is no longer vertical but horizontal:[11] the subjects are at the same time the objects of toleration. Here, a state of mutual tolerance is preferred to conflict as a matter of practical necessity; thus co-existence toleration does not lead to a stable social situation in which trust can develop, because once the constellation of power changes, the reasons for being tolerant on the side of the more powerful group disappear.[12] It is, however, possible that over time such a fragile *modus vivendi* can develop into a more stable system of co-existence and cooperation.[13]

The third conception of toleration – the *respect conception* – is one in which the parties tolerating each other respect one another in a more reciprocal sense: on moral grounds they regard themselves and others as citizens of a state in which members of all groups – majority or minorities – should have equal legal and political status.[14] Even though they hold incompatible ethical beliefs about the good and right way of life, and differ greatly in their cultural practices, they respect each other as moral-political equals in the sense that their common framework of social life should – as far as fundamental questions of the recognition of rights and liberties and the distribution of resources are concerned – be guided by norms that all parties can equally accept, and that do not favour one specific 'ethical community'.[15]

There are two models of the respect conception: 'formal equality' and 'qualitative equality'. The former operates with a strict distinction between the political and the private realm, according to which ethical (i.e. cultural or religious) differences among citizens of a legal state should be confined to the private realm, so as to avoid differences and strife in the political sphere. As citizens, all are equal, and as political equals, they transcend their more narrow ethical beliefs. This version is clearly exhibited in the 'secular republicanism' (as I would call it) of the French authorities who held that headscarves with a religious meaning have no place in public schools in which children are educated to be autonomous citizens.[16] But it can also be found in classical liberal views defending the priority and purity of equal subjective rights.

On the other hand, the model of 'qualitative equality' reacts to the problem that certain forms of formal equality favour those ethical-cultural communities whose beliefs and practices make it easier to accommodate the public/private distinction. In other words, the 'formal equality' model tends to be intolerant toward ethical-cultural forms of life that require a certain kind of public presence that others either do not require, or – as is most often the case – that require a public presence that differs from traditional and hitherto dominant cultural forms. Thus, on the 'qualitative equality' model, persons respect each other as political equals with distinct ethical-cultural identities that must be tolerated as (a) especially important for a person and (b) providing good reasons for certain exceptions from or changes to existing legal and social structures, in order to promote material and not just formal equality. Social and political equality and integration are thus seen to be compatible with cultural difference – within certain (moral) limits of reciprocity.[17]

In many debates on toleration, an additional conception is present, which I call the *esteem conception*. This implies an even fuller, more demanding notion of mutual recognition between citizens than that of the 'respect conception'. Accordingly, being tolerant does not mean respecting members of other cultural forms of life or religions as moral and political equals though objecting to their ethical ways of life. Rather, it means having some kind of ethical esteem for them; that is, regarding their beliefs as ethically valuable conceptions that are – even though different from one's own – in some way ethically attractive and held for good reasons.[18] However, this conception must involve something like 'reserved esteem', that is, a kind of positive acceptance of a belief that for some reason one still considers to be less attractive than one's own. As valuable as aspects of the tolerated belief may be, it also has other aspects that are viewed as misguided or wrong, either from one's personal perspective or from a more objective point of view.[19]

The question now is: how do we decide which of these conceptions is the most justifiable? Should we prefer either the least or the most demanding conception in terms of mutuality of recognition? Given what has been said so far, it seems clear that the concept of toleration *itself* cannot provide us with an answer to this question, since we have just seen that there are many conceptions that can be plausibly called conceptions of toleration. Hence, I suggest that neither the concept of toleration nor a concept such as that of recognition can help us to decide this question: they are what I call 'normatively dependent concepts' that are in need of further, independent normative resources in order to have a certain substance and content. My thesis is that the concept of *justice* or, more specifically, a certain conception of justice in accordance with a notion of practical reason, can provide such a content.

Justice and the threshold of reciprocity and generality

The reason for my claim that a conception of justice is necessary in arguing for a conception of toleration is that the context in which the question of toleration between citizens arises is a context of justice: what is at issue here is the just – that is, mutually justifiable – legal and political structure for a pluralistic political community of citizens with different ethical beliefs. Claims for toleration are raised as claims for justice, and intolerance is a form of injustice, favoring one ethical community over others without legitimate grounds.[20] Hence, toleration is a *virtue of justice*. My thesis is that, by considering the question of justice, I shall be in a position to show that, in its form of 'qualitative equality', the 'respect conception' is superior to the others.

To cut a long argument short,[21] I think that at the centre of a conception of political and social justice there should be a theory of the intersubjective justification of norms that can reasonably – that is, with good reasons – claim to be reciprocally and generally valid. The norms that regulate how the most important rights and resources are granted and distributed have to be justifiable with reasons that can be accepted equally by all citizens as free and equal persons.

The theory of 'public justification' that is thereby implied rests upon the criteria of *reciprocity* and *generality*. Reciprocity means that A cannot claim a right or a resource she denies to B and that the formulation of the claim and the reasons given must be open to questioning and not be determined by one party only. If, invoking the principle of reciprocity, A says that it is right to force B to accept what A regards as true, since she herself would be happy to accept such an imposition, if she were in B's position with regard to the truth, she actually violates true reciprocity. A may believe that she knows and acts in favour of the truth – and something good and true for B also – but she puts the truth as she sees it beyond the demand for mutual justifiability, so that her truth claim turns into an attempt to dominate B. But nobody may deny others their basic (moral) *right to justification*, to be given adequate reasons for actions or norms that affect them in their status as free and equal persons. In connection with this, generality means that the reasons that are sufficient to support the validity of norms should not just be acceptable to, say, two dominant parties in a society (Protestants and Catholics, for example), but to every person and party involved. The realm of justification must be identical with the realm of the validity of a norm. This does not mean that there can be no valid norm until everybody has actually been persuaded to agree, for there will always be people who do not want to compromise their views and interests; rather, it means that a norm's validity is insufficiently established as long as the norm can be 'reasonably rejected' with reasons that are themselves reciprocally non-rejectable.[22]

Using the criteria of reciprocity and generality a distinction can be made between, on the one hand, justifiable general *moral norms* and, on the other, *ethical values* that cannot be generalised in this way but that may nevertheless be justifiably held as values guiding persons in many areas of their life.[23] There is no reified distinction between 'value spheres' at work here, but rather a distinction between different 'contexts of justification' separated by what I call *the threshold of reciprocity and generality*. The basic question is whether a person can give reasons for her claims that can cross that threshold into the moral realm, or whether she fails in that because she appeals, for example, to a 'higher' truth that is revealed to her rather than arrived at through intersubjective argument[24] and has to concede that the 'redemption' of her claim is dependent upon a particular ethical self-understanding and therefore not generally valid.[25] Ultimately, the validity of *ethical* values for a person depends upon the affirmation of these values through this person in his or her particular ethical identity, and if this identification is not possible, the argument based on such values has no moral, categorical force to it. In disputes about the validity of a *moral* norm, however, one is required to raise, accept or reject normative claims with reasons that pass the test of reciprocity and generality. Only then can those claims have categorical force. Thus, whereas in the context of ethical justification it is ultimately *you* (on whatever 'higher' ground) who decides about the direction of your life, in the context of moral justification it is *others* to whom you owe good reasons.

Thus, if a particular ethical community tries to generalise some of its specific values and present them as a legitimate basis for general legislation, it must be able to explain why this is justified, given the legitimate interests of all others who have different identities and conceptions of the good. If the members of that community succeed in showing that they are not merely arguing in favour of their ideas of the good, which they want to make or keep socially dominant – forcing others to 'tolerate' their dominance from a minority position while they only want to 'tolerate' the minority as a different, though not politically equal, party – but that they argue in favour of goals all can agree to, then their claim is justified (for the time being). To give an example:[26] arguments for homosexual marriage can be reciprocally justified as an extension of equal rights. In a context of general justification, this claim cannot legitimately be rejected with arguments that deny equal rights on the basis of particular ethical-religious views. Whereas such arguments are clearly reciprocally rejectable in a moral-political context, strong religious objections to certain ways of life are of course legitimate in an ethical context, where answers to the question of the good life are at issue.[27]

Citizens are tolerant if they accept the boundary set by the criteria of reciprocity and generality as both delineating the justifiability of mutually binding norms and the limits of toleration. Tolerant citizens are 'reasonable' in accepting that the 'contexts of justification' for ethical beliefs and general norms are different: they see that an *ethical objection* does not amount to a legitimate *moral rejection*; and they also see that they have a moral duty to tolerate all those ethical beliefs and practices that they disagree with but that do not violate the threshold of reciprocity and generality (trying to force their views on others). Such a denial of the basic right to justification is a form of intolerance that cannot be tolerated. This is where the limits of toleration are reached.

It is in this sense that justice and reason are connected: persons recognise that with respect to questions of justice certain justifiable reasons have to be given according to validity criteria different from the ones in ethical contexts. Persons are tolerant to the extent that, even though they disagree with others about the nature of the good and true life, they tolerate all other views within the bounds of reciprocity and generality. This is why toleration is a *virtue of justice* and a *demand of reason*.

With respect to the four conceptions of toleration discussed above this means the following. As citizens, persons do have a right to have their ethical identity respected equally, yet they do not have a right to their ethical views' becoming the basis of general law. This is the main problem with the non-reciprocal 'permission conception', while the deficiency of the 'co-existence conception' is also that it insufficiently respects the basic right to justification. Potential weaknesses of one of the groups will therefore turn into a disadvantaged social position. Both conceptions fall short of the demand for mutual respect that a morally justifiable conception of toleration should start from.

Law based on reciprocally and generally justifiable norms can only be a 'protective cover' for diverse ethical identities if it is understood according to the 'qualitative equality' conception of respect referred to above. Given the range of differences among ethical beliefs and practices, equal respect does not mean imposing rigid formal equality, thereby relegating 'ethics' to the 'private realm'. Rather, it means that general social practices have to be sensitive to ethical differences – for example, to the particular demands of religious duties. Tolerating ethical difference thus implies mutual respect in this qualitative way – which is less than what is called for by the 'esteem conception'. In terms of justice, however, it calls for more than what the esteem conception allows, since the limits of toleration will not be drawn on the basis of an ethical judgement of the good: such a judgement creates the danger of drawing the limits too narrowly.

Yet at this point the normative discussion of toleration as an issue of justice has to shift and address the question of tolerance as a personal *attitude* of reasonable persons in more detail. How is this attitude possible? What notion of 'reason' is involved here?

The finitude of reason

Every conception of tolerance implies a certain form of ethical self-limitation or 'self-relativisation'; and in the conception that I am proposing this is understood as a 'demand of reason'. But how can reason demand of me that I relativise my deeply held ethical beliefs in this way and accept that the reasons that are good ethical reasons for me are not (yet) good reasons in the context of general justification? Do I have to be a sceptic or a relativist or a 'comprehensive liberal' to accept this? That is, do I have to believe either in no ethical truth, or in the equality of different ethical beliefs, or in the value of ethical autonomy and the 'good life' of being a tolerant person? These are large questions, and I can only attempt to give a brief account of the notion of reason that I think is required to address them. The guiding idea is that such a capacity of reason is characteristic of people who accept the threshold of reciprocity and generality as a reasonable demand, without being sceptics, relativists, or comprehensive liberals. A theory of toleration must not be built upon such particular ethical points of view. Instead, what is needed is an account of reason that also applies to the 'reasonable' believer in some particular – say, religious – truth. What is required is a mild form of ethical self-relativisation as a reasonable attitude, and this must be neither strategically nor pragmatically motivated, nor justified as part of the person's idea of the good in a strong sense.

I call this form of ethical self-relativisation 'mild', because accepting the argumentative threshold of reciprocity and generality does not imply questioning the ethical truth of one's own beliefs, as opposed to a strong, almost schizophrenic, form of self-relativisation, according to which a tolerant person has to look at his or her convictions from an objective standpoint to assess their merits in terms of an 'impersonal' judgement.[28] It is sufficient that a tolerant person be aware that there are different contexts of justification in which different questions (of the good life or of general norms) require different answers that have to satisfy different criteria of validity. Thus, a convincing answer to an ethical question may very well turn out to be a convincing answer to a general question of justice, though, on the other hand, it may not be. In the latter case, it can still be a convincing ethical answer that is not false in this context, even though it is not generally acceptable. It is in the nature of ethical beliefs that they are shaped by a number of particular experiences, which is why it would be unreasonable to assume them to be equally sharable among persons with very different experiental backgrounds. Hence it is unreasonable *both* to assume that there can be no reasonable ethical disagreement between persons capable and willing to seek a common normative answer given the two criteria of reciprocity and generality *and* to assume that the existence of reasonable disagreement in ethical matters makes it unreasonable or morally false to hold certain ethical beliefs, be they religious or not.[29] The realm of the ethical, we may say, is much broader – and maybe also deeper – than the realm of the mutually non-rejectable.[30]

In his recent writings, John Rawls offers a productive explanation of this complex normative-epistemological attitude of reasonable and tolerant persons. According to Rawls, such individuals are aware of the 'burdens of reason' or 'burdens of judgment' that inevitably narrow the realm of what persons can reasonably agree to. Even those who are seeking to reach a normative consensus and who share 'a common human reason' in the sense that 'they can draw inferences, weigh evidence, and balance competing considerations'[31] may not reach a consensus owing to various limits on their capacities for reasonable theoretical and practical judgement. The most important burden Rawls mentions is that the way individuals assess evidence and weigh moral and political values is shaped by their total experience and whole course of life, which will always differ between persons, especially in modern, complex societies. His main point is that reasonable persons – who hold reasonable 'comprehensive doctrines' – are aware that they as well as others are subject to these burdens, which inevitably lead to disagreement between individuals who are influenced by very different experiences, normative backgrounds, and value horizons. Thus, it is not just a pragmatic and empirical insight that disagreement in normative matters may arise even between well-intentioned persons; it is a fundamental insight about the limitations of finite human reason.

The main reason-based argument for tolerance, therefore, is not the idea of a free and open competition of ideas and values that will separate truth from falsity in a process of inquiry.[32] Rather, the insight into the presuppositions and the limits of such a competition constitutes the primary rationale for such an argument: that is, an insight into the irreducible finitude and plurality of human perspectives, and the limits of falsification in areas of beliefs that are not 'beyond reason' in terms of being irrational or not open to reasonable discourse, but that are 'beyond reason' in so far as they are based on reasons that may ultimately be *neither verifiable nor falsifiable* by human reason. One can both reasonably hold these beliefs and accept that others reasonably disagree with them. One believes in their truth while understanding that others do and may see things differently, given their perspective; thus one may try to convince others of one's beliefs, though one cannot force them upon others who are not unreasonable in holding other views. Hence 'being reasonable' includes epistemological as well as normative elements.

The *epistemological* element of being reasonable consists in an insight into the finitude of both theoretical and practical reason in finding 'final' answers to the question of the good that all can agree on. But it also consists in an insight into the possibilities of reason, that is, the capacity of reaching mutually justifiable normative answers. The finitude of reason does not imply the impossibility of reasonable discourse, but rather the task of finding and defending justifiable reasons, because this is what reasonable and finite persons – who cannot avoid raising general validity claims in their social life – owe to each other. This commonality establishes a community of sharable, but not ultimate reasons.[33] Thus the *normative* element of being reasonable implies this form of respect for others as reasonable and worthy of being given adequate reasons; that is, respect for their basic right to justification. Both elements in combination, the epistemological and the normative, are the basis for the acceptance and recognition of the threshold of reciprocity and generality as discussed above. They provide the essential reasons for being tolerant. Being tolerant thus means seeking reasonable justification, accepting reasonable disagreement within the limits of reciprocity and generality, and being aware of the different contexts of justification that persons are part of. It implies tolerating other beliefs within these limits by not rejecting them as unreasonable or immoral, though it does not imply a qualification of the ethical truth of one's own beliefs. Taken together, then, the epistemological and the normative elements explain my definition of toleration as a demand of reason and a virtue of justice.[34]

Resolving the paradoxes

In conclusion, let me briefly return to the two paradoxes of toleration outlined at the beginning and see whether the conception I have proposed can resolve or avoid them.

Briefly stated, the first paradox consists in the problem of how it can be morally right to tolerate what is morally wrong. Given the discussion above, one can say that it is morally required of reasonable persons to justify norms that they think should be generally binding for everyone with reciprocally and generally justifiable reasons. It is in this sense that they must respect the epistemic and moral autonomy of other persons with ethical beliefs different from their own – that is, beliefs that they may disagree with and even find ethically wrong and insufficient as answers to questions of the good life, but that they cannot accuse of violating the boundary set by the criteria of reciprocity and generality. It is *morally* required and right to tolerate what you find *ethically* disagreeable and wrong within the limits of reasonableness and reciprocity that all have to accept; the fact that you find some beliefs and practices ethically wrong does not make them unreasonable to hold or immoral. Thus, the paradox is avoided by clarifying the acceptance, objection and rejection components of toleration with the help of a distinction between moral and ethical justification.

The second paradox says that toleration, as soon as its limits are defined by a certain content, becomes intolerant toward those 'outside'. As an answer to this, everything depends on whether one wants to call both the suppression of any form of dissent and the suppression of this form of suppression 'intolerance'. But this seems a misuse of the term: we cannot call any form of moral critique 'intolerance', because then we lose the concept of toleration completely. Instead, by drawing the 'limits of toleration' with the help of the criteria of reciprocity and generality, we draw them, as I have tried to argue, in the widest possible way given the existence of a large diversity of world-views, without sacrificing one for the sake of the unjustifiable claims of another. Thus there is no arbitrary substantive content that defines the tolerable; this content is open to dispute and argument, and protection is given to those voices in danger of being marginalised.[35] Those who violate the basic form of mutual respect implied by that cannot claim to be the victims of intolerance. For otherwise, not only the concept of toleration, but also the concept of justice would lose its meaning.

Notes

A version of this chapter was published as 'Toleranz, Gerechtigkeit und Vernunft' in R. Forst (ed.), *Toleranz. Philosophische Grundlagen und gesellschaftliche Praxis einer umstrittenen Tugend* (Frankfurt/Main: Campus, 2000), pp. 119–43. For helpful comments on various versions of my argument I want to thank especially Joel Anderson, Dario Castiglione, Richard Dees, Günter Frankenberg, Elisabetta Galeotti, Jürgen Habermas, Axel Honneth, Otto Kallscheuer, Andreas Kuhlmann, Charles Larmore, Catriona McKinnon, Donald Moon and Henry Richardson.

 1 Here I make use of a distinction that John Rawls has suggested concerning the concept of justice: see J. Rawls, *A Theory of Justice* (Cambridge, MA: Harvard University Press, 1971), p. 5.
 2 P. King, *Toleration* (New York: St Martin's Press, 1976), Ch. 1.
 3 The term 'objection' entails a difficult problem that I can only indicate here briefly. The objection needs to be normatively justifiable (though not generally sharable) in some sense, and must not be based on mere prejudice. If, for example, somebody finds members of a different 'race' generally objectionable and inferior, one cannot simply ask him or her to be 'tolerant', since that would mean to accept his racist prejudice as a possible objection. On this, see B. Crick, 'Toleration and tolerance in theory and practice', *Government and Opposition*, 6 (1971) 144–71, and especially J. Horton, 'Toleration as a virtue', in D. Heyd (ed.), *Toleration: An Elusive Virtue* (Princeton, NJ: Princeton University Press, 1996), pp. 28–43.
 4 D. D. Raphael, 'The intolerable', in S. Mendus (ed.), *Justifying Toleration. Conceptual and Historical Perspectives* (Cambridge: Cambridge University Press, 1988), pp. 137–54; S. Mendus, *Toleration and the Limits of Liberalism* (Atlantic Highlands, NJ: Humanities Press, 1989), pp. 18–20. An earlier formulation of this can be found in Julius Ebbinghaus, 'Über die Idee der Toleranz', *Archiv für Philosophie 4* (1950) 1–34.
 5 On this point, I agree with Glen Newey, *Virtue, Reason and Toleration: The Place of Toleration in Ethical and Political Philosophy* (Edinburgh: Edinburgh University Press, 1999), pp. 32–4, from whom I differ fundamentally, however, in the understanding of the nature of the reasons for objection.
 6 See especially S. Fish, 'Mission impossible: Settling the just bounds between Church and State', *Columbia Law Review* 97 (1997) 2255–333; and Martha Minow, 'Putting up and putting down: Tolerance reconsidered', in M. Tushnet (ed.), *Comparative Constitutional Federalism. Europe and America* (New York: Greenwood Press, 1990), pp. 77–113.

7 See B. Williams, 'Toleration: An impossible virtue?', in Heyd (ed.), *Toleration*, pp. 18–27.

8 See M. Walzer, *On Toleration* (New Haven, CT: Yale University Press, 1997).

9 I have analysed such a conflict in my discussion of the so-called 'crucifix-case' decided by the Federal Constitutional Court in Germany in 1995: see R. Forst, 'A tolerant Republic?', in J.-W. Müller (ed.), *German Ideologies since 1945* (New York: St Martin's Press, forthcoming).

10 J. W. Goethe, 'Maximen und Reflexionen', in *Werke 6* (Frankfurt/Main, Insel, 1981), p. 507: 'Toleranz sollte nur eine vorübergehende Gesinnung sein: sie muß zur Anerkennung führen. Dulden heißt beleidigen.'

11 See E. Garzón Valdés, 'Some remarks on the concept of toleration', *Ratio Juris* 10 (1997) 127–38.

12 See J. Rawls, 'The idea of an overlapping consensus', *Oxford Journal of Legal Studies 7* (1987) 1–25, at p. 11; George Fletcher, 'The instability of tolerance', in Heyd (ed.), *Toleration*, pp. 158–72.

13 On the idea of such a development see Richard H. Dees, 'The justification of tolerance', in G. Magill and M. D. Hoff (eds), *Values and Public Life* (Lanham, MD: University Press of America, 1995), pp. 29–56.

14 See T. Scanlon, 'The difficulty of tolerance', in Heyd (ed.), *Toleration*, pp. 226–39; Y. Yovel, 'Tolerance as grace and as rightful recognition', *Social Research 65* (1998) 897–919; N. Bobbio, 'Gründe für die Toleranz', in *Das Zeitalter der Menschenrechte* (Berlin: Wagenbach, 1998), pp. 87–106.

15 See my discussion of neutrality in R. Forst, *Contexts of Justice. Political Philosophy beyond Liberalism and Communitarianism*, trans. J. M. M. Farrell (Berkeley and Los Angeles, CA: University of California Press, 2002), Ch. 2. Note that in this characterisation of the respect conception the main argument for respect is not the liberal one that persons are to be seen as ethically autonomous authors of their own lives and that tolerance is demanded because persons have a right to such a kind of ethical autonomy as a necessary condition for the good life. Such a justification of toleration, I believe, is based on a non-generalisable conception of the good and is caught in the dilemma of either regarding individual choices *per se* as worthy of respect (which leads to an extremely wide view of toleration) or of tolerating only beliefs and practices that are authentically self-chosen (which leads to a very narrow view). As I will argue below, the respect conception should rather be based on the more fundamental notion of moral autonomy (and the right of each moral person to a justification of general norms he or she is subject to). For a discussion of the distinction between various conceptions of autonomy see R. Forst, 'Political liberty: Integrating five conceptions of autonomy', in J. Christman and J. Anderson (eds), *Autonomy and the Challenges to Liberalism: New Essays* (currently in preparation).

16 See A. E. Galeotti, 'Citizenship and equality: The place for toleration', *Political Theory 21* (1993) 585–605.

17 On the justification of these limits see my debate with Will Kymlicka: R. Forst, 'Foundations of a theory of multicultural justice', *Constellations* 4 (1997) 63–71, and W. Kymlicka, 'Do we need a liberal theory of minority rights? A reply to Carens, Young, Parekh and Forst', *ibid.*, pp. 72–87.

18 See, for example, the (very different) views of Z. Bauman, *Modernity and Ambivalence* (Oxford: Polity, 1991); Julia Kristeva, *Strangers to Ourselves* (New

York, Columbia University Press, 1991); and Karl-Otto Apel, 'Plurality of the good? The problem of affirmative tolerance in a multicultural society from an ethical point of view', *Ratio Juris 10* (1997) 199–212.

19 See J. Raz, 'Autonomy, toleration, and the harm principle', in S. Mendus (ed.), *Justifying Toleration*, pp. 155–75, on moral pluralism as a basis for toleration; or Michael Sandel, 'Moral argument and liberal toleration: Abortion and homosexuality', *California Law Review 77* (1989) 521–38, on the toleration of variations of established cultural practices.

20 See esp. Rawls, *A Theory of Justice*, sections 34 and 35, on the relation between toleration and justice.

21 For an extensive discussion see Forst, *Contexts of Justice*.

22 Here I use a phrase by Thomas Scanlon, interpreting it with the help of the criteria of reciprocity and generality, something that Scanlon does not do, at least explicitly; cf. his 'Contractualism and utilitarianism', in A. Sen and B. Williams (eds), *Utilitarianism and beyond* (Cambridge: Cambridge University Press, 1982), pp. 103–128, and *What We Owe to Each Other* (Cambridge, MA: Harvard University Press, 1998), Chs. 4 and 5.

23 This distinction has been suggested by Jürgen Habermas: see especially his 'On the Pragmatic, the Ethical, and the Moral Employments of Practical Reason', in *Justification and Application*, trans C. Cronin (Cambridge, MA: MIT Press, 1993), pp. 1–17. For a recent discussion (which points out the differences with Habermas's view) see Forst, 'Ethik und Moral', in L. Wingert and K. Günther, *Die Öffentlichkeit der Vernunft und die Vernunft der Öffentlichkeit* (Frankfurt/Main: Suhrkamp, 2001), pp. 344–71.

24 See T. Nagel, 'Moral conflict and political legitimacy', *Philosophy and Public Affairs 16* (1987) 215–40, and *Equality and Partiality* (New York: Oxford University Press, 1991), pp. 154ff.; John Rawls, *Political Liberalism* (New York: Columbia University Press, 1993), pp. 58ff.

25 See C. Taylor, 'Explanation and Practical Reason', in M. Nussbaum and A. Sen (eds), *The Quality of Life* (New York: Oxford University Press, 1993), pp. 208–31.

26 I discuss a number of examples in Forst, 'The Limits of Toleration', in I. Creppell, S. Macedo, and R. Hardin, *Toleration and Identity Conflict* (currently in preparation).

27 This does not imply that religious arguments have no legitimate role in public political discourse; it merely says that they should not be the basis of generally binding law if they cannot pass the test of reciprocity and generality.

28 On this point, see Raz's critique of Nagel's view: J. Raz, 'Facing diversity: The case of epistemic abstinence', *Philosophy and Public Affairs 19* (1990) 3–46.

29 See C. Larmore, 'Pluralism and reasonable disagreement', in *The Morals of Modernity* (Cambridge: Cambridge University Press, 1996), pp. 152–74.

30 I therefore disagree with Brian Barry, *Justice as Impartiality* (Oxford: Oxford University Press, 1995), pp. 168–73, who argues that the acceptance of what he calls the 'burden of public justification' presupposes an ethical scepticism such that 'no conception of the good can justifiably be held with a degree of certainty that warrants its imposition on those who reject it' (p. 169). The kind of self-restraint Barry has in mind here first of all seems to be based on a moral rather than a sceptical insight, for one can of course be convinced of the truth of certain beliefs and still not think that one is justified in imposing them on others; the

willingness to impose one's beliefs would be a rather odd criterion for sincere belief. Furthermore, somebody with a certain religious faith need not, it seems to me, assume that the fact that there is so much disagreement in religious matters is an argument either against the truth of his or her beliefs or against the reasonableness of those who disagree. The relation between 'reason' and 'faith' is much more complex than this, as is argued for instance by Montaigne, who was at the same time a sceptic and a fideist. Sebastian Franck, Sebastian Castellio and Jean Bodin are other examples from post-Reformation Europe, to which period Barry refers. I discuss their views on toleration in Chapters 3 and 4 of my forthcoming *Toleranz im Konflikt*.

31 Rawls, *Political Liberalism*, p. 55.

32 See J. S. Mill, *On Liberty*, ed. G. Himmelfarb (Harmondsworth, Penguin, 1974) and K. Popper, 'Toleration and intellectual responsibility', in S. Mendus and D. Edwards (eds), *On Toleration* (Oxford: Clarendon, 1987), pp. 17–34.

33 See C. Korsgaard, 'The reasons we can share', in *Creating the Kingdom of Ends* (Cambridge: Cambridge University Press, 1996), pp. 275–310.

34 This leads to a very important point (which, however, I cannot spell out here). Given the need to apply philosophical concepts to philosophy itself, a conception of toleration can only be justifiable if it is itself tolerant toward the different ethical world-views that persons hold (a point stressed by Rawls); and these world-views imply different accounts of ethical knowledge, value, and reality. Therefore one would have to show that the conception of toleration I have just explained with respect to its normative and epistemological elements is the conception that leaves the widest possible room for various ways of conceiving the moral world and of explaining the reasons for toleration in a more particular way. On this, see my *Toleranz im Konflikt*, Part II.

35 Needless to say, this calls for a theory of democracy as part of a political theory of toleration. See, for example, James Bohman, 'Reflexive Toleration in a Deliberative Democracy', in this volume.

5

Recognition without ethics?

Nancy Fraser

For some time now, the forces of progressive politics have been divided into two camps. On one side stand the proponents of 'redistribution'. Drawing on long traditions of egalitarian, labour, and socialist organising, political actors aligned with this orientation seek a more just allocation of resources and goods. On the other side stand the proponents of 'recognition'. Drawing on newer visions of a 'difference-friendly' society, they seek a world where assimilation to majority or dominant cultural norms is no longer the price of equal respect. Members of the first camp hope to redistribute wealth from the rich to the poor, from the North to the South, and from the owners to the workers. Members of the second, in contrast, seek recognition of the distinctive perspectives of ethnic, 'racial', and sexual minorities, as well as of gender difference. The redistribution orientation has a distinguished philosophical pedigree, as egalitarian redistributive claims have supplied the paradigm case for most theorising about social justice for the past 150 years. The recognition orientation has recently attracted the interest of political philosophers, however, some of whom are seeking to develop a new normative paradigm that puts recognition at its centre.

At present, unfortunately, relations between the two camps are quite strained. In many cases, struggles for recognition are dissociated from struggles for redistribution. Within social movements such as feminism, for example, activist tendencies that look to redistribution as the remedy for male domination are increasingly dissociated from tendencies that look instead to recognition of gender difference. And the same is largely true in the intellectual sphere. In the academy, to continue with feminism, scholars who understand gender as a social relation maintain an uneasy arms-length co-existence with those who construe it as an identity or a cultural code. This situation exemplifies a broader phenomenon: the widespread decoupling of cultural politics from social politics, of the politics of difference from the politics of equality.

In some cases, moreover, the dissociation has become a polarisation. Some proponents of redistribution see claims for the recognition of difference as 'false consciousness', a hindrance to the pursuit of social justice. Conversely, some proponents of recognition reject distributive politics as part and parcel of an outmoded materialism that can neither articulate nor challenge key experiences of injustice. In such cases, we are effectively presented with an either/or choice: redistribution or recognition? Class politics or identity politics? Multiculturalism or social equality?

These, I have argued elsewhere, are false antitheses.[1] Justice today requires *both* redistribution *and* recognition; neither alone is sufficient. As soon as one embraces this thesis, however, the question of how to combine them becomes pressing. I maintain that the emancipatory aspects of the two problematics need to be integrated in a single, comprehensive framework. The task, in part, is to devise an expanded conception of justice that can accommodate both defensible claims for social equality and defensible claims for the recognition of difference.

Morality or ethics?

Integrating redistribution and recognition is no easy matter, however. On the contrary, to contemplate this project is to become immediately embroiled in a nexus of difficult philosophical questions. Some of the thorniest of these concern the relation between morality and ethics, the right and the good, justice and the good life. A key issue is whether paradigms of justice usually aligned with 'morality' can handle claims for the recognition of difference – or whether it is necessary, on the contrary, to turn to 'ethics'.

Let me explain. It is now standard practice in moral philosophy to distinguish questions of justice from questions of the good life. Construing the first as a matter of 'the right' and the second as a matter of 'the good', most philosophers align distributive justice with Kantian *Moralität* (morality) and recognition with Hegelian *Sittlichkeit* (ethics). In part this contrast is a matter of scope. Norms of justice are thought to be universally binding; they hold independently of actors' commitments to specific values. Claims for the recognition of difference, in contrast, are more restricted. Involving qualitative assessments of the relative worth of various cultural practices, traits, and identities, they depend on historically specific horizons of value, which cannot be universalised.

Much of recent moral philosophy turns on disputes over the relative standing of these two different orders of normativity. Liberal political theorists and deontological moral philosophers insist that the right take priority over the good. For them, accordingly, the demands of justice trump the claims of ethics. Communitarians and teleologists rejoin that the notion of a universally binding morality independent of any idea of the good is conceptually incoherent. Preferring 'thick' accounts of moral experience to 'thin' ones, they rank the substantive claims of culturally specific community values above abstract appeals to 'reason' or 'humanity'.

Partisans of the prior claims of the right, moreover, often subscribe to distributive models of justice. Viewing justice as a matter of fairness, they seek to eliminate unjustified disparities between the life-chances of social actors. To identify these disparities, they invoke standards of fairness that do not prejudge those actors' own (varying) views of the good. Partisans of the good, in contrast, reject the 'empty formalism' of distributive approaches. Viewing ethics as a matter of the good life, they seek to promote the qualitative conditions of human flourishing (as they understand them), rather than fidelity to abstract requirements of equal treatment.

These philosophical alignments complicate the problem of integrating redistribution and recognition. Distribution evidently belongs on the morality side of the divide. Recognition, however, seems at first sight to belong to ethics, as it seems to require judgments about the value of various practices, traits, and identities. It is not surprising, therefore, that many deontological theorists simply reject claims for the recognition of difference as violations of liberal neutrality, while concluding that distributive justice exhausts the whole of political morality. It is also unsurprising, conversely, that many theorists of recognition align themselves with ethics against morality; following the same reasoning as their liberal counterparts, they conclude that recognition requires qualitative value judgements that exceed the capacities of distributive models.

In these standard alignments, both sides agree that distribution belongs to morality, recognition belongs to ethics, and never the twain shall meet. Thus, each assumes that its paradigm excludes the other's. If they are right, then the claims of redistribution and the claims of recognition cannot be coherently combined. On the contrary, whoever wishes to endorse claims of both types courts the risk of philosophical schizophrenia.

It is precisely this presumption of incompatibility that I aim to dispel. *Contra* the received wisdom, I shall argue that one can integrate redistribution and recognition without succumbing to schizophrenia. My strategy will be to construe the politics of recognition in a way that does not deliver it prematurely to ethics. Rather, I shall account for claims for recognition as *justice claims* within an expanded understanding of justice. The initial effect will be to recuperate the politics of recognition for *Moralität* and thus to resist the turn to ethics. But that is not precisely where I shall end up. Rather, I shall concede that there may be cases when ethical evaluation is unavoidable. Yet because such evaluation is problematic, I shall suggest ways of deferring it as long as possible.

Identity or status?

The key to my strategy is to break with the standard 'identity' model of recognition. On this model, what requires recognition is group-specific cultural identity. Misrecognition consists in the depreciation of such identity by the dominant culture and the consequent damage to group members' sense of self. Redressing this harm means demanding 'recognition'. This in turn requires that group members join together to refashion their collective identity by producing a self-affirming culture of their own. Thus, on the identity model of recognition, the politics of recognition means 'identity politics'.[2]

This identity model is deeply problematic. Construing misrecognition as damaged identity, it emphasises psychic structure over social institutions and social interaction. Thus, it risks substituting intrusive forms of consciousness engineering for social change. The model compounds these risks by positing group identity as the object of recognition. Enjoining the elaboration and display of an authentic, self-affirming, and self-generated collective identity, it puts moral pressure on individual members to conform to group culture. The result is often to impose a single, drastically simplified group identity, which denies the complexity of people's lives, the multiplicity of their identifications, and the cross-pulls of their various affiliations. In addition, the model reifies culture. Ignoring transcultural flows, it treats cultures as sharply bounded, neatly separated, and non-interacting, as if it were obvious where one stops and another starts. As a result, it tends to promote separatism and group enclaving in lieu of trans-group interaction. Denying internal heterogeneity, moreover, the identity model obscures the struggles within social groups for the authority, and indeed for the power, to represent them. Consequently, it masks the power of dominant fractions and reinforces intragroup domination. In general, then, the identity model lends itself all too easily to repressive forms of communitarianism.[3]

For these reasons, I shall propose an alternative analysis of recognition. My proposal is to treat recognition as a question of *social status*. From this perspective – I shall call it *the status model* – what requires recognition is not group-specific identity but rather the status of group members as full partners in social interaction. Misrecognition, accordingly, does not mean the depreciation and deformation of group identity. Rather, it means social subordination in the sense of being prevented from participating as a peer in social life. To redress the injustice requires a politics of recognition, to be sure, but this no longer means identity politics. In the status model, rather, it means a politics aimed at overcoming subordination by establishing the misrecognised party as a full member of society, capable of participating on a par with other members.[4]

Let me elaborate. To view recognition as a matter of status is to examine institutionalised patterns of cultural value for their effects on the relative standing of social actors. If and when such patterns constitute actors as peers, capable of participating on a par with one another in social life, then we can speak of reciprocal recognition and status equality. When, in contrast, institutionalised patterns of cultural value constitute some actors as inferior, excluded, wholly other, or simply invisible, and hence as less than full partners in social interaction, then we should speak of misrecognition and status subordination.

On the status model, then, misrecognition arises when institutions structure interaction according to cultural norms that impede parity of participation. Examples include marriage laws that exclude same-sex partnerships as illegitimate and perverse, social-welfare policies that stigmatise single mothers as sexually irresponsible scroungers, and policing practices such as 'racial profiling' that associate racialised persons with criminality. In each of these cases, interaction is regulated by an institutionalised pattern of cultural value that constitutes some categories of social actors as normative and others as deficient or inferior: straight is normal, gay is perverse; 'male-headed households' are proper, 'female-headed households' are not; 'whites' are law-abiding, 'blacks' are dangerous. In each case, the result is to deny some members of society the status of full partners in interaction, capable of participating on a par with the rest.

In each case, accordingly, a claim for recognition is in order. But note precisely what this means: aimed not at valorising group identity, but rather at overcoming subordination, claims for recognition in the status model seek to establish the subordinated party as a full partner in social life, able to interact with others as a peer. They aim, that is, to deinstitutionalise patterns of cultural value that impede parity of participation and to replace them with patterns that foster it.

This status model avoids many difficulties of the identity model. First, by rejecting the view of recognition as a valorisation of group identity, it avoids essentialising such identities. Second, by focusing on the effects of institutionalised norms on capacities for interaction, it resists the temptation to substitute the re-engineering of consciousness for social change. Third, by enjoining status equality in the sense of parity of participation, it valorises cross-group interaction, as opposed to separatism and group enclaving. Fourth, the status model avoids reifying culture – without denying culture's political importance. Aware that institutionalised patterns of cultural value can be vehicles of subordination, it seeks to deinstitutionalise patterns that impede parity of participation and to replace them with patterns that foster it.

Finally, the status model possesses another major advantage. Unlike the identity model, it construes recognition in a way that does not assign that category to ethics. Conceiving recognition as a matter of status equality, defined in turn as participatory parity, it provides a deontological account of recognition. Thus, it frees recognition claims' normative force from direct dependence on a specific substantive horizon of value. Unlike the identity model, then, the status model is compatible with the priority of the right over the good. Refusing the traditional alignment of recognition with ethics, it aligns it with morality instead. Thus the status model permits one to combine recognition with redistribution – without succumbing to philosophical schizophrenia. Or so I shall argue next.

Justice or the good life?

Any attempt to integrate redistribution and recognition in a comprehensive framework must address four crucial philosophical questions. First, is recognition a matter of justice, or is it a matter of self-realisation? Second, do distributive justice and recognition constitute two distinct, *sui generis*, normative paradigms, or can either of them be subsumed within the other? Third, does justice require the recognition of what is distinctive about individuals or groups, or is recognition of our common humanity sufficient? And fourth, how can we distinguish those claims for recognition that are justified from those that are not?

How one answers these questions depends on the conception of recognition one assumes. In what follows, I will employ the status model in order to provide a deontological account. Drawing on that model, I shall expand the standard conception of justice to accommodate claims for recognition. By stretching the notion of morality, then, I shall avoid turning prematurely to ethics.

I begin with the question, 'Is recognition an issue of justice, and thus of morality, or one of the good life, and thus of ethics?' Usually, recognition is understood as an issue of the good life. This is the view of both Charles Taylor and Axel Honneth, the two most prominent contemporary theorists of recognition. For both Taylor and Honneth, being recognised by another subject is a necessary condition for attaining full, undistorted subjectivity. To deny someone recognition is to deprive her or him of a basic prerequisite for human flourishing. For Taylor, for example, 'nonrecognition or misrecognition . . . can be a form of oppression, imprisoning someone in a false, distorted, reduced mode of being. Beyond simple lack of respect, it can inflict a grievous wound, saddling people with crippling self-hatred. Due recognition is not just a courtesy but a vital human need.'[5] For Honneth, similarly, 'we owe our integrity . . . to the receipt of approval or recognition from other persons. [D]enial of recognition . . . is injurious because it impairs . . . persons in their positive understanding of self – an understanding acquired by intersubjective means.'[6] Thus, both these theorists construe misrecognition in terms of impaired subjectivity and damaged self-identity. And both understand the injury in ethical terms, as stunting the subject's capacity for achieving a good life. For Taylor and Honneth, therefore, recognition is an issue of ethics.

Unlike Taylor and Honneth, I propose to conceive recognition as an issue of justice. Thus, one should not answer the question 'What's wrong with misrecognition?' by saying that it impedes human flourishing by distorting the subject's 'practical relation-to-self'.[7] One should say, rather, that it is unjust that some individuals and groups are denied the status of full partners in social interaction simply as a consequence of institutionalised patterns of cultural value in whose construction they have not equally participated and that disparage their distinctive characteristics or the distinctive characteristics assigned to them. One should say, that is, that mis-recognition is wrong because it constitutes a form of institutionalised subordination – and thus, a serious violation of justice.

This approach offers several important advantages. First, by appealing to a deontological standard it permits one to justify claims for recognition as morally binding under modern conditions of value pluralism.[8] Under these conditions, there is no single conception of the good life that is universally shared, nor any that can be established as authoritative. Thus any attempt to justify claims for recognition that appeals to an account of the good life must necessarily be sectarian. No approach of this sort can establish such claims as normatively binding on those who do not share the theorist's horizon of ethical value.

Unlike such approaches, the status model of recognition is deontological and nonsectarian. Embracing the spirit of 'subjective freedom' that is the hallmark of modernity, it assumes that it is up to individuals and groups to define for themselves what counts as a good life and to devise for themselves an approach to pursuing it, within limits that ensure a like liberty for others. Thus the status model does not appeal to a conception of the good life. It appeals, rather, to a conception of justice that can – and should – be accepted by those with divergent conceptions of the good life. What makes misrecognition morally wrong, in this view, is that it denies some individuals and groups the possibility of participating on a par with others in social interaction. The norm of participatory parity invoked here is non-sectarian in the required sense. It can justify claims for recognition as normatively binding on all who agree to abide by fair terms of interaction under conditions of value pluralism.

Treating recognition as a matter of justice has a second advantage as well. Conceiving misrecognition as status subordination, it locates the wrong in social relations, not in individual or interpersonal psychology. To be misrecognised, in this view, is not simply to be thought ill of, looked down on, or devalued in others' conscious attitudes or mental beliefs. It is rather to be denied the status of a full partner in social interaction and prevented from participating as a peer in social life as a consequence of institutionalised patterns of cultural value that constitute one as comparatively unworthy of respect or esteem. When such patterns of disrespect and disesteem are institutionalised, they impede parity of participation, just as surely as do distributive inequities.

Eschewing psychologisation, then, this approach escapes difficulties that plague rival approaches. When misrecognition is identified with internal distortions in the structure of self-consciousness of the oppressed, it is but a short step to blaming the victim, as imputing psychic damage to those subject to racism, for example, seems to add insult to injury. Conversely, when misrecognition is equated with prejudice in the minds of the oppressors, overcoming it seems to require policing their beliefs, an approach that is illiberal and authoritarian. For the status model, in contrast, misrecognition is a matter of externally manifest and publicly verifiable impediments to some people's standing as full members of society. And such arrangements are morally indefensible – whether or not they distort the subjectivity of the oppressed.[9]

Finally, by aligning recognition with justice instead of the good life, one avoids the view that everyone has an equal right to social esteem. That view is patently untenable, of course, because it renders meaningless the notion of esteem.[10] Yet it seems to follow from at least one prominent rival account. In Axel Honneth's theory, social esteem is among the 'intersubjective conditions for undistorted identity formation' that morality is supposed to protect. It follows that everyone is morally entitled to social esteem.[11] The account of recognition proposed here, in contrast, entails no such *reductio ad absurdum*. What it does entail is that everyone has an equal right to pursue social esteem under fair conditions of equal opportunity.[12] And such conditions do not obtain when, for example, institutionalised patterns of cultural value pervasively downgrade femininity, 'non-whiteness', homosexuality, and everything culturally associated with them. When that is the case, women and/or people of colour and/or gays and lesbians face obstacles in the quest for esteem that are not encountered by others. And everyone, including straight white men, faces further obstacles if they opt to pursue projects and cultivate traits that are culturally coded as feminine, homosexual, or 'non-white'.

For all these reasons, recognition is better treated as a matter of justice, and thus of morality, than as a matter of the good life, and thus of ethics. And construing recognition on the model of status permits us to treat it as a matter of justice. But what follows for the theory of justice?

Expanding the paradigm of justice

Supposing that recognition is a matter of justice, what is its relation to distribution? Does it follow, turning now to our second question, that distribution and recognition constitute two distinct, *sui generis* conceptions of justice? Or can either of them be reduced to the other?

The question of reduction must be considered from two different sides. From one side, the issue is whether existing theories of distributive justice can adequately subsume problems of recognition. In my view, the answer is no. To be sure, many distributive theorists appreciate the importance of status over and above the allocation of resources and seek to accommodate it in their accounts.[13] But the results are not wholly satisfactory. Most such theorists assume a reductive economistic-cum-legalistic view of status, supposing that a just distribution of resources and rights is sufficient to preclude misrecognition. In fact, however, not all misrecognition is a by-product of maldistribution, nor of maldistribution plus legal discrimination. Witness the case of the African-American Wall Street banker who cannot get a taxi to pick him up. To handle such cases, a theory of justice must reach beyond the distribution of rights and goods to examine institu-tionalised patterns of cultural value. It must consider whether such patterns impede parity of participation in social life.[14]

What, then, of the other side of the question? Can existing theories of recognition adequately subsume problems of distribution? Here, too, I contend the answer is no. To be sure, some theorists of recognition appre-ciate the importance of economic equality and seek to accommodate it in their accounts. But once again the results are not wholly satisfactory. Axel Honneth, for example, assumes a reductive culturalist view of distribution. Supposing that all economic inequalities are rooted in a cultural order that privileges some kinds of labour over others, he believes that changing that cultural order is sufficient to preclude all maldistribution.[15] In fact, however, not all maldistribution is a by-product of misrecognition. Witness the case of the skilled white male industrial worker who becomes unemployed owing to a factory closure resulting from a speculative corporate merger. In that case, the injustice of maldistribution has little to do with misrecognition. It is rather a consequence of imperatives intrinsic to an order of specialised economic relations whose *raison d'être* is the accumulation of profits. To handle such cases, a theory of justice must reach beyond cultural value patterns to examine the structure of capitalism. It must consider whether economic mechanisms that are relatively decoupled from structures of prestige and that operate in a relatively impersonal way impede parity of participation in social life.

In general, then, neither distribution theorists nor recognition theorists have so far succeeded in adequately subsuming the concerns of the other.[16] Thus, instead of endorsing one of their conceptions to the exclusion of the other, I propose to develop an expanded conception of justice. My con-ception treats distribution and recognition as distinct perspectives on, and dimensions of, justice. Without reducing either perspective to the other, it encompasses both dimensions within a broader, overarching framework.

As has already been noted, the normative core of my conception is the notion of *parity of participation*.[17] According to this norm, justice requires social arrangements that permit all (adult) members of society to interact with one another as peers. For participatory parity to be possible, I claim, at least two conditions must be satisfied.[18] First, the distribution of mater-ial resources must be such as to ensure participants' independence and voice. This I call the *objective condition* of participatory parity. It precludes forms and levels of material inequality and economic dependence that impede parity of participation. Precluded, therefore, are social arrange-ments that institutionalise deprivation, exploitation, and gross disparities in wealth, income, and leisure time, thereby denying some people the means and opportunities to interact with others as peers.[19]

In contrast, the second condition requires that institutionalised patterns of cultural value express equal respect for all participants and ensure equal opportunity for achieving social esteem. This I call the *intersubjective condition* of participatory parity. It precludes institutionalised norms that systematically depreciate some categories of people and the qualities associated with them. Precluded, therefore, are institutionalised value patterns that deny some people the status of full partners in interaction – whether by burdening them with excessive ascribed 'difference' or by failing to acknowledge their distinctiveness.

Both the objective condition and the intersubjective condition are necessary for participatory parity. Neither alone is sufficient. The objective condition brings into focus concerns traditionally associated with the theory of distributive justice, especially concerns pertaining to the economic structure of society and to economically defined class differentials. The intersubjective condition brings into focus concerns recently highlighted in the philosophy of recognition, especially concerns pertaining to the status order of society and to culturally defined hierarchies of status. Thus, an expanded conception of justice oriented to the norm of participatory parity encompasses both redistribution and recognition, without reducing either one to the other.

This approach goes a considerable way toward resolving the problem with which we began. By construing redistribution and recognition as two mutually irreducible dimensions of justice, and by submitting both of them to the deontological norm of participatory parity, it positions them both on the common terrain of *Moralität*. Avoiding turning prematurely to ethics, then, it seems to promise an escape route from philosophical schizophrenia.

Recognising distinctiveness?

Before proclaiming success, however, we must take up our third philosophical question: Does justice require the recognition of what is distinctive about individuals or groups, over and above the recognition of our common humanity? If the answer proves to be yes, we will have to revisit the question of ethics.

Let us begin by noting that participatory parity is a universalist norm in two senses. First, it encompasses all (adult) partners to interaction. And second, it presupposes the equal moral worth of human beings. But moral universalism in these senses still leaves open the question whether recognition of individual or group distinctiveness could be required by justice as one element among others of the intersubjective condition for participatory parity.

This question cannot be answered, I contend, by an *a priori* account of the kinds of recognition that everyone always needs. It needs rather to be approached in the spirit of a pragmatism informed by the insights of social theory. From this perspective, recognition is a remedy for social injustice, not the satisfaction of a generic human need. Thus, the form(s) of recognition justice requires in any given case depend(s) on the form(s) of misrecognition to be redressed. In cases where misrecognition involves denying the common humanity of some participants, the remedy is universalist recognition; thus, the first and most fundamental redress for South African apartheid was universal 'non-racial' citizenship. Whereas, in contrast, mis-recognition involves denying some participants' distinctiveness, the remedy could be recognition of specificity; thus, many feminists claim that over-coming gender subordination requires recognising women's unique and dis-tinctive capacity to give birth.[20] In every case, the remedy should be tailored to the harm.

This pragmatist approach overcomes the liabilities of two other, mirror-opposite views. First, it rejects the claim, espoused by some distributive theorists, that justice requires limiting public recognition to those capac-ities all humans share. Favoured by opponents of affirmative action, that approach dogmatically forecloses recognition of what distinguishes people from one another, without considering whether such recognition might be necessary in some cases to overcome obstacles to participatory parity. Second, the pragmatist approach rejects the opposite claim, equally decon-textualised, that everyone always needs their distinctiveness recognised.[21] Often favoured by recognition theorists, this second approach cannot explain why it is that not all, but only some, social differences generate claims for recognition – nor why only some of those claims, but not others, are morally justified. More specifically, it cannot explain why those occupying advantaged positions in the status order, such as men and heterosexuals, usually shun recognition of their (gender and sexual) dis-tinctiveness, claiming not specificity but universality.[22] Nor why, on those occasions when they do seek such recognition, their claims are usually spu-rious. By contrast, the approach proposed here sees claims for the recogni-tion of difference pragmatically and contextually – as remedial responses to specific pre-existing injustices. Putting questions of justice at the centre, it appreciates that the recognition needs of subordinated actors differ from those of dominant actors and that only those claims that promote parity of participation are morally justified.

For the pragmatist, accordingly, everything depends on what precisely currently misrecognised people need in order to be able to participate as peers in social life. And there is no reason to assume that all of them need the same thing in every context. In some cases, they may need to be unbur-dened of excessive ascribed or constructed distinctiveness. In other cases, they may need to have hitherto underacknowledged distinctiveness taken into account. In still other cases, they may need to shift the focus onto dominant or advantaged groups, outing the latter's distinctiveness, which has been falsely parading as universal. Alternatively, they may need to deconstruct the very terms in which attributed differences are currently elaborated. Finally, they may need all of the above, or several of the above, in combination with one another and in combination with redistribution. Which people need which kind(s) of recognition in which contexts depends on the nature of the obstacles they face with regard to participatory parity.

We cannot rule out in advance, therefore, the possibility that justice may require recognising distinctiveness in some cases.

Justifying claims for recognition

Up to this point, I have managed to answer three major philosophical questions about recognition while remaining on the terrain of *Moralität*. By construing recognition on the model of status, I have given it a deontological interpretation. And by expanding the standard paradigm of justice, I have treated redistribution and recognition as two mutually irreducible dimensions of, and perspectives on, justice, both of which can be brought under the common norm of participatory parity. Thus I have so far avoided the turn to ethics and escaped philosophical schizophrenia.

At this point, however, the question of ethics threatens to return. Once we accept that justice could, under certain circumstances, require recognition of distinctiveness, then we must consider the problem of justification. We must ask: what justifies a claim for the recognition of difference? How can one distinguish justified from unjustified claims of this sort? The crucial issue is whether a purely deontological standard will suffice – or whether, on the contrary, ethical evaluation of various practices, traits, and identities is required. In the latter event, one will have to turn to ethics after all.

Let us begin by noting that not every claim for recognition is warranted, just as not every claim for redistribution is. In both cases, one needs an account of criteria and/or procedures for distinguishing warranted from unwarranted claims. Theorists of distributive justice have long sought to provide such accounts, whether by appealing to objectivistic criteria, such as utility maximisation, or to procedural norms, such as those of discourse ethics. Theorists of recognition, in contrast, have been slower to confront this question. They have yet to provide any principled basis for distinguishing justified from unjustified claims.

This issue poses grave difficulties for those who treat recognition as an issue of ethics. Theorists who justify recognition as a means to self-realisation are especially vulnerable to objections on this point. According to Axel Honneth, for example, everyone needs their distinctiveness recognised in order to develop self-esteem, which (along with self-confidence and self-respect) is an essential ingredient of an undistorted identity.[23] It seems to follow that claims for recognition that enhance the claimant's self-esteem are justified, while those that diminish it are not. On this hypothesis, however, racist identities would seem to merit some recognition, as they enable some poor Europeans and Euroamericans to maintain their sense of self-worth by contrasting themselves with their supposed inferiors. Antiracist claims would confront an obstacle, in contrast, as they threaten the self-esteem of poor whites. Unfortunately, cases like this one, in which prejudice conveys psychological benefits, are by no means rare. They suffice to disconfirm the view that enhanced self-esteem can supply a justificatory standard for recognition claims.

How, then, should recognition claims be judged? What constitutes an adequate criterion for assessing their merits? The approach proposed here appeals to participatory parity as an evaluative standard. As we saw, this norm overarches both dimensions of justice, distribution and recognition. Thus, for both dimensions the same general criterion serves to distinguish warranted from unwarranted claims. Whether the issue is distribution or recognition, claimants must show that current arrangements prevent them from participating on a par with others in social life. Redistribution claimants must show that existing economic arrangements deny them the necessary objective conditions for participatory parity. Recognition claimants must show that institutionalised patterns of cultural value deny them the necessary intersubjective conditions. In both cases, therefore, the norm of participatory parity is the standard for warranting claims.

In both cases, too, participatory parity serves to evaluate proposed remedies for injustice. Whether they are demanding redistribution or recognition, claimants must show that the social changes they seek will in fact promote parity of participation. Redistribution claimants must show that the economic reforms they advocate will supply the objective conditions for full participation to those currently denied them – without significantly exacerbating other disparities. Similarly, recognition claimants must show that the sociocultural institutional changes they seek will supply the needed intersubjective conditions – again, without substantially worsening other disparities. In both cases, once again, participatory parity is the standard for warranting proposals for reform.

This represents a considerable improvement over the 'self-realisation' standard just discussed. Focusing on capacities for participation, the status model condemns the institutionalisation of racist values even in cases where the latter provide psychological benefits to those who subscribe to them. Nevertheless, it remains to be seen whether the norm of participatory parity is by itself sufficient to distinguish justified from unjustified claims for the recognition of difference.

Same-sex marriage, cultural minorities, and the double requirement

The problem is that not all disparities are *per se* unjust. Theorists of distributive justice have long appreciated this point with respect to economic inequalities. Seeking to distinguish just from unjust economic disparities, some of them have drawn the line between those inequalities that arise as a result of individuals' choices, on the one hand, and those that arise as a result of circumstances beyond individuals' control, on the other, arguing that only the second, and not the first, are unjust.[24] Analogous issues arise with respect to recognition. Here, too, not all disparities are unjust – because not all institutionalised value hierarchies are unjust. What is

needed, consequently, is a way of distinguishing just from unjust disparities in participation. The key question here, once again, is whether the deontological norm of parity of participation is sufficient for this purpose – and
whether, if not, one must turn to ethics.

To answer this question, let us apply the standard of participatory parity
to some current controversies. Consider, first, the example of same-sex
marriage. In this case, as we saw, the institutionalisation in marital law of
a heterosexist cultural norm denies parity of participation to gays and
lesbians. For the status model, therefore, this situation is patently unjust,
and a recognition claim is in principle warranted. Such a claim seeks to
remedy the injustice by deinstitutionalising the heteronormative value
pattern and replacing it with an alternative that promotes parity. This,
however, can be done in more than one way. One way would be to grant
the same recognition to homosexual partnerships that heterosexual partnerships currently enjoy by legalising same-sex marriage. Another would be
to deinstitutionalise heterosexual marriage, decoupling entitlements such as
health insurance from marital status and assigning them on some other basis,
such as citizenship and/or territorial residency. Although there may be good
reasons for preferring one of these approaches to the other, both of them
would serve to foster participatory parity between gays and straights; hence
both are justified in principle – assuming that neither would exacerbate other
disparities. What would not be warranted, in contrast, is an approach, like
the French PACS or the 'civil union' law in the US state of Vermont, that
establishes a second, parallel legal status of domestic partnership that fails
to confer all the symbolic or material benefits of marriage, while reserving
the latter, privileged status exclusively for heterosexual couples. Although
such reforms represent a clear advance over existing laws and may command
support on tactical grounds, as transitional measures, they do not fulfil the
requirements of justice as understood via the status model.

Such tactical considerations aside, the case of same-sex marriage presents
no difficulties for the status model. On the contrary, it illustrates a previ-
ously discussed advantage of that model. Here, the norm of participatory
parity warrants gay and lesbian claims deontologically, without recourse
to ethical evaluation – without, that is, assuming the substantive judgement that homosexual unions are ethically valuable. The self-realisation
approach, in contrast, cannot avoid presupposing that judgement, and thus
is vulnerable to counter-judgements that deny it.[25] Thus, the status model
is superior in handling this case.

Perhaps, however, this example is too easy. Let us consider some pre-
sumptively harder cases involving cultural and religious practices. In such
cases, the question arises whether participatory parity can really pass muster
as a justificatory standard, whether, that is, it can serve to warrant claims
deontologically, without recourse to ethical evaluation of the cultural and
religious practices at issue. In fact, as we shall see, participatory parity
proves adequate here as well – provided it is correctly applied.

What is crucial here is that participatory parity enters the picture at two different levels. First, at the intergroup level, it supplies the standard for assessing the effects of institutionalised patterns of cultural value on the relative standing of minorities *vis-à-vis* majorities. Thus, one invokes it when considering, for example, whether erstwhile Canadian rules mandating uniform headgear for Mounted Police constituted an unjust majority communitarianism, which effectively closed that occupation to Sikh men. Second, at the intragroup level, participatory parity also serves to assess the internal effects of minority practices for which recognition is claimed – that is, the effects on the groups' own members. At this level, one invokes it when considering, for example, whether Orthodox Jewish practices of sex segregation in education unjustly marginalise Orthodox girls and whether those practices should be denied recognition in the form of tax exemptions or school subsidies.

Taken together, these two levels constitute a double requirement for claims for cultural recognition. Claimants must show, first, that the institutionalisation of majority cultural norms denies them participatory parity and, second, that the practices whose recognition they seek do not themselves deny participatory parity – to some group members as well as to non-members. For the status model, both requirements are necessary; neither alone is sufficient. Only claims that meet both of them are deserving of public recognition.

To apply this double requirement, consider the French controversy over the *foulard*. Here the issue is whether policies forbidding Muslim girls to wear headscarves in state schools constitute unjust treatment of a religious minority. In this case, those claiming recognition for the *foulard* must establish two points: they must show, first, that the ban on the scarf constitutes an unjust majority communitarianism, which denies educational parity to Muslim girls; and second, that an alternative policy permitting the *foulard* would not exacerbate female subordination – in Muslim communities or in society at large. Only by establishing both points can they justify their claim. The first point, concerning French majority communitarianism, can be established without difficulty, it seems, as no analogous prohibition bars the wearing of Christian crosses in state schools; thus, the current policy denies equal standing to Muslim citizens. The second point, concerning the non-exacerbation of female subordination, has proved controversial, in contrast, as some French republicans have argued that the *foulard* is itself a marker of such subordination and must therefore be denied recognition. Disputing this interpretation, however, some multiculturalists have rejoined that the scarf's meaning is highly contested in French Muslim communities today, as are gender relations more generally; thus, instead of construing it as univocally patriarchal, which effectively accords male supremacists sole authority to interpret Islam, the state should treat the *foulard* as a symbol of Muslim identity in transition, one whose meaning is contested, as is French identity itself, as a result of transcultural interactions in a multicultural society. From this perspective, permitting the *foulard* in state schools could be a step toward, not away from, gender parity.[26]

In my view, the multiculturalists have the stronger argument here. (This is *not* the case, incidentally, for those who would recognise what they call 'female circumcision' – actually, genital mutilation, which clearly denies parity in sexual pleasure and in health to women and girls.) But that is not the point I wish to stress here. The point, rather, is that the argument is rightly cast in terms of parity of participation. For the status model, this is precisely where the controversy should be joined. As in the case of same-sex marriage, so in the case of cultural and religious claims, too: participatory parity is the proper standard for warranting claims. Differences in its interpretation notwithstanding, the norm of participatory parity serves to evaluate such recognition claims deontologically, without any need for ethical evaluation of the cultural or religious practices in question.[27]

In general, then, the status model sets a stringent standard for justifying claims for the recognition of cultural difference. Yet it remains wholly deontological. Applied in this double way, the norm of participatory parity suffices to rule out unwarranted claims, without any recourse to ethical evaluation.

Ecology without ethics?

The question remains, however, whether participatory parity suffices in every case, or whether it must be supplemented by ethical considerations in some. In the latter event, not all claims that passed the deontological test would be justified. Rather, only those that survived a further round of ethical examination would be deemed worthy of public recognition. On this hypothesis, participatory parity would be a necessary but not sufficient condition of justification. While serving to filter out claims that are unacceptable on deontological grounds, it would be incapable of supplying the final step, namely, assessing the ethical value of contested practices. Thus, it would be necessary, in the end, to turn to ethics.

This prospect arises when we consider cases that are not amenable to pluralist solutions. These would be cases, unlike same-sex marriage or *l'affaire foulard*, that cannot be handled by institutionalising toleration. In those two cases, people with different ethical views of the good life could agree to disagree and opt for a regime of live-and-let-live. Suppose, however, we encountered a case in which people's ethical visions were so directly antithetical, so mutually undermining, that peaceful coexistence was an impossibility. In that event, the society would be forced to choose between them, and parity of participation would cease to be a relevant goal. With that deontological standard no longer applicable, it would be necessary to evaluate the alternatives ethically. Citizens would have to assess the relative worth of two competing views of the good life.

Certainly, such cases are in principle possible. But they are not as common as those who assign recognition to ethics believe. Consider the hypothetical case of a society committed to ensuring the integrity and sustainability of the natural environment. Let us suppose that the social arrangements in this society institutionalise eco-friendly patterns of cultural value. Let us also suppose that the effect is to disadvantage a minority of members who identify with eco-exploitative cultural orientations. Suppose, too, that those members mobilised as a cultural minority and demanded equal recognition of their cultural difference. Suppose, that is, that they demanded the institutionalisation of a new pattern of cultural value that ensured parity for eco-friendly and eco-exploitative cultural practices.

Clearly, this is a case that is not amenable to a pluralist solution. It makes no sense to institutionalise parity between eco-friendly and eco-exploitative orientations within a single society, as the latter would undermine the former. Thus, society is effectively constrained to opt for one orientation or the other. The question is what can justify the choice. Proponents of ethics assume that the grounds must be ethical. As they see it, citizens must decide which orientation to nature better conduces to a good form of life; and they must justify their choice on such ethical grounds. If citizens opt for environmentalism, for example, they must appeal to value judgements rooted in an ecological world-view; if they opt for anti-environmentalism, on the contrary, they must appeal to anti-ecological values. Such appeals are problematic, however, for reasons we have already noted. Both invoke justifications internal to a world-view that the other side explicitly rejects. Thus, neither side can justify its position in terms that the other could in principle accept. And so neither can avoid casting the other outside the circle of those entitled to such justification.[28] Yet that is itself a failure of recognition – of one's fellow citizens *qua* citizens. In general, then, if no other – non-ethical – justification is available, misrecognition, and therefore injustice, cannot be avoided.

Fortunately, the difficulty is less intractable than it first appears. In fact, a non-ethical resolution is available, as the anti-ecologists' claim violates the deontological standard of participatory parity – well before ethical evaluation has to kick in. Specifically, it violates the second prong of the double requirement, which holds that proposed reforms must not exacerbate one disparity of participation in the course of remedying another. In this case, the anti-ecologists seek to remedy their own disparity *vis-à-vis* their eco-friendly fellow citizens – but they would do so at the expense of future generations. By instituting parity now for practices that would worsen global warming, they would deny their successors the material prerequisites for a viable form of life – thereby violating intergenerational justice. Thus, the anti-ecologists' claim fails the test of participatory parity. And so this case, too, like same-sex marriage and *l'affaire foulard*, can be adjudicated on deontological grounds. No recourse to ethics is necessary.

The moral here is that one should proceed cautiously before turning to ethics. Ethical evaluation, after all, is problematic. Always contextually embedded, it is subject to dispute whenever divergent evaluative horizons come into contact. Thus, one should take care to exhaust the full resources of deontological reasoning before taking that step. In fact, as this example shows, cases that seem initially to require ethics can often be resolved by deontological means. This is not to say that cases requiring ethical evaluation are impossible in principle. But it is to insist that the determination that one has in fact encountered such a case can be made only at the end of a long line of moral reasoning. To fail to complete that chain is to turn prematurely to ethics. In that event, one embarks on a dubious enterprise. Appealing to substantive horizons of value that are not shared by everyone concerned, one sacrifices the chance to adjudicate recognition claims definitively – in ways that are binding on all.

Conclusion

For this reason, as well as for the others I have offered here, one should postpone the turn to ethics as long as possible. Alternative approaches, favoured, alas, by most recognition theorists, turn prematurely to ethics. Foreclosing the option of developing a deontological interpretation of recognition, they miss the chance to reconcile claims for the recognition of difference with claims for egalitarian redistribution. Thus, they miss the chance to restructure the conceptual terrain that is currently fostering philo-sophical schizophrenia.

Given that unpalatable alternative, it is reassuring to see just how far one can get with a deontological interpretation of recognition. And we *did* get remarkably far here. By employing the status model, with its principle of participatory parity, it was possible to handle apparently ethical questions, such as the recognition of same-sex marriage, on the one hand, and questions of minority religious and cultural practices, on the other, without in fact turning to ethics. Even the seemingly harder case of environmental ethics proved susceptible to deontological resolution.

In general, then, the argument pursued here supports a rather heartening conclusion: there is no need to pose an either/or choice between the politics of redistribution and the politics of recognition. It is possible, on the contrary, to construct a comprehensive framework that can accommodate both – by following the path pursued here. First, one must construe recognition as a matter of justice, as opposed to 'the good life'. This, in turn, requires replacing the standard identity model of recognition with the alternative status model sketched here. Next, one must expand one's conception of justice to encompass distribution and recognition as two mutually irreducible dimensions. This involves bringing both dimensions under the deontological norm of participatory parity. Finally, after acknowledging that justice could in some cases require recognising distinctiveness over and above common humanity, one must subject claims for recognition to the justificatory standard of participatory parity. This, as we saw, means scrutinising institutionalised patterns of cultural value, and proposals for changing them, for their impact on social interaction – both across and within social groups. Only then, after all these steps, *might* one encounter a situation in which it *could* prove necessary to turn to ethics. Apart from such cases, one will succeed in remaining on the terrain of *Moralität* and in avoiding the ethical turn.

It is possible, I conclude, to endorse both redistribution and recognition while avoiding philosophical schizophrenia. In this way, one can prepare some of the conceptual groundwork for tackling what I take to be the central political question of the day: How can we develop a coherent orientation that integrates redistribution and recognition? How can we develop a framework that integrates what remains cogent and unsurpassable in the socialist vision with what is cogent and irrefutable in the new, apparently 'post-socialist' vision of multiculturalism? If we fail to ask this question, if we cling instead to false antitheses and misleading either/or dichotomies, we will miss the chance to envision social arrangements that can redress both economic and cultural injustices. Only by looking to integrative approaches that unite redistribution and recognition can we meet the requirements of justice for all.

Notes

Portions of this chapter are adapted and excerpted from my essay, 'Social justice in the age of identity politics: Redistribution, recognition and participation', in N. Fraser and A. Honneth, *Redistribution or Recognition? A Political-Philosophical Exchange* (London: Verso, 2003). I am grateful to the Tanner Foundation for Human Values for support of this work, an earlier version of which was presented as The Tanner Lecture on Human Values at Stanford University, 30 April–2 May 1996. I thank Elizabeth Anderson and Axel Honneth for their thoughtful responses to the Lecture and Rainer Forst for his probing comments on a previous draft of the present essay.

1 See Fraser, 'Social justice'; N. Fraser, 'From redistribution to recognition? Dilemmas of justice in a "postsocialist" age', *New Left Review*, 212 (July/August 1995) 68–93; reprinted in N. Fraser, *Justice Interruptus: Critical Reflections on the 'Postsocialist' Condition* (London: Routledge, 1997); and N. Fraser, 'Adding insult to injury: Social justice and the politics of recognition', in a forthcoming volume edited by K. Olson.
2 For a fuller discussion of the identity model of recognition, see N. Fraser, 'Rethinking recognition: Overcoming displacement and reification in cultural politics', *New Left Review* 3 (May/June 2000) 107–20.
3 For a fuller critique of the identity model, see Fraser, 'Rethinking recognition'.
4 For fuller accounts of the status model of recognition, see Fraser, 'Rethinking recognition', and 'Social justice'.

5 C. Taylor, 'The politics of recognition', in *Multiculturalism: Examining the Politics of Recognition*, ed. A. Gutmann (Princeton, NJ: Princeton University Press, 1994), p. 25.

6 A. Honneth, 'Integrity and disrespect: Principles of a conception of morality based on the theory of recognition', *Political Theory*, 20:2 (1992), pp. 188–9.

7 A. Honneth, *The Struggle for Recognition: The Moral Grammar of Social Conflicts*, trans. Joel Anderson (Cambridge: Polity Press, 1995) and 'Integrity and disrespect'.

8 I am grateful to Rainer Forst for help in formulating this point.

9 As I noted, the status model eschews psychologisation. However, what this means requires some clarification. The model does not suppose that misrecognition never has the sort of psychological effects described by Taylor and Honneth. But it maintains that the wrongness of misrecognition does not depend on the presence of such effects. Thus, the status model decouples the normativity of recognition claims from psychology, thereby strengthening their normative force. When claims for recognition are premised on a psychological theory of 'the intersubjective conditions for undistorted identity formation', as in Honneth's model, they are made vulnerable to the vicissitudes of that theory; their moral bindingness evaporates whenever the theory turns out to be false. By treating recognition as a matter of status, in contrast, the model I am proposing avoids mortgaging normative claims to matters of psychological fact. One can show that a society whose institutionalised norms impede parity of participation is unjust even if it does not inflict psychic damage on those it subordinates.

10 Here I am assuming the distinction, now fairly standard in moral philosophy, between respect and esteem. According to this distinction, respect is owed universally to every person in virtue of shared humanity; esteem, in contrast, is accorded differentially on the basis of persons' specific traits, accomplishments, or contributions. Thus, while the injunction to respect everyone equally is perfectly sensible, the injunction to esteem everyone equally is self-defeating.

11 Honneth, *The Struggle for Recognition*.

12 This point can be restated as follows: although no one has a right to equal social esteem in the positive sense, everyone has a right not to be *dis*esteemed on the basis of institutionalised group classifications that undermine her or his standing as a full partner in social interaction. I owe this formulation to Rainer Forst (personal conversation).

13 John Rawls, for example, at times conceives 'primary goods' such as income and jobs as 'social bases of self-respect', while also speaking of self-respect itself as an especially important primary good whose distribution is a matter of justice. Ronald Dworkin, likewise, defends the idea of 'equality of resources' as the distributive expression of the 'equal moral worth of persons'. Amartya Sen, finally, considers both a 'sense of self' and the capacity 'to appear in public without shame' as relevant to the 'capability to function', and hence as falling within the scope of an account of justice that enjoins the equal distribution of basic capabilities. See J. Rawls, *A Theory of Justice* (Cambridge, MA: Harvard University Press, 1971), §67 and §82; J. Rawls, *Political Liberalism* (New York: Columbia University Press, 1993), p. 82, p. 181, and p. 318ff.; R. Dworkin, 'What is equality? Part 2: Equality of resources', *Philosophy and Public Affairs*, 10:4 (Autumn 1981) 283–345; and A. Sen, *Commodities and Capabilities* (Amsterdam: North-Holland, 1985).

14 The outstanding exception of a theorist who has sought to encompass issues of culture within a distributive framework is Will Kymlicka. Kymlicka proposes to treat access to an 'intact cultural structure' as a primary good to be fairly distributed. This approach was tailored for multinational polities, such as Canada, as opposed to polyethnic polities, such as the United States. It becomes problematic, however, in cases where mobilised claimants for recognition do not divide neatly (or even do not divide so neatly) into groups with distinct and relatively bounded cultures. It also has difficulty dealing with cases in which claims for recognition do not take the form of demands for (some level of) sovereignty, but aim rather at parity of participation within a polity that is crosscut by multiple, intersecting lines of difference and inequality. For the argument that an intact cultural structure is a primary good, see W. Kymlicka, *Liberalism, Community and Culture* (Oxford: Oxford University Press, 1989). For the distinction between multinational and polyethnic politics, see W. Kymlicka, 'Three forms of group-differentiated citizenship in Canada', in S. Benhabib (ed.), *Democracy and Difference* (Princeton, NJ: Princeton University Press, 1996).

15 Honneth, *The Struggle for Recognition*.

16 In the absence of a substantive reduction, moreover, purely verbal subsumptions are of little use. There is little to be gained by insisting as a point of semantics that, for example, recognition, too, is a good to be distributed; nor, conversely, by maintaining as a matter of definition that every distributive pattern expresses an underlying matrix of recognition. In both cases, the result is a tautology. The first makes all recognition distribution by definition, while the second merely asserts the reverse. In neither case have the substantive problems of conceptual integration been addressed. In fact, such purely definitional 'reductions' could actually serve to impede progress in solving these problems. By creating the misleading appearance of reduction, such approaches could make it difficult to see, let alone address, possible tensions and conflicts between claims for redistribution and claims for recognition.

17 Since I coined this phrase in 1995, the term 'parity' has come to play a central role in feminist politics in France. There, it signifies the demand that women occupy a full 50 per cent of seats in parliament and other representative bodies. 'Parity' in France, accordingly, means strict numerical gender equality in political representation. For me, in contrast, 'parity' means the condition of being a *peer*, of being on a *par* with others, of standing on an equal footing. I leave the question open exactly what degree or level of equality is necessary to ensure such parity. In my formulation, moreover, the moral requirement is that members of society be ensured the *possibility* of parity, if and when they choose to participate in a given activity or interaction. There is no requirement that everyone actually participate in any such activity. For a fuller discussion of French parité, see N. Fraser, 'Pour une politique féministe à l'âge de la reconnaissance: approche bi-dimensionnelle à justice entre les sexes', trans. B. Marrec, *Actuel Marx*, No. 30 (September, 2001).

18 I say '*at least* two conditions must be satisfied' in order to allow for the possibility of more than two. I have in mind specifically a possible third class of obstacles to participatory parity that could be called 'political', as opposed to economic or cultural. 'Political' obstacles to participatory parity would include

decision-making procedures that systematically marginalise some people even in the absence of maldistribution and misrecognition, for example, single-member district winner-take-all electoral rules that deny voice to quasi-permanent minorities. The corresponding injustice would be 'political marginalisation' or 'exclusion', the corresponding remedy, 'democratisation'. For a more extended discussion of this 'third' dimension of justice, see N. Fraser, 'Social justice in the age of identity politics'. For an insightful account of single-member district winner-take-all electoral rules, see L. Guinier, *The Tyranny of the Majority* (New York: The Free Press, 1994).

19 It is an open question how much economic inequality is consistent with parity of participation. Some such inequality is inevitable and unobjectionable. But there is a threshold at which resource disparities become so gross as to impede participatory parity. Where exactly that threshold lies is a matter for further investigation.

20 I say the remedy *could* be recognition of difference, not that it must be. In fact, there are other possible remedies for the denial of distinctiveness – including deconstruction of the very terms in which differences are currently elaborated. For a discussion of such alternatives, see N. Fraser, 'Social justice in the age of identity politics'.

21 Both Taylor and Honneth hold this view. See Taylor, 'The politics of recognition', and Honneth, *The Struggle for Recognition*.

22 L. Nicholson, 'To be or not to be: Charles Taylor and the politics of recognition', *Constellations: An International Journal of Critical and Democratic Theory*, 3:1 (1996) 1–16.

23 Honneth, *The Struggle for Recognition*.

24 See, for example, Dworkin, 'What is equality? Part 2'.

25 Let me forestall any possible misunderstanding: I myself have no quarrel with the view that attributes ethical value to homosexual relationships. But I still insist that it cannot adequately ground the claim for recognition in societies where citizens hold divergent views of the good life and disagree among themselves as to the ethical value of same-sex unions.

26 Certainly, there is room for disagreement as to the effects of the *foulard* on the status of girls. Those effects cannot be calculated by an algorithmic metric or method. On the contrary, they can only be determined dialogically, by the give-and-take of argument, in which conflicting judgements are sifted and rival interpretations are weighed.

27 In general, the standard of participatory parity cannot be applied monologically, in the manner of a decision procedure. Rather, it must be applied dialogically and discursively, through democratic processes of public debate. In such debates, participants argue about whether existing institutionalised patterns of cultural value impede parity of participation and about whether proposed alternatives would foster it – without exacerbating other disparities. For the status model, then, participatory parity serves as an idiom of public contestation and deliberation about questions of justice. More strongly, it represents the principal idiom of public reason, the preferred language for conducting democratic political argumentation on issues of both distribution and recognition. For a fuller account of this dialogical approach, see Fraser, 'Social justice in the age of identity politics'.

28 For an argument for 'a basic right to justification' in terms one could in principle accept, see R. Forst, 'The basic right to justification: Toward a constructivist
   conception of human rights', *Constellations*, 6 (1999) 35–60. For a fuller treatment, see R. Forst, *Contexts of Justice. Political Philosophy beyond Liberalism
   and Communitarianism*, trans. J. M. M. Farrell (Berkeley and Los Angeles, CA:
   University of California Press, 2001), especially Chapters II and IV.

Part II

The contexts of toleration

6

Reflexive toleration in a deliberative democracy

James Bohman

Any feasible ideal of democracy must face the unavoidable social fact that the citizenry of a modern state is heterogeneous along a number of inter-secting dimensions, including race, class, religion and culture. If that ideal is also deliberative, and thus requires that citizens commit themselves to making decisions according to reasons they believe are public, then such diversity raises the possibility of deep and potentially irresolvable conflicts. When conflicts do emerge, such a form of democracy requires that all citizens should have equal standing and influence in any deliberation about their resolution. In the circumstances of wide pluralism (that is, of plural-ism along a number of dimensions), toleration would seem to be both part of the ideal of public reason and an important virtue for citizens to exercise in their deliberative institutions. Yet deliberation also demands more of citizens than silent toleration regarding the reasons of those with whom they disagree, especially if they accept that an important goal of public deliberation is to find the best possible mutually acceptable solution to a problem or conflict. It demands the critical engagement of citizens in a delib-erative polity. How can such engagement be critical without being intoler-ant, and tolerant without being uncritical? That is the task of a deliberative theory of tolerance.

When is deliberative tolerance needed? In a democracy, tolerance is exercised in resolving conflicts that are motivated by differences in belief. It would seem, then, that toleration in deliberation requires that citizens adopt some impartial or neutral stance and avoid directly confronting each other on the most contentious issues. At the same time, it is also equally unlikely that citizens would be able to deliberate about the sources of their conflicts and disagreements at all if toleration entails, as Rawls holds, that 'central to the idea of public reason is that it neither criticises nor attacks any comprehensive doctrine, religious or non-religious'.[1] Rawls goes on to offer the following exception: criticism of any such doctrine is permissible 'insofar as it is incompatible with the essentials of public reason and a democratic polity'. Such a doctrine would then be criticised as 'unreasonable', even if in the 'wider background culture of civil society' such doctrines may be criticised without the restrictions of public reason.[2] Is such an account sufficiently tolerant given the fact of pluralism as it is manifested today? Does it provide the correct basis for criticism that would improve the deliberative process while allowing all to participate as free and equal citizens?

Proponents of deliberative democracy might find these restrictions too weak. They might argue that the requirements of public reason are sufficient to exclude any such appeal to comprehensive doctrines at all, since those who do not accept them have no reason to accept such reasons.[3] Suppose that we take the perspective of the proponent of such a doctrine instead of the critic. How else could the proponent challenge any particular law when it is just the conflict with such reasons that is salient? More importantly, citizens who seek to challenge the regime of toleration itself simply have no recourse other than to appeal to their own comprehensive doctrines if they are to show why it is unacceptable to them or to anyone else who holds beliefs similar to theirs. It would seem, then, that it would be best to make it a demand of tolerance that participants in deliberation accept any reason as public, particularly when toleration and its limits are at stake. However, public deliberation cannot be so tolerant as to make citizens unable to make any distinctions at all among better or worse reasons. All reasons must be subject to critical scrutiny, especially by those who do not believe that they are compelling. This requires that comprehensive doctrines be criticised more thoroughly and substantively than the standard of 'reasonableness' permits. It must also, following Kant, be critical of itself, of its own 'essentials', if it is not to become intolerant and violate the political equality of *all* citizens, some of whom properly challenge the current interpretation of the limits and scope of publicity and toleration. If this is the case, then there is nothing special about the essentials of public reason and democracy, since they, too, are proper subjects for deliberation, and indeed part of the continuum of forms of deliberation in public life in a pluralist society.

Even if we may challenge the essentials of any political conception of justice, toleration must still impose some limits on deliberation if it is to support rather than undermine democracy. A reflexive conception of toleration clearly pulls in two directions and reveals tensions in the deliberative ideal under the condition of pluralism. On the one hand, its ideal is democratic, and for that reason accepts that all have equal voice in an inclusive political community. On the other hand, a deliberative ideal seeks the best reasons, and can do so only if some of the reasons citizens offer will have to be revised and even rejected in public discussion. My goal here is to show that this tension can be resolved if toleration becomes reflexive, that is, only if it is an ideal that is itself open to the demands of free and open public deliberation and the qualities of public communication that make that possible. Deliberative toleration is distinctive, I argue, in so far as it is reflexive in two senses at once. First, it opens up standards and regimes of toleration to public deliberation rather than removing them from debate. Second, deliberative toleration is reflexive because it is not concerned directly with freedom of expression or even with the quality of the reasons that others offer in public discussion. Rather, it is reflexive because its object is not the content of speech, but the maintenance of a free and open structure of communication in a pluralist society. Reflexive toleration still has to serve the purpose of promoting public deliberation, and it does so not only by testing its current procedures and substance, but also by being directed at a fundamental democratic value of political equality. Toleration in a deliberative democracy serves to support 'political egalitarianism', broadly understood as the 'equal access for all to influence political deliberation', especially in those decisions that become collectively and legally binding. Intolerant regimes are then rejected on political egalitarian grounds, and the proof that any regime is intolerant is that it is inegalitarian and undermines inclusive deliberation.

The public role of religious expression provides an interesting test case for reflexive toleration, especially since it is tolerated religions that typically challenge the nature and limits of religious toleration. The debate about religion and the public square has largely focused on the wrong problem: the crucial issue in a reflexive and deliberative regime of toleration is not whether religious reasons are public or not, but how it is that standards of public reason and toleration themselves can properly be challenged and widened with the expanding moral and political community. Such conflicts over toleration will be the result of specific sorts of conflicts in which intersecting dimensions and overlapping domains of social and cultural diversity become salient. The conflicts that are the object of reflexive toleration can be resolved only by creating the conditions for an inclusive deliberative community. Thus, toleration is not merely openness to others in discourse, but the capacity to treat them as free and equal members of a community of deliberation and judgement. As a regulative ideal, toleration maintains such a community; it deems intolerant those who deny that conflicts can be solved in such a way as to maintain the equal membership of all.

Toleration, conflict and pluralism old and new

The need for toleration in any modern polity, whether democratic or not, emerges from general facts of modern societies, in particular 'the fact of pluralism'. Just how this fact is characterised has much to do with the contours of a theory of toleration, particularly in dealing with the nature and scope of toleration. For Rawls, 'the fact of pluralism' is simply the diversity of moral doctrines in modern societies, a permanent feature of modern society that is directly relevant to political order because its conditions 'profoundly affect the requirements of a workable conception of justice'.[4] Such facts are permanent, in that modern institutions and ideals developed after the Wars of Religion, including constitutional democracy and freedom of expression, promote rather than inhibit the development of further pluralism. This fact of pluralism alters how we are to think of the *feasibility* of a political ideal under the conditions of pluralism.[5] Since what is established in any such ideal is a system of cooperation, the essentials of political justice concern what anyone could accept regardless of their moral doctrine. In this section I want to develop an alternative account of the need for toleration using examples of intersecting or 'deep conflicts' that characterise a new threshold of diversity that is no longer captured by the model of religious conflict. These examples show that the greatest difficulty is not the everyday challenges to principles and standards of deliberation, but rather those conflicts that intersect at various levels, dimensions and domains in extremely diverse societies. The key to their solution is subjecting the regime of toleration to the regulative principle of equal standing or non-subordination in an inclusive community.

The defining historical moment of the liberal regime of toleration is the emergence of religious pluralism and the distinctive zero-sum character of religious conflict within a particular political community. With the emergence of genuinely multicultural and even global polities, religion has lost its central place, and become only one aspect of pluralism among many. It has at the same time taken on increasing significance between societies, exacerbated today by unprecedented migration and the rise of religious fundamentalism throughout the world. In the light of this historical difference between the newer and the older situations of religious toleration, it is now important to disaggregate the fact of pluralism in two ways if we are to make sense of the need for a new regime of toleration: pluralism now needs to be distinguished according to aspects and dimensions. These distinctions will in turn suggest further differences in types of conflicts according to their complexity and degree of tractability and to the demands of toleration.

Under contemporary social conditions, the fact of pluralism has a number of different aspects having to do with different sorts of diversity. Such aspects can be defined along several axes: cultural, social, and epistemic diversity. Cultural diversity concerns the presence of different groups with different interpretations of their identities; it has been discussed in terms of multiculturalism and recent disputes about 'identity politics', including ethnic and various religious conflicts over the character of national culture. Epistemic diversity is a relatively recent phenomenon having to do with the cognitive division of labour and the emergence of scientific expertise and its claims to authority. Finally, I include social pluralism, which is not the pluralism of self-identified groups but of various social positions, as having a particular place in a structure or process, such as at the periphery of a society or as being a subordinate in a social hierarchy.

Each aspect of diversity can be measured along various deliberative dimensions: in terms of values, opinions and perspectives. These roughly correspond to the main aspects of diversity: diversity in terms of basic moral or political norms (including conceptions of the common good); in terms of different opinions (including beliefs about the way in which beliefs are justified); and in terms of the perspectives afforded by different social positions (primarily emerging with the range and type of experience of one's society). Divergence in values, opinions, and perspectives can be quite wide, and in this way produce conflicts. Taken singly, however, such divergences need not be 'deep'; a conflict is deep only if it occurs along a number of different and overlapping dimensions. It is these deep and overlapping conflicts that best reveal the scope of toleration in pluralist societies, since democracy in general and deliberative democracy in particular is a way of settling differences of value and opinion in ways that make possible solutions that everyone could reasonably accept. Ordinary politics employs the egalitarian norms of democracy to settle disputes and to accommodate even permanent disagreements along one dimension.

Conflicts of opinion are settled in fairly standard ways, using recognised procedures and assumptions. Even when these do not work, toleration of differences of opinion can leave wide disagreements in place. In practices of inquiry, diversity of opinion is instrumentally valuable for the goal that Mill describes as 'having the truth win out in the marketplace of ideas'. But epistemic diversity also has a negative side that produces potential conflicts when it overlaps with other aspects of the fact of pluralism, such as the plurality of values. Epistemic diversity is valuable in the Millian sense only in light of shared commitments to procedures and practices of evidence. In Christian Science refusal cases or disputes about evolution in schools, the conflict is not along a single dimension but involves overlapping disagreements of values and opinion (especially beliefs about how to settle differences of opinion). Diversity of values alone is not problematic given commitments to democracy and its norms of freedom and equality; freedom defines the scope of reasonable disagreement about values, limiting the degree to which one group may impose their values on others and thereby restrict their freedom. Such ideals commit participants in democracy to finding solutions that can be agreed upon by all those affected. But once again this solution becomes problematic when the norms of democracy are called into question by moral values such as cultural self-determination (in terms of which some forms of democracy itself are seen as oppressive) or epistemic values that see little worth in dialogue or discussion (as in the case of religious fundamentalism). Similarly, differences in perspective can be overcome by shared experiences in a wider background culture that bridge the gap; commitment to other values such as democracy may make citizens willing to undergo a democratic process that entails subjecting oneself to such experiences to achieve a shift in perspectives, as was the case in the American Civil Rights Movement.

In the light of the problem of deep conflicts, a democratic pluralism might seem to be self-defeating. On the one hand, democracy seems to be directly challenged by pluralism, since it seems to be a way of settling conflicts along a single dimension according to the single and perhaps abstract aspect of their political significance. On the other hand, democracy seems directly to challenge pluralism by pointing out its possible limits. One way out of this paradox is to eliminate those alternatives that challenge the principles of a democratic polity from the domain of public deliberation. Because such challenges are *ipso facto* 'unreasonable' and as such can be excluded from deliberation, it is hard to see how these criteria are consistent with the 'inclusive view' that Rawls wishes now to profess. While this solution is not obviously self-defeating, it does not solve the problem. The fact of pluralism can no longer be characterised in such a way that any particular conception of justice, liberal or otherwise, can be regarded as reasonable and others not. It is not possible to exclude such challenges as unreasonable, since the fact of pluralism now demands that conflicts be settled by public deliberation on the essentials of democracy themselves. Given the fact of the 'new' pluralism, the only satisfactory way out of this paradox is to offer an account of the basic norms and ideals governing democratic process based on a stronger conception of toleration consistent with wide and deep pluralism. That is, the facts of pluralism demand that we now must transform how we think about basic democratic conceptions and ideals, while preserving their normative core, if they are to be effective regulative principles for deliberation. The problem of a democratic pluralism is then to transform such norms in such a way as to be able to avoid or to resolve overlapping conflicts.

The first task of a democratic pluralism that is at the same time deliberative is to rethink what it means to resolve a conflict in the light of possibly permanent disagreement, even while retaining the ideal of a deliberative community. Such conflicts seem less trenchant once the goal of deliberation in a tolerant democracy is not to resolve disagreements into consensus, but rather to maintain ongoing public communication and egalitarian social relations. Even this more feasible goal requires rethinking basic ideals of publicity, impartiality, and the rule of law. What guides this transformation? Here it is necessary to consider more closely why citizens should be tolerant of each other in a deliberative democracy. The reason why they ought be tolerant is not to avoid conflict by excluding contentious reasons, but rather to provide for respect for all as equal members of a deliberative community. They can do so only if all groups may participate in such a community without domination or subordination. Because of the central roles of political egalitarianism and deliberative responsiveness, such an account of toleration is also able to redraw the limits of toleration consistently by resolving deep and overlapping conflicts that liberal toleration cannot. This alternative can be developed by showing how it solves the paradox of toleration in a democracy while permitting mutual and critical exchange among citizens. I consider the liberal and deliberative views of religious toleration as the test case.

Toleration: liberal or deliberative?

As the product of the specific historical situation of religious pluralism, many now argue that liberal toleration is increasingly inadequate to deal with pluralism along more than one dimension at a time. Depending on the target, critics argue that liberalism is either too thin or too thick. For some critics, liberal toleration is purely negative, having to do with prohibiting arbitrary interference with others rather than with engaging them morally. These critics argue that thin liberal neutrality leads to a 'dynamic of tolera- tion and oppression, sustained by the morally minimal and instrumental nature of liberal toleration'.[6] Instead, a positive or 'liberating' conception of toleration is not based on discovering the functional requirements for stability in a democracy from some observer's perspective, but rather upon taking up the perspective of the citizen who seeks redress from forms of subordination that inhibit her ability to give effective voice to her dissent.[7] Other critics take the opposing side, seeing liberal toleration as based on the culturally specific conception of autonomy and thus as imposing liberal norms and a comprehensive moral doctrine on those deemed intolerant.[8] A deliberative conception is not liberal, in that it too rejects toleration based on neutrality and autonomy. But, like the liberal conception, it asks how it is that toleration could be morally justified to free and equal citizens, each from his or her own point of view.

It has historically been the case that those who are tolerated, rather than those who are tolerating, more often challenge regimes of toleration. For example, current challenges to the liberal regime of toleration now in place come from religious groups, which from the liberal perspective seem to be merely 'the recurrence of sectarian and cultic religiosity and of fundamen- talist theologies'.[9] Contrary to the liberal view, such a religious challenge could very well be legitimate in a deliberative context. More often than not, it takes the form of the contestation of certain regulative principles guiding deliberation. Consider Gutmann and Thompson's principle of reciprocity.[10] The constraint of reciprocity, they claim, putatively undermines claims such as those of religious fundamentalists in Tennessee decided in *Mozert v. Hawkins County Board of Education* not to have their children read various books because they violate their religious beliefs: 'The parents' rea- soning appeals to values that can and should be rejected by citizens of a pluralist society committed to protecting the basic liberties and opportu- nities of all citizens.'[11] In excluding religious reasons as 'non-reciprocal' or 'unreasonable', the substantive principle of reciprocity begins to look very much like either the liberal conception of autonomy or a principle of neu- trality that simply eliminates religious reasons even when they are the con- dition for meaningful participation by some parties in discussion of the issue at hand.

This example raises several issues. Granted that democratic discussion takes place under some constraints, are these sorts of constraints proper and deliberation-promoting? Should citizens (especially religious ones) rationally accept such *ex ante* constraints in order to participate in public deliberation? Reciprocity cannot be invoked as the overriding constraint if the issue is to treat all parties in the deliberation as equal members of the same deliberative community. Joshua Cohen makes the same point about the constraint of reasonableness: 'If one accepts the democratic process, agreeing that adults are, more or less without exception, to have access to it, then one cannot accept as a reason within that same process that some are worth less than others or that the interests of one group are to count for less than others.'[12] If the reasons of some are not to be worth less than those of others, and if we accept that reasonableness as a norm is constrained by such larger democratic requirements, then the parents in Hawkins County, even if unreasonable in Rawls's sense, are owed a justi-fication for the practice they are challenging. Not to offer a justification to the unreasonable is to exclude them from the community of judgement and thus to violate the democratic commitment to political egalitarianism.[13] Thus, even if we may say that the parents' doctrine was unreasonable or non-reciprocal, or even if certain citizens do not themselves engage in tol-erant perspective-taking, these facts in no way undermine their reflexive challenge. A second-order challenge is legitimate only if it shows that the regime of toleration as practised is indeed exclusionary, as when public reasons are considered secular or when religious reasons have no worth in the context of democratic deliberation. Gutmann and Thompson's sub-stantive criterion of reciprocity is exclusionary in just this sense, to the extent that it violates the principle of political egalitarianism.

Such a criticism of criteria such as reciprocity or reasonableness is quite common in any theory based on deeper democratic commitments. The guiding ideal of deliberative democracy shows that fair procedures are insuf-ficient by themselves if democracy demands all participants be given equal standing and have their particular reasons taken seriously. In this way, citi-zens could justifiably contest a deliberative regime of toleration even if it is based on principles of reciprocity and reasonableness. Religious citizens could argue on egalitarian grounds that these principles are interpreted in such a way that (other things being equal) they could not expect their reasons would have any influence on important issues regarding political liberties. When excluded from the community of judgement, citizens can appeal to democratic principles to urge that the regime be revised. In this case it cannot be justified to them as participants in public deliberation, all of whom as citizens are owed a justification whether they are reasonable or not. Accord-ing to this argument, then, toleration in a deliberative democracy is based on the commitment to the principle of political egalitarianism: that is, the equal access to political influence of all citizens over all decisions that affect them.[14] When the issue being contested is that important reasons are being excluded on some disputable epistemic ground or judgement of the nature of the reason, whether citizens are reasonable or unreasonable is irrelevant prior to deliberation on this very point. Thus, even to say that justification is owed to the unreasonable person *qua* citizen does not quite capture the demanding requirements of deliberative toleration.

How might we think of the *Mozert* case given a different account of the fact of pluralism and reflexive toleration based on political egalitarianism? The solution that takes seriously the parents' concerns would seek some form of accommodation consistent with the deeper democratic principles on which the parents implicitly rely. In this way, school officials could seek a principled compromise from a list of mutually acceptable books.[15] While these parents continue to participate in the wider set of economic, social and political practices, groups like the Amish or indigenous peoples seek less cooperation with the wider society and warrant the widest possible accommodation on this issue (as the Court has already decided in many cases). It is not unreasonable for them to adopt a stance toward the terms of social cooperation that they do not believe others will hold. This attitude is not that of 'mere toleration' that Gutmann and Thompson fear will 'leave social divisions intact' and fail to provide 'a positive basis for resolving moral disagreement in the future',[16] since it still regards these groups as members of the inclusive deliberative community. Those groups that deny the deeper democratic principles upon which a reflexive challenge is based will not receive uptake and accommodation, since they reject rather than seek to modify the regulative framework for common deliberation, nor do they seek any positive basis for resolving moral disagreement. Thus, the deliberative conception of tolerance is not less tolerant than the liberal one, just tolerant in a different and more engaged way.

With these debates about reciprocity and reasonableness in mind, the main difference between a liberal and deliberative conception of toleration can then be put this way: those tolerated in a democracy have to be addressed as equals rather than subordinates, however fairly they are treated when they have no capacity to influence decisions. Furthermore, those tolerated in a deliberative democracy must be able to see that their deeply held convictions, when expressed as reasons for others, have the same public worth as the reasons of others. The recognition of their value does not mean that those reasons will or should carry the day, since they, too, must be reflexively acceptable to those for whom they are offered as a justification without subordination. This justification cannot merely be a matter of the self-expression of a sincere belief; nor can it be justified to the community from a third-person perspective as a requirement of social stability or the common good. Neither of these attitudes establishes sustained critical engagement with the reasons of those to whom one has addressed the justification of a regime of toleration.

Why call such a justification reflexive? A deliberative regime of toleration is 'reflexive' precisely because the appeal to a free and open process of public deliberation is able to make sense of and to countenance just such challenges in ways that a liberal regime cannot. It is reflexive in a stronger sense as well; it connects toleration to norms and obligations of public communication, as the medium in which toleration as a standard of critical engagement is contested and deliberated upon. Deliberative toleration is connected to communication in three ways. First, it is an attitude toward the reasons of others; they must be taken seriously, even as they are criticised or rejected. That is, they must be understood and taken up in discussion in a way that the original speakers cannot reject. Second, it is an attitude toward the speakers, who are equals without subordination only if their communication is treated in such a way that it may be effective. Third, it must also be a communicative attitude toward the *perspectives* of those to whom one is attempting to justify a decision in deliberation. In a deliberative context, toleration requires the capacity not merely to let the other person or group alone regardless of our negative attitudes, but to take up their perspective. Intolerance is thus a failure of perspective-taking, so that the limits on the scope of toleration may not be sufficient to maintain the free and open public communication needed for deliberation inclusive of all citizens. Neither demanding that citizens exercise virtues of civility nor prohibiting uncivil speech legally is sufficient to maintain the structure of communication necessary for deliberation among equals.

Toleration, democracy and communication

Depending upon the practices, attitudes of toleration have various potential objects. At the most abstract level, toleration ought to be extended to all persons as bearers of human rights, including rights of self-expression. This may be expressed in duties not to interfere with or to prohibit such expression. But these negative, perfect duties may not be the most appropriate level of description for democratic contexts in which citizens are already engaged in practices of deliberation. The language of rights, permissions and prohibitions is not sufficient, in that we do not violate the rights of others to self-expression when we fail to consider seriously their reasons in deliberation. In order to capture the obligations of public deliberation, Onora O'Neill correctly argues that it is communication itself that is 'the proper object of toleration' in a democracy.[17] In deliberative settings, citizens manifest their equality with each other not only by refraining from interfering with each other's acts of expression; they also do so by sustaining the conditions for communication. How do they do this? They do so reflexively, in their communication with each other in public deliberation and in their attitudes towards others as participants in a public process.[18] This concern of participants with the publicity of communication has special importance when the inclusive character of both discussion and reason-giving are themselves the special object of deliberation. Toleration in this sense is discursive openness.

If publicity is the more general norm and attitude of concern for the structures and processes of communication in a democracy, then toleration demands that citizens be concerned with the structural features of public debate and discussion through which deliberation takes place. Two aspects of such communication are the more specific objects of toleration. First, toleration in a weak sense is directed towards the reasons that others offer in communication: they must be taken seriously and not disqualified *ex ante* (either in principle or in fact). Toleration is needed in the public process aimed at discovering whether a reason is a publicly acceptable one or not. Publicity is in this sense historical rather than formal. If the public character of a reason in this sense is better seen as an outcome of an actual process of discussion, then it is not necessarily significant if the reason is religious or secular.[19] When communicating with an audience as heterogeneous as the citizens of a large and pluralistic polity, such disqualification threatens the public character of political communication in which reasons are considered on their own merits. However, taking a reason seriously does not entail that we refrain from criticising it (even if we think it is reasonable in Rawls's sense). Indeed, the opposite is true: no reason can be expected to receive uptake by others unless it passes their critical scrutiny; that is, a criticism must be addressed to them as one that they could accept. Being tolerant thus does not exclude criticism; it in fact demands it, since without it others will not form the expectation that their reasons as publicly expressed shaped the course of the debate. Toleration is directed both towards policies that might accommodate a minority view and also towards the minority's reasons put forward in deliberation. This inclusion of other citizens' salient reasons, such as they are, is a means toward preserving the public character of communication and the inclusive character of the democratic community of citizens.

This brings us to the second feature of communication that is the object of toleration. Taking reasons seriously is not all that deliberation requires. Toleration in the strong sense does not extend directly to the reasons as such but to the perspectives that inform these reasons and give them their cogency. Before a reason can first be seen as a reason and then potentially as one that passes the critical scrutiny of all citizens, the perspectives of others and the experiences that inform them must be recognised as legitimate; in the light of this inclusion of their perspective, groups recognise themselves as contributing to democratic decisions. The toleration of others' perspectives is then part of recognising them as equal members of a political community, where membership is recognised despite the potential for persistent disagreements and deep conflicts. As Scanlon puts it, what toleration expresses is recognition of common membership that is deeper than these conflicts, recognition of others as 'just as entitled as we are to contribute to the definition of our society'.[20] A regime of toleration is illegitimate if it denies such an entitlement by falsely generalising the perspective of the tolerating group so that they can reject the claims and reasons of the tolerated group. Toleration in this sense is a property of a regime; a regime of toleration is just if it permits citizens to fulfil their obligations to justification to all and respects the entitlement of each to contribute to the definition of their society. The toleration of perspectives is not only a matter of first-order communication, but of the second-order properties of the regime that aim at protecting the integrity of communication and deliberation.

The distinction between reasons and perspectives in deliberation and thus between toleration as an attitude in communication and as a property of a regime is central to understanding the nature of disagreements among free and equal citizens. In the case of conflicts or disagreement, deliberation cannot simply be guided by toleration in the weak sense common when we say 'those are their reasons', any more than we might expect that saying 'these are my reasons' will add any weight to them. First-order conflicts and disagreements about whether this or that reason is best are the normal business of public deliberation, and public communication over such first-order disagreements is preserved by respectful and mutual criticism and scrutiny. In order to do so, the variety of perspectives as such is not the subject of debate. When we say that all are equally entitled to shape deliberation in a democracy, then the clear pragmatic implication is that each perspective must be considered even if the particular reasons tied to it on particular issues do not pass critical scrutiny.[21] In this respect, toleration is a second-order property of the framework that creates the deliberative community: whether the deliberative framework includes enough reasons to grant all citizens equal standing as members of a community that makes binding judgements.

In this section, I have argued that public communication requires a complex set of attitudes of toleration. First, deliberative democracy requires the 'weak' toleration of reasons to make communication possible, as the give and take of reasons in dialogue and their possible uptake by an audience. Second, it is an attitude toward any perspective as necessarily included in a community of all citizens who are all equally entitled to shaping the definition of their society. Thus, the inclusion of reasons requires attitudes of toleration by participants in communication; the inclusion of perspectives requires the justice of the deliberative framework (including its regime of toleration) that creates an inclusive political community. Next, I argue that the traditional 'paradoxes of toleration' themselves have reflexive form: they state that practices of toleration may themselves be intolerant. Far from undermining deliberative toleration, this sort of claim makes perfect sense in a deliberative democracy: democratic deliberation permits formal and informal regimes of toleration to become the topic of public communication and criticism and thus to test its explicit standards of inclusion for reasons and its implicit exclusion of perspectives.

Toleration and participation in a deliberative community

For all its open, inclusive and reflexive character, deliberative toleration still must be able to distinguish the tolerant from the intolerant. Such a distinction might paradoxically be deemed intolerant, especially in the light of the democratic standard of the inclusion of all perspectives in deliberation. What if some citizens refuse to adopt the perspectives of other citizens they deem immoral or simply false? This suspicion might be further reinforced by the fact that while all reasons are admissible in discussion, only those reasons that are able to withstand public scrutiny appear to be favoured. Those reasons will be just those favoured by the views that I have criticised. Even if I have failed to rid such accounts of their inherent difficulties, it is clear that a deliberative procedure clearly ought not to favour intolerant attitudes of whatever kind that undermine the obligations and entitlement of political egalitarianism. In this section, I want to argue that reflexive toleration can solve another paradox of toleration, the need to tolerate what one finds to be false or wrong in some instances. Toleration is an attitude that is for something: for participation in an inclusive and pluralist political community.

Even with such attitudes of toleration so specified, we could still ask why citizens should adopt them in their democratic deliberation, as the fact of the 'new pluralism' suggests that they should.[22] Here the tension in the deliberative ideal could emerge once again. Should they be adopted just because they make it more likely that decisions will be acceptable to more citizens under the circumstances? Or do we have independent reasons to accept such standards, such as fairness or the epistemic value of such procedures? These sorts of second-order questions have to be raised precisely because they must be answered in order that a deliberative regime not be self-defeating. It is not self-defeating given that the aim of a deliberative regime of toleration is to provide the framework for an inclusive democratic community. We tolerate what is wrong and false because it is part of our justificatory obligations to fellow members of a deliberative community. The regime promotes wide toleration because of the entitlements of members as political equals to shape the course of deliberation. Such a regime does not undermine itself, since reflexive challenges to it are legitimate only if they reflexively appeal to the political egalitarianism on which these obligations and entitlements are based, that is, only if the expansion of the limits of toleration advocated makes it such that all members of the society have greater access to political influence and for that reason continue to cooperate.

From the participants' perspective, deliberation begins when there is a commonly perceived problematic situation, such as a conflict or a problem to be resolved. In deliberation these conflicts or problems may be manifested in a variety of ways, such as in disagreements over the cogency of various reasons. Deliberation under democratic constraints is not simply about which reasons are better or more likely to be correct; it is rather the attempt to find a solution that is best and acceptable to all those involved. From an observer's perspective, we could always say that some type of reason is better than another, perhaps because it is stated in a general fashion and thus is more likely to be acceptable to a broader audience or perhaps because it takes certain facts into account that others do not. Even if true, this feature does not mean that any particular universal reason or appeal to facts will be acceptable to everyone in the discussion. The same could be said for epistemic properties: for example, some reasons might be better because they support a policy that experts agree is more likely to achieve commonly accepted goals. For some participants will reject defining the problem as a matter for experts. In the face of such conflicts, David Estlund argues that a deliberative procedure must take the epistemic 'quality' of the reasons into account rather than simply egalitarian considerations such as equal access or availability of influence over a decision.[23] Despite his proper insistence that such a standard should not be based upon 'invidious comparisons', I argue that it is still intolerant of the diversity of citizens' perspectives, and any principle that justifies considerations of epistemic quality over equal access to influence is open to the same sort of reflexive objections as I raised earlier to Gutmann and Thompson's use of the principle of reciprocity.

A closer look at Estlund's argument shows that it is based on the claim that all citizens could accept that 'the epistemic advantages of wider discussion might outweigh the disadvantages of some degree of unequal influence'.[24] This concern seems to resemble reflexive toleration in that maintaining the structure of public communication is its main object. Does extensiveness alone capture the requirements of toleration? Since it is doubtful that extensiveness alone ensures that all in fact share the advantages of wider discussion, it is reasonable for some to reject it (as might be argued in unlimited private campaign finance in the United States). Nor does extensiveness capture 'the epistemic value of equality', since a discussion is more extensive in quantity even if the same messages are repeated over and over. Quantity then is insufficient to capture the epistemic value of diversity. It is only when more speakers are included that more discussion increases the epistemic value of deliberation. *Pace* Estlund, there is, then, no conflict between epistemic quality and political egalitarianism, since both depend on the quality of communication in a society. The corrective value of diversity is essential particularly in the case of second-order questions concerned with the effectiveness of participation in a political community.

It is not clear that those whose perspective has been excluded would accept either 'the epistemic value of quantity' ('a greater quantity of input at the same level of equality') or 'the epistemic difference principle' (which permits each to gain 'more input' at the price of inequality).[25] The increase is in overall input, and thus without the correlative expectation that such extensive discussion also increases the opportunity for being heard and hence for the equal exercise of influence. Otherwise, participants are asked by Estlund's epistemic difference principle to accept not only the dispersal of influence in a wider body of citizens but also that some quantity of 'epistemic compensation' is sufficient for them to exchange for the lesser worth of their political liberty. But this difference principle can no more pass the reflexivity test than could reciprocity, since it would demand that some citizens surrender their potential influence without any process of collective authorisation. Such authorisation usually depends on a prior agreement about what counts as a good reason in a particular context. Citizens could then enjoy the same epistemic gains through authorising experts without any loss of access to influence, particularly if they can challenge the appropriateness of the authorisation of experts in some given cases, as often occurs in issues of risk and safety.

In this way, any consideration of epistemic quality either rides piggyback on the diversity of perspectives or is acceptable to all only if each could reflexively endorse the division of labour from their own point of view, not by some independent standard identified from an observer's perspective. As is the case with average utility, such standards do not respect the differences among persons. Whatever the intrinsic merits of some independent standard or intrinsic value (whether it be reasonableness, reciprocity or epistemic value), it may be reflexively challenged as intolerant from the participants' perspective of disadvantaged citizens.[26] The difference principle does not apply when disadvantaged participants have no reason to accept the justification that they have benefited from the inequality, except through the illicit and intolerant generalisation of the perspective of those who do exercise influence. This dependence of any application of the difference principle on the perspective of those disadvantaged by it does not leave us without standards. Those standards are rather the regulative ideals of a democratic community.

With these resources it is possible to solve another potential paradox of toleration. It is not only equal membership, but also the regulative ideal of an inclusive democratic community that provides the basis for tolerating those whom we judge to be wrong or immoral.[27] But this community is not the actual political community, in which the tolerated and the tolerator may stand in a social relationship of inequality or subordination. Rather, such a democratic community has a just regime of toleration to the extent not only that it promotes the proper attitudes of communication, but that it also organises a framework for deliberation that makes possible participation in a pluralist political community. Although Rawls accepts that each can accept such ideals for their own reasons, he sees such a framework as 'essentials', as having a special place that then becomes the basis for all further deliberation. Habermas makes deliberation more open and dynamic by arguing against Rawls that citizens cannot employ norms of publicity determining in advance what reasons are likely to be accepted in deliberation. Nonetheless, he insists that mutually acceptable reasons will have to be impartial and general such that 'the consensus brought about through argument must rest on identical reasons that are able to convince the parties in the same way'.[28] Both either suggest a more substantial unity than a deliberative community requires or are insufficiently robust to solve the problems of deep conflict. Instead, it is better to appeal to the regulative ideal of an inclusive community in both challenging and setting the limits on deliberative toleration.

The central place of the deliberative community points towards another sort of case that evades this reflexive solution and thus falls outside the deliberative ideal of toleration. Some tolerated groups may even ask not to be tolerated in the sense that they do not wish to be part of an inclusive community, as is the case for the Amish and many indigenous peoples. Here the appeal is to some other ideal, such as the recognition of their equal freedom to pursue their definition of their own society. Such groups are accommodated though the right not to be included in the common life of a community in which they do not wish to have the entitlement to define and in this way change the dynamic away from tolerant inclusion to the differentiation of citizenship. How might such differentiation enter into a just regime of toleration?

I argued earlier that the Amish and indigenous groups do not enter into a close cooperative relationship with the larger tolerating community and thus accept being democratically unequal in influence over some decisions, in exchange for the maximum degree of non-interference possible. It is important to see that this is an exception. The existence of such groups does not challenge the ideal of toleration, but presents limits to its capacity to solve problems of difference in a highly heterogeneous society. They attempt to create a different sort of social relationship of non-subordination outside rather than within a democratic society. In contrast, intolerant groups cannot claim to offer a reflexive challenge, since the purpose of the regime of toleration is precisely to protect the integrity of communication in the deliberative process and in doing so to create a pluralistic community. Challenges to toleration and its legal regime are constrained by the regulative ideal of an inclusive deliberative community that informs the regime of toleration, as one might imagine in the case of certain demands of moral constraint on expression proposed by some non-accommodationist fundamentalist religious groups or by racial or ethnic separatists. Such groups violate the demands of toleration, since they cannot intelligibly be construed as widening the deliberative community. As opposed to the Amish, they do not gain their own religious or cultural non-subordination for the toleration of the larger community's democratic ideals. Multiple memberships of a certain kind are thus consistent with citizenship.

The second-order character of toleration, the proper object of which is public communication, is in this way sufficient to accommodate reflexive challenges to the ideal and regime of toleration without falling into contradiction or paradox. But because it seeks to expand the democratic community of equal citizens and maintain its structures of free and open communication, it is pluralist without being morally neutral. Because it permits the mutual criticism of reasons offered in deliberation, it is also not epistemically abstinent. Neither the standards of public reason nor those of toleration are themselves fixed points beyond critical scrutiny. Indeed, public reason can improve deliberation and reliably perform its role of solving problems and conflicts 'only when it is itself subject to revision and correction in light of public standards that are open, accessible and available to all'.[29] The possibility of such self-correction itself requires not only public standards, but also the openness and accessibility demanded by the normative attitudes and instituted in egalitarian practices of toleration. The practices in which such attitudes are exercised require the regulative framework of an expansive deliberative community.

Conclusion: challenging toleration, extending political community

The superiority of the deliberative over a liberal regime of toleration consists in its ability to deal with the main problems of wide pluralism: second-order challenges and overlapping and intersecting deep conflicts. In a deliberative democracy, debates about the basic principles of governance and shared political life belong on one end of the continuum of deliberative problem-solving. Far from being avoided, appeals to the interpretation of fundamental principles are an everyday occurrence in a deliberative democracy, especially when pluralism produces conflicts along a number of dimensions (as is the case in debates about the wall of separation of church and state and the accommodation of religious minorities in schooling). Such debates can become pitched conflicts, whose constant recurrence indicates a lack of problem-solving capacity in the current deliberative framework. The community that this framework creates is not one that is pluralistic across sufficient dimensions. Spurred by persistent deep conflicts (and not merely everyday persistent disagreement), debates about the framework for deliberation and the ideal of democratic community can lead to a period of 'constitutional politics' such as was the case in the Reconstruction period and the New Deal in United States history, when the deliberative framework of rights and powers had to shift to solve problems and conflicts.[30] The deliberation that occurs in periods of constitutional politics is much more fundamental than the development of acceptable exemptions and privileges typical of current calls for 'differentiated citizenship'. Rather, it demands rethinking the normative framework that operates in the background of democratic deliberation and provides the basis for deciding to which reasons institutions must be responsive. The regulative ideal of an inclusive political community is the basis for deliberating about such a transformation of the obligations and entitlements of citizenship.

Religious toleration has played a crucial role in the emergence of modern citizenship. It became the basis for a distinctly universal identity within the political community of a modern nation-state that united citizens across social and cultural differences. Both multiculturalism and cosmopolitanism challenge the adequacy of this universal identity. Deliberative toleration looks at the problem of inclusion from the other way around. Precisely because of the successful inclusion of ever more citizens in a non-naturalistically or culturally based community of principle, the conflicts inherent in wide pluralism challenge the institutional framework that made this inclusion possible. Once again, current religious conflict over toleration provides a ready example. The emerging challenges to the liberal regime of toleration even in its expanded multicultural form are increasingly transnational, given the fact that global migration has spurred new levels of pluralism in liberal democratic societies. This migration will call into question the requirements of citizenship, as people no longer live their lives within the boundaries of a particular nation-state. Here we might consider the extent to which traditional liberal and republican conceptions can provide the basis for mutual toleration among diverse citizens. As Rawls put it, liberal toleration applied in the international sphere 'asks of other societies only what they can reasonably grant without submitting to a position of inferiority or domination'.[31] Given the fact of wide pluralism, cosmopolitanism begins at home. It may well be that the deliberative framework in societies characterised by migration and wide pluralism will have to incorporate interactions among many different inclusive communities. The laws of an inclusive community would have to protect and regulate a variety of different statuses surrounding citizenship.

By now it should be clear exactly how reflexive toleration is different from other conceptions. Broadly understood, it belongs to a family of conceptions related to the standards of justification in a deliberative democracy. In this way, it bears family resemblances to many of the views criticised here, such as those of Rawls, Gutmann and Thompson, and Habermas. The differences emerge in response to the various levels of the challenges entailed by the deep conflicts engendered by the fact of the new pluralism. At the level of the joint activity of common deliberation about such conflicts, reflexive deliberation has the integrity of communication as its main object, where each perspective is given a full hearing without prior constraints on the publicity of a reason. Intolerance is evidenced in the inability of citizens to raise vital and significant concerns in deliberation, by excluding them as acceptable reasons or by illicitly generalising the dominant or majority perspective. Second, reflexive toleration establishes a different ideal, not merely of mutually granted rights and immunities from interference, but of a shared community of deliberation and judgement. In justifying toleration, a deliberative conception of political community not only provides for the nature and limits of challenges to the regime of toleration, but also provides toleration with its aim or purpose. Guided by its practical orientation to successful public communication and the ideal of an inclusive community, reflexive toleration is both a means and an end for furthering democratisation in a situation of undiminished pluralism. If such ideals are to be maintained, then the contemporary facts of pluralism require a more reflexive understanding of norms that guide deliberation and a wider variety of institutional settings in which citizenship is exercised and conflicts are resolved.

Notes

1 J. Rawls, 'The idea of public reason revisited', reprinted in *Collected Papers* (Cambridge, MA: Harvard University Press, 1999), pp. 573–615, at p. 574.
2 Rawls, 'The idea of public reason revisited', p. 576.
3 J. Habermas, 'Reconciliation through the public use of reason', *Journal of Philosophy*, 3 (1995) 109–32, at p. 124.
4 J. Rawls, 'The idea of an overlapping consensus', in *Collected Papers*, p. 424.
5 Rawls, 'The idea of an overlapping consensus', p. 425.
6 B. Herman, 'Pluralism and the community of moral judgment', in D. Heyd (ed.), *Toleration: An Elusive Virtue* (Princeton, NJ: Princeton University Press, 1996), pp. 81–105, at p. 61; on 'positive tolerance' as distinguished from the repressive character of purely negative toleration, see H. Marcuse, 'Repressive tolerance', in *A Critique of Pure Tolerance* (Boston, MA: Beacon, 1965); specifically, a positive or liberating conception has for Marcuse an epistemic connotation, since 'the telos of toleration is truth' (p. 90). Marcuse's criticism of liberal toleration makes one of the points that I am stressing here, that toleration need not be sceptical or even non-epistemic. For an epistemic criticism directed at Rawls's idea of 'toleration extended to philosophy', see D. Estlund, 'The insularity of the reasonable: Why political liberalism must admit the truth', *Ethics*, 108 (1998) 252–75. Estlund's criticism also relies on a reflexive argument, to the effect that political liberalism must admit the truth of its own view. This argument is insufficiently reflexive, however, because it does not make clear that the necessity of admitting truth and overcoming insularity is from the participants' point of view. In contrast, my argument accepts reflexivity in order to show that both the constraints and the insularity of the reasonable are inconsistent with the inclusive conception of public reason that Rawls now endorses. Toleration by public reason requires that we may publicly criticise others' doctrines, or they ours. The limits of toleration are rather the limits of an inclusive deliberative community.
7 Marcuse, 'Repressive tolerance', p. 95. The 'liberating' feature of democracy is not mere or 'pure' toleration, but 'the chance it gave to social dissent' to change circumstances.
8 See Rawls's criticism of arguments for liberal neutrality based on autonomy as a moral doctrine; for Rawls, liberalism as a moral doctrine itself 'fails to satisfy the criterion of reciprocity'. See J. Rawls, *Political Liberalism* (New York: Columbia University Press, 1996), pp. xliv–xlv; also pp. 77ff. Such a form of autonomy-based liberalism would include Kymlicka's arguments for the basis of toleration.
9 M. Walzer, *On Toleration* (New Haven, CT: Yale University Press, 1997), p. 71.
10 Just as he criticises Kymlicka's autonomy-based argument for toleration, Rawls criticises Gutmann and Thompson's view of deliberative democracy for treating reciprocity as a substantive norm in the sense of a 'comprehensive doctrine'. See Rawls, 'The idea of public reason revisited', p. 578.
11 A. Gutmann and D. Thompson, *Democracy and Disagreement* (Cambridge, MA: Harvard University Press, 1996), p. 65.

12 J. Cohen, 'Procedure and substance in deliberative democracy', in *Democracy and Difference*, ed. S. Benhabib (Princeton, NJ: Princeton University Press, 1996), p. 101. Note that for Cohen this is a matter of freedom of expression, not a matter of entitlement to contribute to the common definition of a society. Freedom of expression permits religious reasons to be used in public discourse as acts of testimony; this is a defence of toleration as non-interference.

13 E. Kelly and L. McPherson, 'On tolerating the unreasonable', *The Journal of Political Philosophy*, 9 (2001) 38–55. However 'strong' their conception of toleration, it leads Kelly and McPherson to the opposite conclusion to that I defend here: 'Our position in favour of extending public justification to the unreasonable implies, however, that philosophical discussion in the public sphere should ideally be kept to a minimum' (p. 51). This is because they defend and extend a liberal notion of non-interference with clearly anti-deliberative consequences. Second, the argument in favour of extending justification to the unreasonable continues to hold that the category is relevant to discussions of toleration. The proper conclusion is that since justification is owed to the reasonable and the unreasonable alike for exactly the same democratic reasons, judgements of reasonableness are simply irrelevant to the aims of toleration.

14 Views that endorse political egalitarianism as essential to deliberative democracy include Joshua Cohen, Thomas Christiano, Jack Knight and James Johnson, and myself. See the essays in *Deliberative Democracy: Essays on Reason and Politics*, ed. J. Bohman and W. Rehg (Cambridge, MA: Massachusetts Institute of Technology Press, 1997); I shall consider David Estlund's argument against political egalitarianism below. To the extent that his epistemic alternative is based on principles that can be reasonably rejected, it results in political intolerance.

15 The parents actually accepted such an accommodation, but some school officials rejected it. See W. Galston, 'Diversity, toleration and deliberative democracy: Religious minorities and public schooling', in *Deliberative Politics*, ed. S. Macedo (Oxford: Oxford University Press, 1999), pp. 39–48. Galston defends 'mere toleration', limited only by 'the minimum necessary social unity'. A deliberative theory does not defend such a minimum unity, since it locates toleration within the regulative ideals of a democratic community.

16 Gutmann and Thompson, *Democracy and Disagreement*, p. 62.

17 O. O'Neill, 'Practices of toleration', in *Democracy and the Mass Media*, ed. J. Lichtenberg (Cambridge: Cambridge University Press, 1990), p. 167.

18 On the variability of norms of publicity as related to their problem-solving capacity, see J. Bohman, 'Citizenship and norms of publicity: Wide public reason in cosmopolitan societies', *Political Theory*, 27 (1999) 176–202.

19 Robert Audi has long identified public with secular reasons. See his initial article and subsequent ones thereafter, 'The separation of Church and State and the obligations of citizenship', *Philosophy and Public Affairs* XX (1989) 259–96. For Rawls's criticisms of this view, see 'The idea of public reason revisited', pp. 587ff.

20 T. M. Scanlon, 'The difficulty of toleration', in Heyd (ed.), *Toleration: An Elusive Virtue*, p. 231.

21 On the distinction between reasons and perspectives, see I. Young, 'Difference as a resource for democratic communication', in *Deliberative Democracy: Essays on Reason and Politics*, ed. J. Bohman and W. Rehg (Cambridge, MA:

Massachusetts Institute of Technology Press, 1997). Young argues that the primary resource that such differences offer for democratic communication 'is not a self-regarding identity or interest, but rather a perspective on the structures, relations, and events of a society' (pp. 393–4).

22 W. Kymlicka, *Multicultural Citizenship* (Oxford: Oxford University Press, 1995), pp. 174ff. It is interesting to note that most proponents of such citizenship are implicitly cosmopolitan, in that the differentiation of citizenship is modelled on the mutual recognition by states of each other's legitimacy and rights to determine membership.

23 D. Estlund, 'Political equality', *Social Philosophy and Policy*, 17 (2000) 127–60. The conception of toleration that I am defending here is precisely a species of the 'political egalitarianism' that Estlund is criticising there: deliberative toleration requires the 'equal availability of power or influence over collective choices that have legal force' (p. 127). This form of substantive political equality follows from the basic requirement of toleration that everyone is equally entitled to shape the definition of the society in which they live. Epistemic obligations follow from this entitlement, as citizens who attempt to influence this definition open their reasons to public criticism.

24 Estlund, *ibid.*, p. 132.

25 For 'the epistemic value of quantity', see *ibid.*, p. 144; the 'epistemic difference principle' is formulated on p. 147. More input is valuable from the participants' perspective only if it increases the possibility of each perspective being heard. Increasing input would be justified to the worst off only by increasing the number of perspectives in discussion. For the difference principle to apply, the relevant epistemic value is diversity, not quantity.

26 S. Mendus, *Toleration and the Limits of Liberalism* (Atlantic Highlands, NJ: Humanities Press, 1989), pp. 8–9. Mendus sees these circumstances as having to do with various relations between the tolerator and the tolerated, given diverse and potentially conflicting ways of life. Whatever they are, the circumstances of toleration hold whenever there is democracy, in which the social relationships among diverse citizens are defined by ideals of freedom and equality.

27 On the impact of the fact of pluralism on the way 'regulative principles constitute a community of moral judgment', see B. Herman, 'Pluralism and the community of moral judgment', p. 69. While Herman discusses her Kantian account of moral community in terms of 'engaged moral judgment', my account owes more to Habermas's conception of an inclusive communication community. Both are inadequate in the face of deep pluralism and must be supplemented by reflexive challenge to the deliberative framework.

28 J. Habermas, *Between Facts and Norms* (Cambridge, MA: Massachusetts Institute of Technology Press, 1996), p. 339. For a such a theory of toleration, see R. Forst, 'Toleranz, Gerechtigkeit und Vernunft', in *Toleranz*, ed. R. Forst (Frankfurt: Campus Verlag, 2000), pp. 118–43.

29 D. A. J. Richards, 'Toleration and the struggle against prejudice', in Heyd (ed.), *Toleration: An Elusive Virtue*, p. 135.

30 B. Ackerman, *We the People, Vol. I* (Cambridge, MA: Harvard University Press, 1991).

31 J. Rawls, *Law of Peoples* (Cambridge, MA: Harvard University Press, 1999), p. 121.

7

City life and community: complementary or incompatible ideals?

Andrew Mason

The words 'city' and 'community' conjure up very different images. The city is often pictured as an arena where diverse social groups or networks may co-exist in an atmosphere of mutual toleration, while the community is seen as a cohesive unit where conformity is fostered at the expense of diversity, thereby breeding intolerance. So understood, community is an unattractive ideal, unlikely to endear itself to those with liberal sympathies. It may be able to meet the needs of its members to feel that they belong; but it does so at a high cost to them and to others. Cities, in contrast, promise to provide their inhabitants (and indeed their visitors) with a diverse range of possibilities that, even if they do not represent options that can be combined harmoniously, may nevertheless co-exist together.

My aim is to assess whether this picture of city life and community, and their relative merits, can be sustained. Some may find it hard to believe that it can withstand critical scrutiny: on the one hand it seems to idealise the city, while on the other ignoring the possibility of communities that are open to difference and respectful of it. But there are those such as Iris Young who think that this picture does represent a deeper truth that can be given philosophical defence. Without glamorising actually existing cities, Young argues that city life contains within it a liberating promise. In contrast, community in her view is a deeply flawed ideal: it manifests what she calls the logic of identity, which entails excluding or repressing difference.

Community is a complex notion, however. Against Young I shall maintain that her picture of city life is compatible with the ideal of community when the latter is properly conceived. Young's real target is a form of communitarianism that envisages a network of self-contained groups in which relations are face-to-face and wholly transparent. But those who value community need not be offering this vision. They can allow that communal relations may exist between those who do not know each other and do not fully understand each other. They can also acknowledge the value and importance of non-communal relations, and celebrate the way in which, in the context of the city, members of different communities can learn from each other while at the same time coming to appreciate the limits of their own understanding and experience.

Following a path that has been well trodden, I shall also suggest that city life and community can be complementary ideals in another way. Not only may cities permit and encourage a variety of different communities to flourish, they may also themselves constitute communities of a kind that could facilitate an activist local politics committed to urban renewal, coupled with modest redistributive programmes.

Community and difference

Young has three main complaints against the ideal of community.[1] First, she contends that it requires full and complete mutual understanding and identification. As such, she believes it is valued as a means to satisfy a rather infantile desire for fusion, or as a way of accommodating 'a longing for harmony among persons, for consensus and mutual understanding'.[2] She maintains that in so far as full mutual understanding and identification are possible at all, they are likely to occur only between those who are alike in terms of history, cultural background, or point of view on the world.[3] Therefore in practice community can be realised only by excluding some from membership or by repressing difference.

Second, Young maintains that those who value community are in the grip of a false ideal of face-to-face relations, conceiving these relations as transparent, unmediated and harmonious. Young argues that face-to-face relations cannot be transparent in the way required by ideals of community, for an individual is never fully present to herself let alone to others.[4] These relations are necessarily mediated, since, for example, they involve the interpretation of speech and gestures. Furthermore, face-to-face relations are not necessarily harmonious, because they contain the possibility of separation and violence.[5]

Third, Young argues that the privileging of face-to-face relations inherent in the ideal of community serves to devalue non-communal encounters and divert our attention away from their importance. Relations between those who are not personally acquainted are judged to involve some degree of alienation simply because they are mediated. But, Young maintains, non-communal relations need not involve alienation and can be mutually enriching. In virtue of their commitment to the value of face-to-face relations, communitarians often envisage a society that consists of small decentralised units. But, Young maintains, this is unrealistic and fails to confront the political question of how different communities should relate to one another.[6]

In Young's view, city life provides a much more attractive social and political ideal than community, for it can allow difference to be truly respected. (When she talks of city life, she intends to include living in what we ordinarily call 'towns'; her ideal is not restricted to the huge metropolis.)[7] City life, as she conceives it, is a form of being together with strangers that involves encountering those with different cultures, histories and points of view.[8] Modern cities can thereby cultivate a sense of difference: dwellers in them come to appreciate that there are forms of experience beyond their own, occurring in or near public spaces, and that as a result they will never be able fully to grasp the city as a whole.[9] In cities there can be social differentiation without exclusion;[10] individuals can be members of groups that overlap and intermingle, the character of which may change over time and the boundaries of which are porous. According to Young, this ideal of city life, unlike the ideal of community, does not require face-to-face relations, nor does it require full mutual understanding: relations in the city are often mediated by time and space, and we are made constantly aware of the limits of our understanding of others.

In Young's view, city life potentially incorporates the ideal of 'openness to unassimilated otherness'.[11] Young does not fully unpack this notion, but it is safe to infer that openness of this kind goes beyond what is required by toleration, although it is not incompatible with the latter ideal.[12] Toleration is called for only in contexts where one person or group disapproves of what others do. Openness to others, in contrast, is needed primarily when understanding is lacking. It is an ideal that should enter in before toleration becomes an issue, and in that sense is prior to it. It is manifested as a willingness to learn from others and to refrain from judging them when one lacks full understanding; as an appreciation that there may be valuable modes of being that one cannot fully grasp given the limits of one's own experience; and as a refusal to deny difference by illegitimately assimilating it to something familiar and already understood.

In order to evaluate Young's critique of community, and her proposal that city life can provide us with an alternative ideal, we need to be clear about what she means by 'community'. She points out that there are normative and non-normative uses of the term, and that her concern is with its normative use: for example, she has no objection to the sociological use of the term in the context of community studies, where it usually means something like a 'small town' or 'neighbourhood'.[13] Here I agree with Young that some distinction needs to be drawn, but I think that more needs to be said about it.

'Community' is a much over-used term, both in ordinary language and in academic debates. So much so that we are entitled to some degree of scepticism about whether it can serve any useful analytical purpose. In my view, however, it is worth retaining the term, so long as we are clear about the different notions it is used to express.[14] To develop my argument against Young, I propose to distinguish between an ordinary and a moralised sense of community by reference to two ideal types.[15] According to the first ideal type, which I shall refer to as the ordinary concept or ordinary sense, a community is a group of people who share a range of values and a way of life, whose members identify with the group and its practices, and acknowledge each other as members of that group. This account of community in the ordinary sense does not specify precise necessary conditions: a group of people may constitute a community in this sense even if, for example, they share only some of the same values, and the way of life in which they participate is not all-encompassing. As a result, community may be realised in degrees, and the ordinary concept of community is inherently vague: its application requires a judgement about whether members of a group share enough values, whether they participate in a way of life that is sufficiently encompassing, whether they identify sufficiently strongly with the group, and whether there is sufficient agreement amongst them concerning who counts as a member of the group.

According to the second ideal type, which I shall refer to as the moralised concept or moralised sense, two further conditions need to be met before a group can constitute a community. First, its members must be mutually concerned. What counts as mutual concern depends on the nature and scale of the group; but minimally it means that they must give each other's interests some non-instrumental weight in their practical reasoning. Second, there must be no systematic injustice or, at least, no systematic exploitation occurring between them. Like my account of community in the ordinary sense, however, this does not provide a precise list of necessary conditions for a group to be a community in the moralised sense, because it allows that people may constitute such a community even if, for example, they do not share a wide range of values. So, like the ordinary concept, the moralised concept allows for degrees of community. It also allows that communities may be of different kinds and exist at different levels.[16] (The moralised concept is to be found particularly in the socialist tradition; but there are liberal, feminist, and conservative variants that provide their own distinctive interpretations of what counts as mutual concern, exploitation or injustice.)

It is clear, I think, that Young's critique is directed against ideals of community in the moralised sense.[17] She in effect argues that they are incoherent: she maintains that it is impossible for communities to be free from exploitation and oppression in the way advocates of the ideal maintain, because they must inevitably repress or deny difference. But this argument cannot get off the ground without the premise that community requires its members fully to identify with each other and fully to understand each other. Young believes that this is impossible, and that striving for it results in either exclusion or the repression of difference. But full mutual identification and understanding is not essential for community as I have characterised it, even according to the moralised sense. A person can be concerned for the well-being of others without being in a face-to-face relationship with them and without identifying with them in the way that Young thinks the ideal of community requires. Nor do communal relations in the moralised sense need to be transparent or harmonious. Community does require some degree of shared values and some shared way of life, but these minimal requirements can be satisfied in the face of considerable divergences in values and considerable variations in the way members lead their lives.

Young might argue that I have misunderstood the main thrust of her argument. In her view community is valued as a means to satisfy a desire for fusion, and that desire could only be met by repressing difference. At best I think this is a partial truth. Many communitarians have valued community for other reasons. They have argued that it satisfies a widespread desire to belong or to be recognised by others. (Some of them would say that this is a human need rather than simply a widely held desire, but they do not have to make such an extravagant claim.) Although a person might acquire a secure sense of belonging by fusing with other members of a group, such a sense might also be obtained without abandoning one's independence in the way that fusion would require. Recognition by others is not merely compatible with retaining one's independence, but appears to require it. For part of what it is to be recognised by others is to receive acknowledgement of one's own separate existence and independent worth.

Even if the attractions of community life cannot be explained by the idea that it is valued as a means to fusion, could it nevertheless be true that it is valued because of its (ultimately unrealistic) promise of harmony and consensus? In a critique of community that resonates with Young's, Elizabeth Frazer argues that 'the aspiration to community is an aspiration to a kind of connectedness that transcends the mundane and concrete tangle of social relations'.[18] She maintains that such an experience of transcendence will be fleeting at best, and that the longing for it may be politically dangerous because it diverts attention away from the material conditions that are necessary for successful political organisation and action.[19] Frazer is surely right that experiences of fully-fledged community in its moralised sense are likely to be rare and brief (even though communities of this sort may be realised in a truncated form more frequently). But it would be a mistake to suppose that the ideal of community requires complete harmony and consensus for its realisation. And although I do not want to deny that an exclusive preoccupation with ideals of community can have the damaging consequences that Frazer fears, it is hard to see why a commitment to these ideals cannot be coupled with a hard-headed appreciation of their limitations and material preconditions.

In some sense communities must exclude. Putting aside the possible exception represented by the ideal of global community, it is part of the logic of community that it will never be fully inclusive and there will always be insiders and outsiders.[20] But even Young must accept that this is true of the groups that will encounter each other in cities. The question is: why must communities, unlike these groups, exclude in an objectionable way, or stand opposed to her ideal of openness to unassimilated otherness? Communities too may overlap and intermingle; their membership may be fluid and their boundaries porous. And in principle there is no reason why members of a community shouldn't acknowledge, struggle to understand,

and even celebrate, the existence of diversity within their community, or the existence of other communities with different histories involving different values or ways of life.

Are there any arguments of a more empirical kind that might show that communities are likely to repress difference or fail to be open to it in one way or another? Young declares that self-identification as a member of a community 'often occurs as an oppositional differentiation from other groups, who are feared, despised or at best devalued'.[21] It is not hard to find examples of communities in the ordinary sense that are in conflict with one another, dismissing each other's achievements and ways of life without making any genuine attempts to understand. But is there any general reason to think that relations between communities (in either the ordinary or moralised sense) will tend to be like this or worse? Joseph Raz appears to think so. He argues that even though communities founded upon very different ways of life may each be worthwhile because they realise incompatible values, individuals who are part of one way of life will tend to devalue the others because commitment to their way of life will encourage a dismissive attitude towards the genuine values contained in the others: 'pluralists can step back from their personal commitments and appreciate in the abstract the value of other ways of life and their attendant virtues. But this acknowledgement co-exists with, and cannot replace, the feelings of rejection and dismissiveness towards what one knows is valuable'.[22] If Raz is right, members of a community will tend to repress or deny the reality of valuable difference when they encounter it, even when they have some appreciation of it. In effect, Raz's argument throws into question the extent to which Young's ideal of openness can be realised.[23]

But even if there is an inevitable tension in practice between being committed to a way of life that realises one set of values, and admiring or respecting ways of life that realise different values, the nature of this tension will surely vary. One can participate in different ways of life and indeed be a member of a number of communities. Under such conditions, the tendency to devalue, which Raz claims is inevitable, may be relatively insignificant. It may be that it is acute only under adverse conditions, for example, when ways of life are geographically separated from each other or under threat in some way, or when there is a conflict of material interests between them. It is not naive to suppose that under relatively hospitable conditions city life may provide a good antidote to any tendency to devalue other ways of life, especially given the proximity of these ways of life and the likelihood that they will become interwoven.

City life and voluntary community

I would not want to exaggerate my disagreement with Young. I think that she fails to appreciate what many regard as the main source of the value of community, namely the way in which it satisfies a widely shared desire to belong or to be recognised by others, and that this failure is reflected in the account of community she gives. But I do not deny that her critique is successful against *some* ideals of community.[24] Like her, I think that a vision of a society 'composed of decentralized, economically self-sufficient, face-to-face communities functioning as autonomous political identities' is deeply flawed and 'wildly utopian'.[25] And I agree with her that city life can provide us with an ideal of social existence. But I would put the point rather differently in order to draw out the way in which the ideal of city life and belonging to communities can be compatible. In my terms, city life could in principle be the setting for a vibrant civil society, in which a multiplicity of voluntary associations and communities *in the ordinary sense* flourish (existing alongside more transient networks of social relations), enriching each other in the process.

Civil society potentially provides an important sphere in which people might find fulfilment. As Michael Walzer points out, this conclusion is reinforced when we contemplate the main alternatives.[26] Work will provide some with fulfilling lives; but given the limits imposed by the division of labour, it is surely too optimistic to hope that it could do so for all. There are ways in which work could be reorganised so as to provide greater opportunities for self-realisation, perhaps even without compromising efficiency. But it would be unrealistic to expect such changes to eliminate boring or repetitive jobs, or even make them scarce. Political activity is sometimes held up as a practice within which individuals can transcend the realm of necessity and find fulfilment. But a life of political participation is not to everyone's taste, and it would be unjustifiable to regard it as an essential ingredient of a good life for everyone. In short, work and politics can provide fulfilment for some, but not for everyone. When there is a healthy civil society, the network of communities and voluntary associations that constitute it provide an important alternative source of fulfilment.

The idea that city life can be valuable in virtue of providing people with the space to form and join associations or communities that enable them to lead fulfilling lives might be questioned by some communitarian thinkers, on the grounds that civil society can provide only impoverished forms of community, or what Robert Bellah and his co-authors call 'lifestyle enclaves'.[27] Expressed in terms of language whose meaning is familiar from the work of Ferdinand Tonnies, these communitarian thinkers believe that only *Gemeinschaft* – something that one is born into and grows within – and not *Gesellschaft*, can meet our needs.[28] According to this view, the communities that are really important to us are those into which we are born rather than those we join, for only those we enter at birth are truly ours; only our ancestral communities, such as our families or ethnic communities, can satisfy our deeply felt need to belong or be recognised by others, and give depth to our practical reasoning.[29]

To some extent at least this scepticism about the ability of civil society to respond to out deepest needs is misconceived. Even if civil society is viewed as a network of *voluntary* associations and communities, this does not mean that it excludes the communities into which people are born. These can properly be regarded as voluntary so long as their members are free to leave, even if they had no choice in the first place about whether to become members. What constitutes freedom to leave is, of course, a hard question. The mere possibility of leaving does not seem sufficient to justify saying that a person is free to leave. For that to be the case, she must have meaningful alternatives available to her. She must also be in a position to assess the risks of leaving, at least in some rough and ready way, which requires that she have the capacities and information to do so. If these conditions are satisfied for the members of a community, they would seem to possess the freedom to leave it, and the community can properly be regarded as voluntary.

In any case, forms of communitarianism that attach overriding importance to people's ancestral communities seem to involve considerable exaggeration: people can often satisfy their need to feel that they belong, or to be recognised by others, by joining communities and associations, and their decision to join can be based upon deep commitments and need not be arbitrary. But we should not recoil from these exaggerated forms of communitarianism to the opposite extreme, namely, the idea that cities are valuable because they make space for the *only* authentic form of existence in the modern world, 'the cosmopolitan life'. The cosmopolitan in this context is someone who shops around, appropriates different cultural materials, and adapts them for his own purposes in the light of his own conception of what is worthwhile.

Jeremy Waldron presents this vision of the cosmopolitan in the following passage:

> The cosmopolitan may live all his life in one city and maintain the same citizenship throughout. But he refuses to think of himself as *defined* by his location or his ancestry or his citizenship or his language. Though he may live in San Francisco and be of Irish ancestry, he does not take his identity to be compromised when he learns Spanish, eats Chinese, wears clothes made in Korea, listens to arias by Verdi sung by a Maori princess on Japanese equipment, follows Ukranian politics, and practices Buddhist meditation techniques.[30]

I do not deny that such an individual can flourish, and that he may represent the realisation of something genuinely valuable.[31] But I have reservations about the provocative thesis that Waldron toys with, that the way of life of 'the cosmopolitan individual' is the only authentic one for us nowadays.[32] For many people, the communities into which they are born exert a powerful attraction, and continue to provide deep sources of fulfilment. It is not obvious why their lives must be inauthentic if they see themselves as partly defined by membership of those communities and seek to protect and preserve what they regard as the best in them, by whatever legitimate means are at their disposal.

Giving clear content to the notion of what it is to be defined, or to think of oneself as being defined, partly or wholly, by one's membership of some community, is not easy. But it does not seem to preclude giving due weight to the fact that the community (or communities) that define a person's identity are likely to be fluid. These will evolve in the face of changing circumstances, and in the process the identity of their members will be transformed. Nor does the idea that a person's communal membership is constitutive of her identity imply that she cannot be true to herself whilst learning from other ways of life and seeking to change her own. Indeed she may remain authentic whilst striving to realise Young's ideal of openness to others.

The model of city life and civil society I have been presenting must steer a path between the two extremes I have described. It must acknowledge the importance many people attach to their ancestral communities, and accept that these communities co-exist and may sometimes interact in mutually enriching ways with other communities in the city, even permitting their members to carve out untraditional lives within them. But the model must also recognise the value of being able to reject one's inherited communities more radically, by ceasing to define oneself in terms of them and living a cosmopolitan life: when these communities allow their members genuine freedom to leave, city life can provide access to a range of cultural materials, social networks and ways of life. So cities can in principle provide a space in which individuals come to terms with their various inheritances, remain open to difference, and determine within limits their own mode of being with others.

Of course, this is a description of an ideal. No one – especially not Young – is claiming that cities as we know them always (or indeed ever) provide the respectful and open environment that would allow a variety of different associations and communities to flourish, and that would make possible a meaningful and enriching encounter between these communities. But we can see the way in which cities could provide a unique setting for this to happen, since they concentrate together a large and diverse group of people. What other conditions would be required to facilitate this is a complex issue. Social justice is no doubt important, and forms of civic education that cultivate not only respect for others but also openness to other ways of life.[33]

Cities as communities

I began by drawing attention to two contrasting images projected by the terms 'city' and 'community': cities as a context of choice where diversity and toleration can thrive, and communities as claustrophobic, fostering uniformity at the expense of diversity. I have spent some time trying to dislodge the second of these images in order to make space for the thought that community and city life might provide us with complementary ideals.

But I have not yet entertained the idea that cities could themselves *be* communities. This idea has been presupposed by a number of those who defend the importance of a vibrant and activist local politics.

One feature of the concept of community, the importance of which has often been ignored by communitarian thinkers, is that community can, in principle at least, be realised at different levels. For example, it might be realised below the level of the state, between groups of its citizens, or at the level of the state, between all or most of its citizens; and there may be transnational communities that cut across the borders of states. In the context of the city, therefore, we can hardly avoid the question of whether it is possible to make sense of the idea that the inhabitants of a city might together form an overarching community.

Young would no doubt respond that this is a dangerously 'totalising' vision – that a community of this sort would have to deny difference. The diversity present within cities means that it would be rash to dismiss such a response out of hand. How could those who differ in terms of race, ethnicity, sexual orientation, class and income be bound together in a single community? How could individuals residing in new housing developments, protected by gates and security systems, be in community with those who live in impoverished circumstances beyond those gates, perhaps under the daily threat of violence?

Divisions of these kinds act as a serious barrier to the idea that the inhabitants of really-existing cities might constitute communities. But we should not forget that community can be a matter of degree (and co-exist alongside voluntary associations and social networks of various kinds). Many cities seem already to be communities, in what I have called the ordinary sense, to some degree and in some respects. The inhabitants of a city often identify with it and describe themselves with pride as, for example, Londoners, Glaswegians or Geordies. Identification with the city may be strengthened by support for its football team, or where there is more than one, through local rivalries. Cities often support a distinctive way of life for their inhabitants, perhaps partly in virtue of the climate they suffer and their geographical setting, or perhaps in virtue of their festivals and their use of public spaces. Indeed cities may go some way towards satisfying the need to belong that communitarian theorists have claimed is important.

By partly defining the identities of their inhabitants, cities might also provide a locus for the realisation of other values. Some philosophical nationalists have maintained that a shared *national* identity makes feasible active citizenship and a politics of the common good. By extension, could it be argued that a shared local or civic identity provides the foundation for an activist local politics of a kind that seems badly needed if urban renewal or regeneration is to be more than just rhetoric in the mouths of politicians? This is the question I propose to explore briefly in the remainder of the chapter.

The philosophical nationalists I have in mind argue that only if citizens have a sense of belonging together will they attach importance to active citizenship. David Miller, for example, says that 'nationality gives people the common identity that makes it possible for them to conceive of shaping their world together'.[34] Miller also believes that in practice a shared national identity is important for the cultivation of social trust. That trust is necessary for a politics of the common good, since without it people will meet as advocates of particular groups, rather than 'as citizens whose main concerns are fairness between the different sections of the community and the pursuit of common ends'.[35] By extension it might be claimed that a shared *civic* identity makes possible active participation in *local* politics, and the successful implementation of policies that look to the good of the inhabitants of the city as a whole rather than a particular group of them, perhaps giving priority to the needs of the worst off, for example, by subsidising services of various kinds for the local homeless or unemployed.

I have not defended the value of participation in local politics or the legitimacy of redistribution of resources within the city.[36] And even those who share these normative commitments might regard the extension of the philosophical nationalist's position from nations to cities as far-fetched. The reason why some nationalists have thought that a shared national identity is important in a polity is precisely because it provides its citizens with a sense of belonging together. When citizens share a national identity there is a widespread belief amongst them that there is some reason why they should associate together other than that they happen to have ended up in the same polity. And it is just that which is missing in cities. Given the movement to and from cities, often driven by the labour market, it would require a massive dose of self-deception for city dwellers to believe that there is some special reason why they should associate together other than that they happen to have ended up in the same city. It might be replied that conationals as well require self-deception to sustain their belief that they belong together. But there is surely a difference in degree here, for movement across national borders is controlled in a way that movement to and from cities within the same state is not. The myths that play a role in binding together nations often cannot survive close scrutiny; but they are not usually manifestly false.

There is nevertheless a potential objection to the nationalist position, which makes possible a re-thinking of the conditions that are required for active citizenship and a politics responsive to the common good. This objection can be cast in the form of a question: why cannot politics take this shape when people have a sense of belonging *to* the appropriate political unit, even if they lack a sense of belonging *together* in the relevant sense? I do not propose to explore this question in the depth it would require to give it a proper answer; but let me explain the distinction it presupposes between a sense of belonging together and a sense of belonging to some political unit.[37]

Suppose we stipulate that a person has a sense of belonging to some political unit, such as a polity or a city, if and only if she identifies with some
of its major institutions and practices and feels at home in them. In principle at least, the inhabitants of a polity or city could identify with some of
their institutions and practices, and feel at home in them, without believing that there was any deep reason why they should associate together of
the sort that might be provided by the belief that they shared a culture,
history, or particular conception of the good. In other words, the inhabitants of a city, or the citizens of a polity, might have a sense of *belonging
to it* without thinking that there was any real sense in which they *belonged
together*. People may move to a city for a variety of different reasons, for
example, employment or easier access to the place where they already work,
better leisure facilities, higher quality-schools – but they may nevertheless
all come to feel that they belong to it. So the suggestion is that a participatory politics at the local level, involving a commitment to urban regeneration and modest forms of redistribution, might be possible without local
inhabitants' possessing a sense of belonging together so long as they shared
a sense of belonging to the locality.

This is hardly a novel idea. Many advocates of more robust forms of
local democracy have said something similar. It is an empirical claim,
however, and cannot be justified by armchair reflection alone, despite the
attraction to the philosophically inclined of doing what Robert Nozick
calls 'normative sociology'. Proper research on these matters appears, at
best, inconclusive. William Hampton in his study of the connection between community and political activity in Sheffield concludes that a sense
of belonging to a given area 'is connected only very tenuously to the
enhanced civic consciousness which might be expected'.[38] In their study of
six localities in Britain, Geraint Parry, George Moyser and Neil Day express
some scepticism towards the idea that a sense of belonging to an area fosters
participation in its political life, concluding that the best which can be said
is that it is 'not proven'.[39]

Though existing research does not support the idea that a sense of belonging to a locality fosters political participation, it is not sufficiently advanced
to undermine the intuitive plausibility of that idea or some refined version
of it. Indeed this research appears to leave open the possibility that some
suitably qualified claim (of the form, 'under certain specifiable conditions,
a sense of belonging to a locality will facilitate participation') might be
sustained in the face of the evidence. A hypothesis of this kind can allow
that other social conditions, including various non-communal relations (for
example, social networks or coalitions formed around shared interests) are
often more important for facilitating local political participation, and can
concede that participation of this kind does not necessarily require a shared
sense of belonging to a locality.

If a sense of belonging to a city can, under some circumstances, play a
role in facilitating an activist local politics, this leaves open the question of

what conditions are conducive to fostering such a sense of belonging. Some of these conditions seem uncontroversial. It will be harder for those who live on housing states where they experience constant threats to their person or possessions to feel a sense of belonging to the city that fails to provide them with adequate security. Those who are constantly at the receiving end of racist abuse will also find it difficult to identify with the city in which they live. To the extent that the character and way of life of a city exclusively reflect the concerns of the dominant cultural community, this will make it difficult for those from other cultural communities to feel at home in it. In principle, however, none of these threats to a widespread sense of belonging is impossible to counter. In practice, whether they are countered will depend to a large extent on the existence of the necessary political will.

Conclusion

Far from being incompatible with the realisation of community, cities could in principle provide the setting for a robust civil society in which voluntary associations and communities offer important sources of fulfilment, and in which their individual members display what Young calls 'an openness to unassimilated otherness'. The notion of community is far less hostile to difference than Young maintains. Indeed, cities may themselves be communities in the ordinary sense, and under some circumstances fostering a sense of belonging to them may facilitate a vibrant local politics informed by a concern for the common good.

Notes

I would like to thank Dario Castiglione, David Owen and Graham Smith for their helpful comments. I also benefited from comments to a paper, on which this chapter is based, when I presented it to the Centre for Post-Analytic Philosophy at the University of Southampton and to the conference on 'The Culture of Toleration' held at the University of Exeter.

  1 See I. Young, 'The ideal of community and the politics of difference', in L. Nicholson (ed.), *Feminism and Postmodernism* (London, Routledge, 1990); *Justice and the Politics of Difference* (Princeton, NJ: Princeton University Press, 1990), Chapter 8.
  2 Young, *Justice and the Politics of Difference*, p. 229.
  3 Young, 'The ideal of community', p. 311.
  4 Young, *Justice and the Politics of Difference*, p. 232.
  5 Young, 'The ideal of community', p. 314.
  6 Young, *Justice and the Politics of Difference*, p. 233.
  7 Young, 'The ideal of community', p. 318.
  8 *Ibid.*
  9 *Ibid.*
 10 Young, *Justice and the Politics of Difference*, pp. 238–9.
 11 Young, 'The ideal of community', p. 319.

12 See C. McKinnon, 'Tolerance and the character of pluralism', chapter 3 in this volume.

13 Young, 'The ideal of community', p. 320n1. Young believes that this sociological use of the term is also present in ordinary speech: see *Justice and the Politics of Difference*, p. 234.

14 See E. Frazer, *The Problems of Communitarian Politics* (Oxford: Oxford University Press, 1999), Chapter 2, for a recent analysis of the concept of community that has some similarities with, but also some differences from, the one I proceed to offer.

15 I present this argument in more detail in my *Community, Solidarity and Belonging: Levels of Community and Their Normative Significance* (Cambridge: Cambridge University Press, 2000), Chapter 1.

16 See my *Community, Solidarity and Belonging*, pp. 61–3.

17 Young, 'The ideal of community', p. 320n1.

18 Frazer, *The Problems of Communitarian Politics*, p. 83.

19 *Ibid.*, pp. 83–4, 167–8, p. 220.

20 See also *ibid.*, pp. 166–7.

21 Young, *Justice and the Politics of Difference*, pp. 234–5.

22 J. Raz, 'Multiculturalism: A liberal perspective', in *Ethics in the Public Domain* (Oxford: Oxford University Press, 1994), p. 165.

23 See McKinnon, 'Tolerance and the character of pluralism', chapter 3 in this volume.

24 Cf. Young, 'The ideal of community', p. 320.

25 *Ibid.*, p. 316.

26 For this argument, see M. Walzer, 'The civil society argument', in R. Beiner (ed.), *Theorizing Citizenship* (Albany, NY: State University of New York Press, 1995).

27 R. Bellah *et al.*, *Habits of the Heart: Individualism and Commitment in American Life* (Berkeley, CA: University of California Press, 1985).

28 See F. Tonnies, *Community and Association*, trans. C. P. Loomis (New York: Harper and Row, 1963).

29 Michael Sandel comes close to presenting this sort of view: see his *Liberalism and the Limits of Justice* (Cambridge: Cambridge University Press, 1982).

30 J. Waldron, 'Minority cultures and the cosmopolitan alternative', in W. Kymlicka (ed.), *The Rights of Minority Cultures* (Oxford: Oxford University Press, 1995), p. 95.

31 For some worries about whether the cosmopolitan life really can offer a stable vision of human flourishing, see S. Scheffler, 'Conceptions of cosmopolitanism', *Utilitas*, 11 (1999) 255–76, at pp. 270–1. Scheffler argues that communities, societies and cultural groups provide an 'infrastructure of responsibility' that sets out the responsibilities of their members as well as provides institutional mechanisms through which they can be discharged. Those who lead freewheeling cosmopolitan lives are deprived of these structures and therefore may be 'cut off from the forms of social support that structure and sustain individual responsibility' (*ibid.*, p. 271). Although this worry is not wholly misplaced, Scheffler does not seem to me to give due weight to the possibility that the cosmopolitan may be a member of various associations and participate in practices that carry with them responsibilities and provide their own forms of support. Social life is not exhausted by membership of communities and cultural groups.

32 J. Waldron, 'Minority cultures and the cosmopolitan alternative', pp. 100–1. Scheffler also notes the way in which Waldron flirts with this extreme thesis: see Scheffler, 'Conceptions of cosmopolitanism', p. 261. Waldron has now distanced himself from this thesis and I am not sure whether there is any residual disagreement between the position I develop here and the one he now advocates. See J. Waldron, 'What is cosmopolitan?', *Journal of Political Philosophy* 8 (2000) 227–43, at pp. 231–3.

33 On the kind of education required to cultivate the former, see D. Heyd, 'Education to toleration: Some philosophical obstacles and their resolution', this volume.

34 D. Miller, *Market, State, and Community: Theoretical Foundations of Market Socialism* (Oxford: Oxford University Press, 1989), p. 189.

35 D. Miller, 'Socialism and Toleration', in S. Mendus (ed.), *Justifying Toleration: Conceptual and Historical Perspectives* (Cambridge: Cambridge University Press, 1988), p. 247.

36 In Britain the last twenty years have seen much controversy over the best way of securing urban renewal or regeneration, with the New Right arguing that it needs to be market-driven, leaving local authorities to play at best an enabling or facilitating role. See D. Hill, *Citizens and Cities: Urban Policy in the 1990s* (Hemel Hempstead: Harvester Wheatsheaf, 1994), esp. Chapter 7, for a discussion of the relevant policies and debates. The idea that a more participatory local politics might be needed for urban regeneration of a desirable kind is premised on at least a partial rejection of these New Right ideas.

37 This distinction is developed further in my *Community, Solidarity and Belonging*, Chapter 5, and in my 'Political community, liberal-nationalism, and the ethics of assimilation', *Ethics*, 109 (1999) 261–86.

38 W. Hampton, *Democracy and Community: A Study of Sheffield* (London: Oxford University Press, 1970), p. 121.

39 G. Parry, G. Moyser and N. Day, *Political Participation and Democracy in Britain* (Cambridge: Cambridge University Press, 1992), p. 344.

8
Social ethos and the dynamics of toleration

Jonathan Wolff

'The difficulty with toleration', writes Bernard Williams, 'is that it seems to be at once necessary and impossible.'[1] Toleration is necessary if groups with fundamentally different and conflicting values and beliefs are to live in peace together, but, so it is said, *prima facie* impossible under such circumstances. Why so? The idea of toleration only seems appropriate when a conflict of values or beliefs goes so deep that groups may think that 'they cannot accept the existence of each other'. Williams sums up: 'Toleration, we may say, is required only for the intolerable. That is its basic problem.'[2]

Although Williams, unlike many others, refrains from calling this the 'paradox of toleration', there is something of a genuine puzzle here. As Williams indicates, formulating the apparent conditions under which toleration is required makes it rather difficult to see how those conditions could be satisfied. After all, it is not the case that all differences call for toleration.[3] Under normal circumstances differences in hair colour do not call for toleration (although this is not to say that one cannot think of abnormal circumstances). Nor is it the case that all differences in beliefs, or values, call for toleration. Only differences of a certain kinds require toleration, so it seems; perhaps differences of a certain depth or fundamental nature. And it may be that when we spell out the nature of such differences the possibility of toleration may be remote.

The supposition that there is a puzzle or paradox here seems to presuppose what we could call the 'toleration presupposes repugnance' view. This is the view that the question of whether I should tolerate something only arises when I find myself revolted or otherwise offended by it. If I am untroubled, so it is said, toleration is not at issue.

It is not clear, though, that this is correct, at least in all cases. Is there anything wrong with the language of the person who says 'I'm a pretty tolerant sort of person: I don't find any beliefs or practices offensive or revolting'? Some will say that toleration lies between 'indifference' and 'empathy', and so this apparently super-tolerant person is not tolerant at all, but either indifferent or abundantly empathetic. Behind this verbal squabble, though,

there is something of importance. There is no doubt that there is a normative element to toleration. It only makes sense to say that one tolerates
beliefs or practices that fall into a certain class. Yet it is less clear that that
class is 'the beliefs and practices I personally find revolting'. The alternative is to say that it is 'the beliefs and practices that often, or normally, are
found revolting around here, or have been until recently (or if not here,
then in places similar to this one)'. Thus, we can agree that overcoming, or
somehow suspending, personal revulsion will often be part of the process
of toleration; but it need not be.[4] And, as has often been noted, when toleration of a practice becomes widespread enough – of interracial friendship, for example – describing this in terms of toleration normally loses its
point.

It is probably important, though, to distinguish the issue of toleration as
an individual virtue from that of the nature of a tolerant society, which is
our central concern here. Yet there are bound to be some similarities (I will
return to this later), and I think we have seen enough to be sympathetic
to the idea that, in general, toleration requires an 'overcoming'. Thus,
although it doesn't follow that we must see things this way, it makes sense
to think of toleration as a particular process, and of a tolerant society as
one that develops in a particular way. In other words, a tolerant society is
one that has a certain dynamics. To bring this out it will be helpful to contrast it with another view. The view I question in its pure form – and
whether anyone has ever explicitly held it is not at issue here – asserts that
a tolerant society is the same thing as a politically liberal society, and that
a politically liberal society is a society that is neutral between competing
conceptions of the good. In sum, then, on this view, a tolerant society is a
neutral society.

There is, no doubt, much to be said in favour of such a view, and it may
well be that the alternative perspective I shall offer differs primarily only in
emphasis. But note first that if we define a tolerant society in terms of
whether or not it is neutral between certain competing conceptions of the
good we seem to be looking at what we could call a structural feature of
that society. We look at it not so much in its development but in its statics;
what Nozick calls a 'current-time slice'.[5] We take an inventory of laws and
practices and examine them to see whether they are neutral or not.

What it means to pass this test will depend on the notion of neutrality
at play. According to 'outcome neutrality' the essence of whether a society
is tolerant depends on the consequences of its laws and practices for people's
ability to live according to their own conceptions of the good. According
to 'justification neutrality' the test will be whether or not assumptions about
the relative superiority or inferiority of one conception of the good, or a
range of conceptions, explicitly or implicitly enter into the justification of
a society's laws and practices.[6]

Is there anything wrong with the claim that a tolerant society is a (justi-
fication-) neutral society? One obvious flaw is that we have never encoun-

tered an entirely neutral society; indeed, on many views, no actual society has ever remotely come close. Yet we think we have encountered tolerant societies. Should we say, then, that social tolerance comes in degrees, and a society is tolerant to the degree that it is neutral? Perhaps, but let us look at a richer characterisation of a tolerant society; one that more centrally judges a society in terms of how it responds to change – in the dynamics of the system. An analogy from epistemology might help. Consider the question: how might we define a rational believer? One, apparently trivial, necessary condition of being rational is to have a set of consistent beliefs: the 'statics' of a rational believer. But this encounters one important problem: as a matter of fact, no one does. When the logical implications of everything a given person believes are fully spelt out, inconsistencies will be revealed. We have never encountered a truly consistent believer. Now we could try to define degrees of rationality, so that some inconsistencies of belief are still compatible with being rational to a high degree. However, a number of epistemologists have responded in a different way: by trying to define rationality at least in part in terms of the processes by which one updates one's beliefs in the light of new evidence. Thus, there are books called *Knowledge in Flux*,[7] *Change in View*,[8] and *The Dynamics of Belief*[9] (which was also the working title of *Knowledge in Flux*!).

There are, as with any analogy, limits to this one, which I introduce just to illustrate the possibility, and the possible advantages, of a shift of emphasis from statics to dynamics. My question is whether this shift might help us understand the nature of a tolerant society. The idea would be to say that a tolerant society should be understood not as neutral society but as a society that responds in certain ways to certain challenges. But challenges to what? And what are these challenges? And how should it respond? These are our questions.

Social ethos

If we are to take seriously the idea that a tolerant society is one with certain dynamics, then we need to come to an understanding of what it is that changes or, at least, is threatened with change. Here I want to appeal to the idea of a 'social ethos'. In general I want to say that everything that we would recognise as a society has a social ethos. This is not, however, intended as a definition of a society (as smaller groups too can have an ethos), but as one necessary condition. Some societies have a tolerant social ethos, and some do not, although this is going to be a matter of degree. But what, it will be said, is a social ethos?

It will be helpful, I think, to start with a model case, and then try to apply the lessons learnt there back to the case of an entire society. The case I want to consider is that of a big city firm of accountants,[10] who pride themselves on the idea that 'here we work hard, but we play hard too', perhaps stating as much in their recruitment material on their website. This slogan, or principle, is likely to be exemplified in certain practices. The staff are likely to get to work early and stay late, and work through their lunch break. But on Friday nights they go out for drinks together, and at weekends they play team sports for the company against similar companies.

The 'work hard–play hard' slogan may seem at the core of the company's corporate ethos, but is itself expressive of some underlying values: profitability and collegiality, most likely. The company wants to make money, but it also, either for the same reason or independently out of goodwill, wants a workforce who get on with each other and identify with the company. So we can see here we have three levels to the company's ethos: first, fundamental values; second, slogans or principles; and third, practices. No doubt there are intermediate levels too, but for simplicity let us ignore them for now. My claim is that the corporate ethos is constituted by all three levels: each of values – which may only be implicit – principles and practices must all be in place for us to say that there is a genuine 'work hard–play hard' ethos. For consider another firm, which says exactly the same on its website, and the workers believe that they work hard and play hard, but in fact they don't: they get in late, do the easy crossword before starting work, and always get their regular trains home. Here we may say that there isn't so much an ethos in place as an ideology. Indeed, although there are no doubt many other uses of the term 'ideology', one important sense seems to be 'degenerate ethos'. An ideology, in this sense, is a deformed ethos where the principles and the practices do not match. (We might also consider whether an ethos could be deformed in other ways, but I will leave this to one side.)

When should we say that an individual shares the social ethos? One sufficient condition, presumably, would be when she values the values, believes and recites the principles, and follows the practices that exemplify the principles. Each of these, again, will be a matter of degree, and may allow us room to make a distinction between a strong and a weak social ethos. There are at least two dimensions by which a social ethos can be judged strong or weak. The first is that of those individuals who hold the ethos, how strongly they do so. With how much conviction do they recite the slogans, and how directly motivated are they to act on them? I say 'directly' motivated as a way of making Kant's distinction between acting *from a principle* and acting *in accordance with it*, perhaps out of the fear of the consequences of not doing so. Strength of an ethos is measured, in part, by action from the principle, governed by the values, rather than merely in accordance with it.[11]

The second dimension of strength is the proportion of the population of the society who adhere to the ethos. Thus it is obvious that an ethos can be strong according to one dimension and weak according to another. We might also add a third dimension of strength, which we could call pervasiveness. To explain, suppose we view a society as a complex set of relations, and suppose that an ethos is a set of norms to govern those relations:

which relations should it govern? There are, for example, relations between citizens *qua* citizens; between citizens *qua* economic actors; between citizens and the state; between the state and individuals outside the state; between the state and other states, and so on, and so on. If a society that, say, in other ways values equality of opportunity nevertheless enforces fairly rigorous trade barriers we could say that this ethos is less pervasive than it might be. Whether we treat this as a third dimension of strength, or as an independent feature, may be a merely terminological question.

The mechanics of toleration

We introduced the idea of a social ethos as a way of pursuing the dynamic account of toleration: in effect the idea is that a tolerant society is one that has a social ethos that responds to challenges in a certain, tolerant, way. What I mean by a 'tolerant way' of responding will be clarified, but it is worth noting that 'tolerance' is, itself, sometimes, a mechanical, or at least an engineering, term. We talk about certain measurements having a degree of tolerance, meaning a margin of error, and to extend this use we could use the term 'tolerant' as the opposite of 'highly tuned'. A highly tuned engine, we might say, is one that responds badly to interference, or 'noise': it is intolerant, or unforgiving. This is exactly what so many people find so infuriating about computers. A more tolerant machine might still manage to do what it is meant to, even if the wrong key is pressed, or a little sand gets in the works. In other words, a tolerant machine is one that can fulfil its function even in the face of some dysfunctional elements. An intolerant machine, on the other hand, needs a sterile environment and operators wearing white gloves.

Should we say that a tolerant society is merely a society with a weak ethos; one that is held by few people, or by many people but only to a low degree? This, I think, is quite wrong. What is correct is that a tolerant society can have a weak ethos; and sometimes it can be tolerant because it has a weak ethos; but it seems to me just as likely that a society will be *intolerant* precisely because it has a weak ethos. That is because the ethos would crumble if it were not protected; it has to be protected from challenges through intolerance. This, indeed, may be how some totalitarian regimes have acted: because the ethos was so weak, no one is permitted to consider alternatives, for fear that alternatives would prove too attractive. If this is right, then tolerance is independent of strength.

So how should we model tolerance? Consider again the firm of accountants, happy in their 'work hard–play hard' ethos. Suppose, now, someone who does not share this ethos miraculously gets through the selection process. Suppose that this person subscribes to the 'family values' ethos. This means not routinely getting in early and routinely staying late, not socialising with workmates after hours or at weekends, but generally working efficiently enough that normal work tasks can be completed in normal working hours, in order to make room for a strong family life. How will the company respond?

Clearly there are several ways that the company may behave. It may well be said, for example, that this person is not a 'team player' and does nothing to contribute to an attractive working environment. Indeed, they may even be considered a disruptive influence by setting a bad example. If so, it may well be that they will be frozen out: perhaps they will not survive the probationary period. If such a decision is taken for this reason, we should say that this firm is extremely intolerant.

Of course they need not act this way. Another possibility is that, while strongly disapproving of the person's behaviour, they may decide not to dismiss them. This could be for various reasons: a feeling that to do so would be unfair – after all the person's work is adequate – or a feeling that this would draw a certain type of unwelcome attention on the firm. Rather than bring the issue to a head by firing this worker, perhaps they would adopt a different strategy: making the workplace discouraging enough to encourage them to leave of their own accord, but not doing anything to force the issue. This would mean passing them over for promotion, finding reasons why bonuses went to others, and so on. There must be many real-life examples of this. This is a form of toleration; but not the only form: if Marcuse hadn't taken the term for other uses we could call it repressive toleration; but here I shall call it 'grudging' tolerance. Toleration is adopted as a type of defensive strategy.

There is, though, another possible line of response. When confronted with the example of someone who works effectively, but to a different model, perhaps the senior management will take pause. It may be that they will reflect on the idea that there is more than one way of getting what they most want – profit – and feel that they should reconsider their principles and/or practices. After reflection they may start to review such things as their recruitment material, the type of activities they sponsor, and the general image they present. In other words they will treat the alternative working style on its merits, and come to appreciate and welcome it as a valuable alternative. To act this way is to be 'accommodatingly tolerant'.[12]

I said that we might define a tolerant society in terms of how it responds to certain challenges. We had three questions: what is it that is challenged; what are the challenges, and how does a tolerant society respond? We have seen answers in the accountants example: the ethos is constituted by the values, principles, and practices of the firm; it is challenged by someone who does not share the working principles, and it responds by recognising that there are other valid ways of working. Before trying to apply the lessons of this model back to the case of a whole society, it is worth bringing out the point that this model also shows something about the limits of toleration.

Recall that the model of an ethos involved a three-way distinction between values, principles and practices. At any time some collection of values, principles and practices constitutes the ethos of the group. We have examined the example of a person who joins the group but wishes to live by alternative principles. But why should we assume that all challenges appear at the level of principles? There could be challenges to practices and challenges to values too. Suppose someone comes up with the idea that everyone should get in an hour earlier in the morning for a group session in the gym, or that some other modification of sporting or social arrangements should take place. Again the three responses are possible: intolerance, grudging toleration or accommodating toleration. Facing such challenges is likely to put very little strain on the organisation, and the evaluation will simply be a question of whether this is a more effective way of putting the 'work hard–play hard' slogan into practice. Thus, the organisation needs to decide whether it will get more or less work out of its workers if they have the extra gym session, and whether encouraging this behaviour will improve morale or have the reverse effect.

At the other extreme consider another employee who, after gaining the confidence of the firm, proposes that the company should make many more charitable donations, and that it should seek out worthwhile organisations it can help at reduced or no fees, and who personally declines to work for clients whose activities he or she finds morally dubious, advocating very publicly that the company should drop these clients irrespective of the effect on profitability. This employee may, however, thoroughly approve of the 'work hard – play hard' part of the ethos. The conflict in this case is not at that level, but at the level of fundamental values. In this case the employee wishes to modify 'profitability' with 'social responsibility' at the level of core value.

Again the three responses are possible; however, in this case intolerance appears overwhelmingly likely to be the response. Grudging toleration is just about conceivable, provided a method of containment for this employee can be found, but accommodating tolerance seems unlikely in the extreme. It would be a complete rethinking of corporate goals, and why should the company do that? This is not to say that there cannot be large accountancy firms for whom social responsibility is important; but change is much more likely to be top-down than bottom-up.

Yet need it be that in order to be considered tolerant the firm has to change? A firm that gives serious consideration to the question of whether it should be more socially responsible – even if it ultimately rejects the proposal – is surely more tolerant than a firm that rejects the suggestion out of hand, other things being equal. Indeed, firms or organisations that make important changes without serious consideration would seem not to be so much tolerant as irresponsible. But what does it mean to give a challenge 'serious consideration'? In the case of challenges to practices or principles this is relatively easy to understand. Each is evaluated in terms of how it coheres with, develops or interprets some aspect at a more fundamental level within the ethos. So a proposed new practice may be evaluated by how well it exemplifies the principles, and a new principle by how well its implementation will realise the values. But how can we evaluate a challenge to the values? It seems that there is nothing more fundamental to which we can appeal, and if we take literally the idea that a value must be assessed on its own merits it will always win.

This is too quick, though. First, the idea of a three-level structure to an ethos is an over-simplification. In reality there are an indefinite number of levels and some values will be subordinate to others. Therefore, a similar structure of evaluating the less fundamental in terms of the more fundamental is possible. Second, we can evaluate values in the light of other values, even values at the same level. We can consider how well they mesh or cohere, or – a point of great importance – fall into an apparently natural pattern of change. Third, in some cases certain influences or pressures reflecting 'the spirit of the age' may be relevant. If a proposed new value is assessed in these, or other, ways, but is considered to be taking things 'too far', or in the wrong direction, it seems a bit hard to call the society that made this decision flatly intolerant. Perhaps we could introduce a category of 'reasoned intolerance'. This is a way of applying Mill's distinction between rejecting a view because it has been defeated after a full and fair hearing, and refusing to consider it altogether. However, although reasoned intolerance generally seems at least a step in the right direction, there may nevertheless be cases where this form and degree of calculation comes over as rather sinister, and may be found less excusable than mere bigotry.[13] But clearly cases will differ.

Back to society

So much for the accountants. What, though, do we learn about the nature of a tolerant society as a result of this discussion? Earlier, I contrasted the view I favour with the view that, ultimately, a tolerant society is a neutral society. I suggested that a problem with this view is that we have never seen a fully neutral society. Yet, there is a more basic shortcoming with the neutralist view. The trouble is that we simply don't know how to be neutral until we know what we are meant to be neutral between. Neutralism requires us to be ready for anything, but who was prepared for the challenges Western societies have faced in recent times? We have discovered numerous ways in which our political and social institutions have turned out to be non-neutral in unexpected ways with respect to gender, race, sexual orientation, religion, disability and so on.

In reply it will be said that although we may have found our societies to be 'outcome non-neutral' it does not follow from this that they are 'justification non-neutral'. For this would be to say that the justification of its laws and/or practices depends implicitly or explicitly on assumptions about the relevant merits of different conceptions of the good. Clearly it is right that such a case needs to be made out more carefully, and cannot be inferred from the mere observation of non-neutral outcomes. But nevertheless, the claim still seems obviously true. For example, a great deal of recent and current law rests on assumptions about the 'ideal' family, and a certain amount of recent legal reform has been the consequence of the struggle to try to eliminate such assumptions in many areas of law. Thus, our societies are both outcome non-neutral and justification non-neutral. Yet we believe Western societies to be tolerant, and broadly I think we are correct.

But whatever we think about its desirability, I do not think that the goal of making societies justification-neutral is a reasonable one. We cannot predict what future challenges will be made to our unthinking assumptions. And even if we could, it will be both very difficult and very wasteful to make preparations to allow a place for new life styles or beliefs before we know whether any or many people will show much interest in living that way. The dynamic approach, by contrast, encourages us to react to what exists, including what has just come into being, rather than what is merely possible.

One good example of the dynamic approach is the way in which liberal societies are slowly adapting themselves to the existence of gay life styles. Although the nature of the challenge is different in different places, it seems fairly clear that a large proportion of people in Western societies were, and perhaps still are, revolted by the idea of homosexuality, and this had been encoded in various repressive laws. Toleration takes the form, first, of non-enforcement of law, and then repeal. Yet, as Mill and Marx both point out, the law can be tolerant without society being so, and discrimination continues to take many unofficial and indirect forms. Nevertheless, the situation is largely such that Western democracies have accepted the obligation of trying to work out ways in which gay people can be accommodated into society while overcoming or at least allaying the fears of those non-gays who, somehow, feel threatened. This may well be a case where society is more tolerant than the average of its people.

Now change is a long process, and is not complete. But this is something we should expect on the dynamic view. Because we have an existing ethos, and one that is not standing ready to plug in just any new life style or beliefs, whatever they are, change can take a long time. It is a way of working out how to fit different things together. This is, in part at least, an experimental question and can be solved in different ways in different places. Some moves may be seen to be counterproductive and unhelpful, and may be withdrawn. The lesson is that toleration can hardly mean instant acceptance.

How do these comments, though, relate to the 'accountancy' model? What insight does that model give us with this case, and others like it? I would prefer to approach this question from the other direction. Clearly, I would have not introduced it unless I thought it does a great deal to help illustrate the nature of social ethos; what it is for a social ethos to be strong or weak; and what it is for a social ethos to be tolerant or intolerant. But others may not be as charitable to my analogy as I am myself, and may argue that it fails to be illuminating. The main criticisms will centre on the claim that it is simply incorrect to say that contemporary liberal societies have an ethos in any way comparable to that of a firm of accountants, however large the firm, or small the society.

The most obvious difficulty, it will be noted, is at the level of fundamental values. If, as is sometimes said, liberal society does not attempt to advance fundamental values then, ultimately, the idea of new life styles presenting challenges does no work: there is nothing to challenge.

The equally obvious answer is that it simply isn't true that liberal society promotes no values in particular. This becomes particularly clear when we look at the theorists of liberalism. Early on in the *Second Treatise*, Locke makes the claim that human beings are naturally free, equal and independent. Other triads of rights or values are offered. Locke also gives us life, liberty and estate. We are also familiar with the calls for life, liberty, and the pursuit of happiness; and liberty, fraternity and equality. Rawls worries that leaning too hard on these, or similar, values would make liberalism 'but another sectarian doctrine',[14] but it seems to me that Rawls (with his followers) are the exception to the tradition. As Rawls himself notes, by this standard the doctrines of Locke, Kant, Mill, and contemporary theorists such as Raz, are not properly forms of liberalism. Yet, however desirable one finds Rawls's position, it seems to me best to view it as a possible aspiration for society, rather than an account of existing liberal theory or practice. Liberal society does have some particular root values, although they tend to be rather vague and inclusive, and held 'implicitly'.[15]

Although it has played little explicit role in the philosophical tradition, the idea of 'the pursuit of happiness' may be central to our liberal ethos. Each individual has the right to pursue happiness[16] in their own way, subject to constraints concerning harm to others, and, possibly, the use of resources. Conventional life styles embody folk wisdom about where happiness, and perhaps other values, are to be found. We might say, for example, that part of this conventional wisdom is the implicit principle that 'every man should have a wife, kids, and a job'. Now I cannot recall anyone actually saying this to me, but one can hardly doubt that it has determined many people's expectations for many generations.

Typically, conventional patterns of life or belief tend to become ossified and become treated as values in themselves, independently of the question of how well they realise the values to which they are instrumental. There is very good reason for this, for we generally do better by following traditions than by re-inventing the wheel. However, conventional patterns will not suit everyone equally well, and those who more easily find happiness in other ways may attempt life styles that we may at first find threatening. Why are they threatening? I don't find that this is an easy question to answer; but perhaps they are threatening because comparisons with difference require us to think and reflect upon our own lives and values, which is often an uncomfortable experience.

The story so far, then, is this. Central to the liberal social ethos is the idea that each person has a right to pursue happiness. As a historical achievement we have found certain ways of living, in general, more conducive to happiness than others. These become conventional life styles, and the underlying assumption that these ways of living are preferable to others shapes many of our laws and practices. From time to time certain individuals find certain of these laws and practices overly constraining, and rebel by attempting to live in a way that allows them to pursue happiness in their own fashion, but does not coalesce with our existing laws and practices. This, then, provides a challenge to our social ethos.

Thus challenged, the model proposed suggests that we can respond in any of at least four ways: with intolerance (refusing to think); with grudging tolerance (acceptance as a way of avoiding the issues); with accommodating tolerance (coming to understand the value of the alternatives and making room for them); and with reasoned intolerance (being prepared to consider accommodation but finding that this is not possible without 'too much' revision). Accordingly, then, once we understand that existing liberal societies value the pursuit of happiness, we have a necessary core value with which to run our dynamic model of toleration.

It might be argued that if an ethos is to be adaptable in the way I suggest then it must have a special underlying value, perhaps 'live and let live'. If so, then this opens up two important challenges. First, the contrast between the dynamic and static disappears, for a society will be tolerant in virtue of one aspect of its social ethos. Second, the notion of 'live and let live' is so close to the idea of 'tolerate diversity' that the analysis becomes circular, presupposing the idea it is trying to explain.

Now the possible collapse of the distinction between statics and dynamics was always a threat. In brief, any disposition needs a 'categorical base' so ultimately the distinction between statics and dynamics is, as I have said, one of emphasis. But the problem of circularity is more troubling. However, my reply is that there is no single, special, value that all tolerant societies must endorse. A society might be tolerant, for example, purely because it is based on a strong doctrine of individual rights. Or it might be committed to the exercise of public reason. Or because its people are just naturally open-minded. The essence of toleration continues to depend on the process by which challenges are met, rather than any particular value or values underlying the process (even though some value or other must be present).

A different problem in applying the model, it will be said, is that the values of a liberal society are so thin and inclusive that there is no room for intolerance unless some sort of clear harm, to individuals or to public order, is threatened. But even if this is so, it is not an objection. A liberal society should hope, eventually, to be able to find room for all ways of life that do not damage third parties. But in addition this objection ignores the element of time-scale. Change may have to be slow. Thus, there may be reasoned intolerance of particular practices, where the proposed rate of change is too much, too soon. We cannot expect the overturning of conventional wisdom to be swift.

Finally, I have claimed that a tolerant society is one that responds to certain challenges in particular ways; but what should we say about a society that, as a matter of fact, faces no challenges? Does it not make sense to ask whether or not such a society could be tolerant, nevertheless?

Here it is tempting to say that we need to consider certain counter-factuals: how would it respond in the face of challenges? However, the truth or falsity of such counter-factuals will depend on existing features of the society; i.e. its statics. In this respect, then, the contrast between the dynamic view and static view is again one of emphasis rather than deep philosophical difference. Nevertheless, it does seem, generally, to put the emphasis in the right place.

Toleration as an individual virtue

The dynamic analysis of toleration as a social virtue was initially motivated by the thought that toleration as an individual virtue typically requires some sort of 'overcoming'. Thus, the question arises of whether we should apply the dynamic model to individuals as well.

There is reason for disquiet here. The obvious way of developing the view is that an individual is tolerant only if she has a disposition to react in certain ways in the face of the experience of new life styles. Here, though, we meet the objection that someone could have, and espouse, extremely bigoted views, yet nevertheless has the right dispositions. It is simply that she has never faced the challenging circumstances, and so her tolerant dispositions remain unrealised. But on my analysis this bigoted person would be classed as tolerant.[17]

Now, of course, we will not discover that she is tolerant unless she faces a challenge, so her virtue may lie dormant. But this is not a problem. One can be musical without ever having played a note, for example, so we are generally prepared to recognise the existence of yet-unrealised dispositions. Rather the problem is, so it is claimed, that the bigot is not tolerant at all. So the analysis fails.

However, I think we need to press this further. Imagine a case of a person who expresses extremely bigoted views; perhaps virulently anti-gay. But, by hypothesis, he has never knowingly met a gay person, and so has never had a chance to put his bigotry into action in any concrete fashion. Now suppose a gay couple moves in next door. After his initial extreme unease our subject finds himself going out of his way to make them feel welcome, and to include the newcomers into the neighbourhood. His behaviour takes him, and others, by surprise. His bigoted remarks about gays in general may not have changed, but when it comes to a real challenge he behaves in a tolerant fashion.

Now we need to ask, has this person suddenly become tolerant, or was he tolerant all along, 'underneath', without knowing it? Of course we now have evidence of tolerance, which we did not have before; but that it is not the question. It seems to me that we should say that he was always a tolerant person, but never had a serious chance to show it, or even find out for himself. So, just as there may be mute Miltons, there may also be bigoted tolerators.

Notes

I would especially like to thank Simon Evnine and Catriona McKinnon for extremely valuable written comments on a draft of this chapter. Versions of a paper on which this chapter is based were given at the University of Exeter, the University of Reading, the University of St Andrews, the University of Stirling, the University of Chicago at Illinois, and Columbia University. I would like to thank the audiences of those occasions for many difficult questions, and for not tolerating easy answers.

1 B. Williams, 'Toleration: An impossible virtue?', in D. Heyd (ed.), *Toleration: An Elusive Virtue* (Princeton NJ: Princeton University Press, 1996), p. 18.
2 *Ibid.*, p. 18.
3 Indeed, it is not obvious that *only* differences call for toleration: for example 'she could not tolerate another child doing as well as her on the maths test'; 'she could not tolerate her secretary turning up at the party wearing the same dress'.
4 David Heyd's well-made point that toleration involves a shift of perspective from the evaluation of beliefs or values to an evaluation of the person holding them does, I think, provide an analysis of one type of toleration. It is less clear, though, that this is the only type of 'tolerance proper', even when tolerance is considered as an ethical, rather than a political, virtue, which is my focus here. See D. Heyd, 'Introduction', in *Toleration: An Elusive Virtue*, pp. 3–17.
5 R. Nozick, *Anarchy, State, and Utopia* (Oxford: Basil Blackwell, 1974).
6 See J. Raz, *The Morality of Freedom* (Oxford: Oxford University Press, 1986), pp. 110–62; and W. Kymlicka, 'Liberal individualism and liberal neutrality', *Ethics*, 99 (1989) 883–905.
7 P. Gärdenfors, *Knowledge in Flux: Modelling the Dynamics of Epistemic States* (Cambridge, MA: Massachusetts Institute of Technology Press, 1988).
8 G. Harman, *Change in View: Principles of Reasoning* (Cambridge, MA: Massachusetts Institute of Technology Press, 1986).
9 P. Forrest, *The Dynamics of Belief: A Normative Logic* (Oxford: Basil Blackwell, 1986).
10 Here I extend an example first used in J. Wolff, 'Fairness, respect, and the egalitarian ethos', *Philosophy and Public Affairs*, 27 (1998) 97–122.
11 It is interesting to note that when it is remarked that someone believes in certain values 'implicitly' this is often taken to indicate the strongest possible level of belief. This seems odd, for surely 'explicit' is generally stronger than 'implicit'. However, it makes perfect sense. If values are held implicitly they are not subject to the type of reflection and questioning that can cast doubt on explicitly held values. The strongest social ethos, therefore, may well be one where the values are held implicitly. This may also make it very hard for people to say what the

ethos of their own society is. What, in detail, is the ethos of contemporary British society? This is a question to be asked, not of a British citizen, but, say, of a French sociologist long-resident in Britain (just as a native language speaker can rarely formulate the grammatical rules of their own language, without special training).

12 There may be other responses too; toleration for different types of reason. I do not mean to say that grudging toleration and accommodating toleration are the only possibilities. There may be further possibilities between the two.

13 I owe this point to Simon Evnine.

14 J. Rawls, 'Justice as fairness: Political not metaphysical', *Philosophy and Public Affairs*, 14 (1985) 223–51.

15 See Note 11.

16 Is 'happiness' the right word? It is becoming a philosophical commonplace that individuals may rationally and knowingly seek goals that make them unhappy. Yet, however well-established this point is in philosophical circles, it does not yet seem to have filtered down into folk wisdom.

17 I owe this observation to Catriona McKinnon.

9

Toleration and *laïcité*

Cécile Laborde

> France is an indivisible, *laïque*, democratic and social republic. It ensures equal-
> ity of all citizens before the law with no distinction made on the basis of origin,
> race or religion. It respects all beliefs.
>
> (Article 2 of 1958 Constitution)

In September 1989, three schoolgirls wearing the traditional Muslim head-
scarf were barred from entering a school near Paris, and later expelled. The
headmaster claimed to be applying a long-established republican rule prohibiting religious symbols in secular state schools. The incident quickly
sparked a hotly contested national debate about the principle of religious
neutrality in republican schools. A decade later, everything, it seems, has
been said about the 'headscarves affair', and the way in which, in quite an
exemplary fashion, it crystallised latent national anxieties. These concerned,
notably, the contested status of public education in a fragmented society,
the problematic legitimacy of traditional norms of authority and social
integration, the protracted liquidation of the colonial heritage, fears about
a 'conflict of civilisations' pitting the West against 'illiberal' cultures, and a
sense of a diffuse but multifaceted threat to French national identity.

Fewer attempts, however, have been made to take seriously the debate
surrounding the headscarves affair as a form of philosophical engagement
with general principles of toleration, neutrality, and citizenship.[1] The headscarves debate has generally been perceived as too embedded in a particular socio-political context – too French, in a way – to be compatible with
any familiar or plausible understanding of justice and citizenship. This relative neglect of French debates by Anglo-American political theorists
undoubtedly stems both from lack of familiarity with the type of political
argument favoured in France *and* from genuinely diverging normative commitments. If we are to make sense of a local debate about justice, such as
that surrounding the headscarves affair, we should try to delimit, as far
as possible, linguistically mediated misunderstandings from substantive
disagreements.

I take a tentative step in this direction in this chapter through an elucidation of the meaning of the pivotal concept invoked throughout the headscarves debate, *laïcité* – for which the best (if unsatisfactory) translation
remains 'secularism'. Although the word itself did not appear until the end
of the nineteenth century, the origins of *laïcité* are usually traced back to
the French revolution, which brutally accelerated a century-long process of
autonomisation of the civil government from the Catholic Church. After a
century of veiled confrontation and failed compromise between the two
institutions, *laïcité* became the official doctrine of the Third Republic
(1870–1940), symbolised by such landmarks as the generalisation of secular
state primary education in the 1880s and the disestablishment of the
Catholic Church in 1905.[2] However, it would be a mistake to reduce *laïcité*
to a conception of the proper relationship between state and religion, with
particular attention paid to matters of education. *Laïcité* is a broader moral
and social philosophy, a complex set of ideals and commitments that
constitutes the closest equivalent in France – or perhaps direct alternative
– to the liberal philosophy of toleration.

In this chapter I suggest that *laïcité* is a confusing concept because it is
internally complex, and appeals to values and concerns that tend to be kept
separate in Anglo-American liberal political theory. I identify three main
strands of *laïcité*: neutrality (*laïcité* A), autonomy (*laïcité* B), and community (*laïcité* C). I attempt to situate each of them in the historical context
of its emergence, and to offer an analytical elucidation of its relevance to
the issues raised by the headscarves affair and to wider debates about
toleration. In the conclusion I suggest that the wearing of headscarves in
schools was problematic in France because it questioned the normative
relevance of all three interpretations of *laïcité* at the same time. I also raise
some questions about the coherence of the concept, and point towards an
alternative conceptualisation of *laïcité* that would do justice to the republican – rather than liberal – language in which it is embedded.

Laïcité as state neutrality

Laïcité A refers to the institutional separation between church and state.
According to the Law of Separation of 1905, 'the state neither recognises
nor subsidises any religion' (Article 2). This establishes a regime of mutual
independence: freedom of religion (in its individual and collective dimensions) is guaranteed in the private sphere, while state policies are pursued
and justified without reference to religious values. *Laïcité* A is therefore a
form of state neutrality. There are, however, two senses in which a state
policy can be said to be 'neutral' towards religion. The first, which roughly
corresponds to the 'non-establishment' clause of the First Amendment of
the US Constitution ('Congress shall make no law respecting an establishment of religion or prohibiting the free exercise thereof') forbids all forms
of governmental assistance to any religion. The second, which roughly cor-

responds to the 'free exercise' clause of the First Amendment, may compel the state to step in to ensure that all groups have effective means to exercise the rights associated with freedom of religion.[3]

The first interpretation of neutrality captures the dominant spirit of the 1905 Separation Law. State abstention, on the *laïcité* A interpretation, is the best way to accommodate the fact of pluralism. By suppressing the privileges enjoyed by the Catholic Church, the Separation Law established the principle of equal treatment between believers, and between believers and non-believers. This principle requires that members of religious minorities, as well as non-religious citizens, not simply be tolerated, but be fully recognised as bearers of the same rights as members of the dominant Church. These rights are universal rights attached equally to all individuals, rather than to groups. The process of institutional dissociation between state and church was thus complemented by the privatisation and individualisation of religion. Catholics were, in a sense, 'refused everything as a nation, and granted everything as individuals', as Jews had famously been during the 1789 revolution.[4] The neutrality of the state, understood as the privatisation of religious matters, was seen as a guarantee of inclusiveness. All citizens – Catholics and Protestants, Jews and atheists – could identify *equally* with a shared, non-discriminatory public space where religious beliefs and allegiances were 'bracketed off'. Thus, *laïcité* has recently been defined as 'the political philosophy that best entrenches in law the combination of freedom of conscience and state neutrality'.[5] Countries where there is an official inequality of treatment between established and non-established religions – such as Britain – or where there is a non-secular public culture – such as the US – are seen by advocates of *laïcité* A as falling short of this ideal of neutrality *qua* abstention.[6]

In practice, however, the Catholic Church has not been reduced to the status of a merely private association in France. The dominant interpretation of *laïcité* A as a strict principle of absolute separation between the state and a wholly 'privatised' church must be qualified. After all, Article 2 of the Separation Law also proclaims that 'the republic . . . guarantees the exercise of religious freedom', and such a guarantee can be understood to require an 'active neutrality'.[7] In practice, the French state does subsidise private religious schools, provide financial help towards the maintenance of religious edifices, respect the internal structure of authority within religious associations, and make possible the exercise of religious liberties in prisons and state boarding schools. 'Active' neutrality, in contrast to 'abstentionist' neutrality, raises tricky issues concerning equality of treatment between religious groups. There are, for example, significant disparities in the degree of state support to 'older' religions such as Christianity and religions such as Islam that have been established more recently in France.[8] This is because the public funding of religion has in fact rarely been articulated as the consequence of a principled commitment to freedom of religion but was, rather, the outcome of a pragmatic compromise between the state and the Catholic Church in 1905.[9] Prudence and precedent, rather than abstract norms of justice, have underpinned the French policy of active neutrality, which turned out, in practice, to be a policy of active partiality towards the Catholic Church. No wonder therefore that the dominant view of *laïcité*, that of secular republicans, has been inclined to present the (relatively modest) instances of state funding of religion as an unfortunate *exception* to, not an application of, the principle of *laïcité*.[10] Many Catholics, by contrast, accepted *laïcité* only in so far as it was defined as an active commitment to the actual exercise of freedom of religion. Abstract liberties, they wryly reminded their opponents on the Left, are not worth having if they cannot be exercised.[11] Nevertheless, the Catholic attempt at conceptual redefinition failed to displace the dominant philosophical interpretation of *laïcité* A, that of the separation between the public and the private sphere, and the strict abstention by the state from interference in religious matters.

On this view, the boundaries of the public sphere must be strictly policed, and its secular character preserved, in order for citizens to be able to address one another as equals. In recent years, this interpretation of neutrality as abstention, which was originally elaborated in the context of deep-seated conflicts between state and church, has been extended to the question of the appropriate response to demands for the public recognition of cultural diversity. *Laïcité* A, in a sense, has become a blueprint for the contemporary management of multiculturalism in France. The neutrality of the state requires that it neither promote nor hamper the expression of religious and cultural identities. Whereas citizens are free to practise their religion and culture within civil society, they should disregard their special memberships in the public sphere. The public sphere, crucially, includes state schools; pupils and teachers are therefore expected to leave behind their particular commitments and identities when they pass the gates of the school. Only then can schools be open to all 'with no distinction made on the basis of opinion or religion', as proclaimed by the 1884 Education Law, which established the principle of free, compulsory and secular primary education. In turn, children are entitled to an education that does not infringe on their private beliefs. *Laïcité* A, therefore, promotes an 'abstentionist' philosophy of education. In the words of the inspirer of the 1884 law, Jules Ferry, 'the republic stops where conscience begins': teachers have a duty of religious and political neutrality. Not only should they refrain from disturbing the 'sacred conscience' of children but, in addition, they should be careful not to impart values and attitudes likely to offend parental beliefs.[12] Schools should eschew morally controversial topics and concentrate on the inculcation of so-called 'elementary' notions based on morally neutral, scientific truths. The purpose of public education is to diffuse a corpus of objective knowledge, while 'neutralising all partisan opinions'.

Laïcité A, in sum, offers a broadly liberal response to the problem of toleration, based on a 'wall of separation' between a neutral political sphere and the diverse conceptions of the good held by individuals. However, *laïcité* in France is more than an institutional arrangement designed to accommodate the fact of pluralism. From the start, it was also, perhaps primarily, an attempt to disentangle political institutions from the grip of the Catholic Church, and to substitute democratic civic loyalty for religious and traditional allegiances. In contrast to countries that experienced a slow, incremental process of secularisation, whereby the state progressively shed its non-secular attributes and the established Church slowly relinquished its political and social power to make way for religious pluralism, France experienced the brutal – or at any rate confrontational – assertion of an autonomous civil power struggling to impose a secular, republican order against the claims of religious supremacy made by the Catholic Church.[13] In the light of this historical heritage, it would be 'reductive'[14] to understand *laïcité* exclusively through the concern for freedom of religion and state neutrality. From its inception, *laïcité* was less a consensual compromise than a fighting creed. The separation between public and private implied a distinct *re-evaluation* of the public sphere, compounded by the *relegation* of religious beliefs to the private sphere.[15] Citizens were required, not only to leave behind, but often to transcend, their particularisms by endorsing a superior public identity. *Laïcité*, therefore, often appealed to a comprehensive liberal ideal of autonomy from religion (*laïcité* B) or to a communitarian concern for civic unity (*laïcité* C).

Laïcité as promotion of individual autonomy

Laïcité B refers to the promotion by the state of the value of secular autonomy, not only in public deliberation but also in the conduct of the good life. It reflects a comprehensive liberal view that the good life consists in autonomy, as well as a perfectionist belief that the state must encourage the pursuit of autonomy-orientated ways of life. *Laïcité* B differs from *laïcité* A in claiming to be 'a philosophy of human emancipation', instead of a philosophy of neutrality,[16] and in explicitly attributing to state education the function of promoting the skills associated with the exercise of autonomy.

Historically, *laïcité* B can be seen as a stage in the forcible liberalisation of society undertaken by the French state, at a time when republican liberalism was a militant fighting creed rather than the consensual ideology it became during the twentieth century. Liberalising society meant coming into direct confrontation with a conservative Catholic Church, which deemed democratic self-determination an aberration, found repugnant the idea that the identity of the citizen could be separated from that of the believer, claimed to define moral norms for the whole society, and was reluctant to give up its social power – notably in the sphere of education.[17] It is in a context of strong opposition to established religious authorities that the republicans in power sought to disseminate the principles and practices of democratic citizenship. As Claude Nicolet has put it, the republican citizen 'is neither a natural given, nor a product of history. It only exists – in the full sense – through the conquest and exercise of his [or her] reason.'[18] Citizenship consecrated the human capacity for freedom – its ability to shake off all obstacles to the expression of the autonomous rational will. Such sources of heteronomy were diverse, ranging from the holding of unre-flected-upon beliefs to blind obedience to traditional authorities, through to instinctive loyalty to particularist groups. The attribution of citizenship, therefore, was conceived as a process of individual emancipation from tra-ditional, oppressive, and obscurantist institutions. Of these, the Catholic Church was the most prominent, and republican citizenship was an instru-ment of emancipation from religious dogmatism. Individuals were to be encouraged to think of themselves as citizens first, through the inculcation of what the Protestant educationalist Ferdinand Buisson ambiguously called a *foi laïque* (*laïque* faith).[19] *Laïcité* was like a religion in the etymological sense: it provided a foundation for individual morality and a sense of col-lective belonging. But this was a non-transcendental, non-clerical religion, which appealed to human reason alone, and substituted for the mystical, conservative and hierarchical ethos of the Church the Enlightenment values of individualism, egalitarianism and rationalism. On this view, progress was identified with the progressive emancipation of human reason from its shackles: ignorance primarily, but also ancestral traditions and unexamined beliefs. As the republican leader Léon Gambetta put it, 'we only have one religion, namely, intellectual culture for all the French'.[20] Only autonomous individuals could be enlightened citizens – hence the crucial autonomy-promoting function of state education. That autonomy should be promoted by the state was not seen as a paradox. In the French political tradition, the state shapes, rather than regulates, liberal society, and modern individ-ualism is seen as intimately linked to the civilising power of social and polit-ical institutions.[21] The perfectionist strand of *laïcité*, therefore, fitted neatly into a tradition less wary of state paternalism than the Anglo-American tradition.

    Laïcité B was therefore originally articulated as the official liberal ideol-ogy of the French republic. In the early years, however, there was a debate between what we would now call 'political' and 'comprehensive' liberals. The former hoped that *laïcité*, if construed strictly as a principle of political morality, could be endorsed even by non-liberals – such as traditional Catholics. The challenge was then to define a non-religious moral alterna-tive to religion, which would nonetheless be acceptable to religions. In the words of the sociologist Emile Durkheim, *laïque* morality should 'seek to capture the truth inherent in every religious or non-religious moral view'[22] – for example, a certain conception of the person. To use John Rawls's terms, *laïcité* should be grounded in an overlapping consensus between reasonable moral doctrines. As for the latter, more 'comprehensive' liberals, they argued, first, that there was a basic incompatibility between republican and Catholic world-views and, second, that the state should not refrain from promoting specifically liberal conceptions of the good life, even if these offended non-liberals. In their view, republican *laïcité* should not be made compatible with religion simply for the sake of stability. Rather, as the Kantian philosopher Renouvier put it, *laïque* morality should explicitly aim to 'take minds away from superstitious beliefs, and above all from doctrines which contradict [the ideal of] justice'.[23] Under the double influence of Enlightenment critical rationalism and nineteenth-century positivism, many republicans believed that a secular, critically orientated life was more valuable than a religious and conformist one. As political anticlericalism merged with philosophical secularism in the post-Dreyfus years, *laïcité* became a fighting creed for the promotion of a distinctive conception of human well-being. The conservative teachings of the Catholic Church came to be seen as the main obstacle to social and intellectual progress. Religion, in a word, embodied heteronomy. Republicans sought to promote what they called freedom of thought (*la liberté de penser*) – free rational enquiry and self-determination – instead of freedom of conscience (*la liberté de conscience*) – the freedom to believe whatever one feels inclined to.

In so far as the republicans in power did endorse a more 'comprehensive' than 'political' understanding of *laïque* morality, this was translated almost exclusively – though crucially – into a distinctive philosophy of education. On the republican view, it is the chief mission of state schools to inculcate children with the skills essential to the exercise of autonomy. Now, it is true that in matters of education, the distinction between political and comprehensive liberalism is elusive.[24] Liberal education promotes individual autonomy without necessarily being *ipso facto* comprehensively liberal – that is, without controversially promoting a particular conception of the good life. This is for three main reasons. First, education always involves a degree of paternalist authority, because it is addressed to individuals who have not yet formed their conception of the good. Second, education involves inculcating general autonomy-related skills such as the capacity to identify causes and reasons, to exercise critical judgement, to reflect on one's beliefs, and the like. Third, although education may teach the value of choice, it does not have to discriminate between the various ways of life that can be objects of autonomous choice – even if these amount to 'voluntary servitude'. Proponents of *laïcité* B have often insisted that what matters is not so much the content of the conception of the good held by individuals as the fact that it is autonomously chosen. *Laïcité* is then defined as a 'culture that provides the means to orient oneself freely in the question of [the] meaning [of life]'.[25] *Laïque* education may encourage children to reflect on the religious beliefs they were brought up with, but does not forbid them from autonomously endorsing them again at the end of a process of careful critical attention. As Claude Nicolet puts it, 'a republican can think what he wishes, provided he thinks by himself'.[26] On this view, *laïcité* B does not go beyond providing individuals with the skills associated with the exercise of autonomy, that is, it does not stipulate the particular ways in which autonomy may be used to the good.

However, it is undeniable that in its exclusive emphasis on the development of critical skills and its denial that the function of education can in any sense be to preserve children's sense of cultural coherence, *laïcité* B can be said, ultimately, to involve a comprehensive – rather than narrowly political or instrumental – interpretation of education. Education has more a transformative (or substantive) than a formative (or instrumental) quality. Schools are sometimes presented as the only sphere in which – not only through which – genuine liberty is possible, because they are insulated from the inegalitarian, oppressive structures of civil society. The clearest exposition of *laïcité* as a comprehensive philosophy of emancipation through education is by a neo-Kantian educationalist, Catherine Kintzler. Writing in the midst of the headscarves affair, she argues that to educate a child is to encourage her to distance herself from her family or community beliefs and to reflect critically on them. As Kintzler puts it, children should 'forget their community and think of something other than that which they are in order to think by themselves'. On this view, social structures essentially alienate individual liberty: only if individuals stand back from received values will they achieve freedom, conceived as rational self-determination. In a society characterised by ubiquitous relationships of domination – cultural, religious and economic – state schools are a privileged locus for the inculcation of the habit of independence through the exercise of critical judgement.[27] Republican education, Kintzler concludes, is quite literally 'anti-social': it substitutes for non-voluntary forms of social membership a rational capacity for individual self-determination.[28] On this view, schools should not 'reproduce' social diversity: autonomy is gained, not by exposing children to a range of different ways of life, but by fostering their capacity to abstract from the bonds of social life itself. The near-absence of exposure to basic religious knowledge in French state schools certainly betrays a specific view of the conceptions of the good life that can be the object of legitimate choice.

One should however take the exact measure of the claims made about the emancipatory potential of the republican public sphere. *Laïcité* B is essentially a philosophy of education: the perfectionist ambitions of the French state, it should be stressed, hardly extend beyond the school gates and the protection of under-age children. Significantly, the legal battle against 'harmful sects' (*les sectes nocives*) in France has focused on the dangers of the mental manipulation of vulnerable children and adolescents, rarely of adults. The well-publicised 'anti-sect' *Vivien Report* of 1983, for example, while underlining the risks of 'alienation of moral autonomy' involved in membership of 'irrational' movements, reaffirmed France's central commitment to freedom of conscience and association, and centred its proposals on better information and prevention. Typically, it advocated a reform of *laïque* education in schools.[29] So, while it is legitimate for the state to foster the *capacity* for autonomy – through education – the promotion of its actual *exercise* by mature adults – through paternalist coercion – is found to be hardly compatible with other republican intuitions. Significantly too, autonomy-related arguments were sometimes used to oppose the wearing of headscarves by young Muslim girls, but not by older students or teachers.[30] *Laïcité* B, in a word, has stopped short of legitimating an all-out struggle against all forms of heteronomy and domination. Only socialists, from Jaurès onwards, developed an expansive understanding of *laïcité* as a comprehensive philosophy of non-domination. Their *laïcité* was associated with a progressive, rationalist humanism that promoted a conception of social regeneration and comprehensive emancipation from the reactionary structures both of traditional and modern capitalist society. *Laïcité* became one integral component of a progressive, militant creed inspired by visions of a transparent, rationally organised, domination-free, self-governing egalitarian society. The official doctrine of *laïcité*, for its part, rarely questioned structural power relationships in bourgeois civil society, centrally imbued as it was with the Enlightenment view that individual flaws such as ignorance, irrationality and unreasonableness were the only significant obstacles to a 'free' society. Yet despite this narrowly individualist, educationalist and intellectualist bias, long stigmatised by Marxists, there is no denying that *laïcité* B still offers a distinct alternative to the Anglo-American liberal philosophy of toleration. In its commitment to the promotion of individual autonomy, it is centrally concerned with the legitimate limits to toleration, and its advocates often show puzzlement at the idea that the toleration of non-liberal practices of domination can ever be a liberal virtue. *Laïcité* B, in a word, provides a perfectionist solution to the paradox of liberal toleration.

More in line perhaps with a less perfectionist, more narrowly 'political' liberalism, another justification for autonomy-promoting *laïque* education is its contribution to education for democratic citizenship. Here, a certain level of education is seen as essential to the practice of political deliberation; in Condorcet's terms, it serves to 'enlighten men to make them citizens'.[31] Historically, this concern for education to citizenship stemmed from the French experience of democracy as a radical experience of self-government. Democracy implies the de-legitimisation of all transcendental or non-rational sources of authority – divine, customary, charismatic – and the exclusive reliance on the will of the citizenry as the only legitimate foundation of power. The 1789 Revolution is often defined as *laïque* in this sense. Interestingly, the etymological origin of *laïcité* is the Greek *laikos*, literally – and as opposed to *klerikos* – that which characterises the people as a whole, not only a section of it.[32] Democracy means government by discussion between equal individuals who only recognise the authority of Reason or, as we would say in post-Kantian, post-metaphysical terms, who only wish to be convinced by each others' reasons and to exercise their critical judgement. Education is crucial in inculcating the skills required to be able to question the normativity of existing institutions and norms. As Condorcet put it: 'the goal of instruction is not to make men admire a legislation fully completed, but to render them capable of evaluating and correcting it'.[33] More broadly, *laïcité* B is often defended as the political counterpart of the commitment to autonomy; as a practice of free, unconstrained democratic deliberation within a 'pluralist public space' that welcomes 'uninterrupted questioning'.[34] A *laïque* political space is a space of radical collective self-determination, a space whose autonomy it is crucial to protect from the encroachments of non-democratic powers – theocratic, traditional or technocratic. *Laïcité* B, therefore, establishes a strong connection between individual autonomy and democratic deliberation; in both cases, it reflects a concern to preserve and enhance the human capacity for self-determination – both individual and collective.

Laïcité as civic loyalty

What I propose to call *laïcité* C is undoubtedly the most difficult to grasp, because it is least amenable to liberal thought. The intuition behind it is best captured by the following statement by a contemporary republican philosopher – that 'one cannot be *laïque* in France unless one accepts an important part of our national-republican heritage'.[35] On this view, *laïcité* calls not so much for a neutral state respectful of religious difference, nor for a perfectionist state committed to the promotion of individual autonomy, but, rather, for a communitarian state fostering a civic sense of loyalty to a particular historical community. Historically, *laïcité* C underlaid the republican ambition to substitute for traditional Catholic-inspired sociability a new civic bond, which would unite citizens in common love of the secular republic. The pro-active policy of *laïcisation* was therefore two-pronged: it simultaneously sought to reduce the pervasive and multifaceted influence of Catholic norms on French society and to anchor the liberal, individualistic principles of the revolution in an alternative republican public culture. The proponents of *laïcité* C believed that a nation founded on abstract, disembodied principles of human rights would be quite unable to replicate the level of affective mobilisation achieved by the hegemonic Catholic *Zeitgeist*. On this view, a society whose only public commitments are to neutrality, individuality or autonomy would be inherently fragile and incapable of sustaining a sense of mutual concern and solidarity between its citizens. In other words, the new *laïque* civic bond should not be solely based on *liberté* and *égalité*: it would also have to inspire feelings of *fraternité*. Republican society should foster, not the minimal virtue of toleration, but the more demanding virtues of mutual empathy and even altruistic devotion to the community of citizens. *Laïcité* C supplements the liberal emphasis with rights and procedures with a concern for the dispositions and attitudes of citizens and the content of the public culture. Abstract citizenship must be complemented with allegiance to a republican public culture, which provides the motivational anchorage essential to the legitimacy and stability of a liberal society.

This republican public culture is centred on the cultivation of the traditions and memories of the national civic community.[36] Since the Third Republic, one explicit purpose of secular, *laïque* education has been to promote national unity and social cohesion, and to effect the cultural integration of the masses. The regime engaged in an ambitious programme of nation-building that was famously designed to transform 'peasants into Frenchmen' through cultural uniformisation and the diffusion of the values of egalitarian, democratic, patriotic citizenship.[37] Late eighteenth-century revolutionaries – and a distinguished line of thinkers before and after them, Rousseau and Tocqueville notably – had wondered whether democracy required a civil religion as a functional equivalent to Catholicism. In the course of the nineteenth century, a state-promoted, secularised national identity came to provide this functional equivalent. The elites of the Third Republic, influenced partly by the republican civic tradition and by positivist sociology, sought to establish a new 'civil religion' – as *laïcité* C is sometimes described to[38] – complete with founding myths, revolutionary rituals and patriotic celebrations, and promoting an ethically-charged feeling of national belonging and a consensualist conception of democracy. State schools during the Third Republic were often likened to secular churches dedicated to the diffusion of the religion of the *patrie*. The philosophy of education promoted by advocates of *laïcité* C tended to emphasise the centrality of schools in fostering basic moral education, civic loyalty and social conformity, in contrast to *laïcité* B's preferred emphasis on the role of education in promoting 'a-social' individuality, autonomy and critical spirit.[39]

It is, therefore, very fitting that *laïcité* C should have been dubbed *catholaïcité* by its critics. Republican ideology undoubtedly moulded itself to the structures of Catholic society and mentality, only to secularise its symbols and rituals.[40] Crucially, it also inherited a powerful state tradition permeated by an overriding concern for national unity, a tradition revived by the legacy of the revolution of 1789, which had in effect destroyed all intermediary groups between state and individuals. The communitarian inspiration of *laïcité* C cannot be understood unless one takes the measure of this long-standing anxiety towards the individualistic fragmentation of society and the concomitant obsession with social cohesion. *Laïcité* C must be interpreted as an explicit attempt to transcend pluralism, mainly through civic education. In today's society, where growing cultural and ethical pluralism has become as much a normative value as a sociological fact, a 'communitarian' education of that sort is bound to raise questions about the extent of the republican tolerance of diversity. As Meira Levinson concisely puts it, 'the French model shifts the brunt of democratic education from teaching toleration of private *others* to inculcating mutual respect for public *similars*'.[41] The question here is whether, by focusing exclusively on

equal membership in a civic community, *laïcité* C actually fosters intolerance of private differences. On the one hand, it must be noted that *laïcité*
C claims to found a liberal community: it, notably, endorses *laïcité* A's insistence that equal rights must be protected through a rigid separation between
the public and the private sphere, as well as *laïcité* B's emphasis on individuality and autonomy as the central values of the republican public
culture. On the other hand, it is undeniable that there is a risk that individuals' differences are in practice swallowed up rather than protected by
a homogenising national public character'[42] and that members of minority
cultures find themselves forced to assimilate into the ways of life of the
majority.

Conceptual coherence in context

At the end of this inquiry we are in a better position to understand why
the wearing of Muslim headscarves in state schools was seen as so problematic in France. This is because, I would suggest, it questioned the normative relevance of *laïcité* in its three dimensions at the same time. In
contrast to other high-profile public debates on *laïcité* (about the funding
of private schools or the content of school curricula, for example) that
touched only on one aspect of *laïcité*, the headscarves affair was exemplary
in the complexity of the issues it raised. First, as state schools are seen as
extensions of the public sphere, the 'ostentatious' expression of religious
belief that headscarves were deemed to represent was interpreted as an
encroachment on the neutrality of the public sphere and on the separation
between public and private (*laïcité* A). Second, as veil-wearing is gender-
specific and was seen as imposed on the schoolgirls by their parents, it could
be construed as a symbol both of inequality and of heteronomy, and therefore as justifying paternalistic state intervention in the interests of the girls
(*laïcité* B). Lastly, in a context of mutual hostility between the French state
and sections of the Muslim community (fed by a wave of Algerian fundamentalist terrorism and a general sense of social alienation felt by second-
generation immigrants) the intrusion of headscarves in schools was
interpreted as a symbol of the fragmentation and break-up of society under
the centrifugal pressure of multiculturalism (*laïcité* C). Interestingly, it
should be noted, *laïcité* was also the central concept invoked by advocates
of the Muslim girls' position. They too endorsed *laïcité* A's concern for
neutrality, but interpreted it primarily in terms of the entrenchment of the
superior principle of freedom of religion. They too invoked the value of
individuality and autonomy central to *laïcité* B, but contested their opponents' definition of what qualifies as an obstacle to autonomy, and pointed
out the value of communal membership to individuality. They shared the
concern for social unity highlighted by *laïcité* C, but argued that *laïcité*
should provide a framework for a pluralist social unity, allowing for the
mutual recognition of a diversity of cultural groups. In sum, they defended

'open' *laïcité* (*laïcité ouverte*) against the 'hardline' *laïcité* of opponents of veil-wearing.[43]

In quite a striking way, therefore, both advocates and opponents of veil-wearing were involved in a multi-layered debate about what may appear to be an essentially shaky concept. For the account given here might be taken to imply that *laïcité* really refers to three different things (neutrality, autonomy, community) that are only confused and conflated in French usage. Yet there is a sense in which my way of recasting the 'headscarves affair' and *laïcité* in general, while it may satisfy the broad intellectual references of Anglo-American liberalism, fails to do justice to the French debate. For, it might be rightly objected, *laïcité* works in French public discourse precisely as a complex, historically grounded articulation of its various levels of meaning. While the semantic meaning of *laïcité* has always been a matter of intense dispute, the concept is explicitly accepted by all French participants as a useful, relevant and reasonably coherent concept. To conclude, let me venture three brief remarks about the complex issue of conceptual coherence.

First, all political concepts are to some extent contested concepts.[44] This is most obviously true of *laïcité*, which has always been a practical slogan rather than an abstract philosophy. *Laïcité* has never really formed part of an autonomous juridical, political or philosophical theory, isolated from concrete historical moments, and has always been intimately linked to the republican project of the entrenchment of the modern liberal society born out of the French revolution. The semantic meaning of the concept emerged out of political processes of ideological contestation, not out of careful philosophical enterprises of analytical clarification. It is, in fact, a defining feature of political ideologies – of which French republicanism is one – that they tend to accommodate a certain level of conceptual indeterminacy.[45]

Second, the coherence of a concept does to some extent depend on its capacity to make sense of the 'reality' that it claims to describe. The lively debates about *laïcité* in France undoubtedly reflect growing uncertainty about its contemporary meaning and relevance, an uncertainty that is itself a symptom of the disintegration of the 'republican synthesis' forged under the Third Republic. In the nineteenth century, when nation-building and liberalisation went hand in hand, little tension was felt between the struggle for private freedoms and equal rights (*laïcité* A), emancipation from traditional and religious identities (*laïcité* B), and the embrace of a new public identity (*laïcité* C). It could even be argued that it is precisely the congruence between the three that has defined modern democratic citizenship. In today's France, the conditions that made possible what Marcel Gauchet calls the convergence between 'the exercise of personal rights and the production of collective unity through the state machine'[46] have all but disappeared. There is now a vast literature on the theme of the 'crisis of *laïcité*'.[47] This crisis is rooted in a number of complex recent trends: the collapse of comprehensive ideologies (notably *laïcité*'s main adversary, Catholicism), the displacement of citizenship as individuals' central identity, the rise of consumerist individualism, the discredit of shared public moralities, the broad questioning of Western universalist rationalism, growing pluralism and demands for the recognition of difference, and the multifaceted crisis of the nation. It is in this context that the tensions intrinsic to the concept of *laïcité* – between state neutrality and state perfectionism on the one hand, and between individual autonomy and civic loyalty on the other – are most acutely felt.

Third, the possibility must at least be raised that such conceptual tensions are, at least in part, embedded in the analytical language that has been used to make sense of French *laïcité* throughout this chapter. I have explicitly sought to 'translate' French debates into the language of Anglo-American liberal philosophy, using such concepts as state neutrality, political and comprehensive liberalism, autonomy-promoting perfectionism, universalist and communitarian ethics. Such conceptual combinations have suggested an analytical decomposition of *laïcité* into three distinct components, and allowed a more rigorous understanding of its political implications. It might be the case, however, that these conceptual combinations also hide from view other semantic connections, which might be absent from the ordinary (English) language in which analytical philosophy is rooted, but central to alternative political philosophies. After all, the dominant language of politics in France is republicanism, not liberalism (even if republicanism has historically occupied the ideological space of liberalism). If we recast *laïcité* in ways that make it consistent with the distinct understanding of liberty favoured by French (liberal) republicans – liberty as non-domination – we might be able to soften some of the tensions that exist between its three analytical components of neutrality, autonomy and community. The contradiction between *laïcité* A's commitment to equal rights and freedom of religion and *laïcité* C's commitment to a state-promoted public culture, for example, dissolves if it is conceded that liberty is not a 'natural' condition but a fragile social status that must be upheld by public institutions. Similarly, the tensions between the ideals of comprehensive emancipation (*laïcité* B) and state neutrality (*laïcité* A) can be eased somewhat if neutrality (and *laïcité*) is seen as an ideal of non-domination rather than an ideal of non-interference. Clearly, more needs to be done to specify the conceptual ways in which a republican account can transcend the dichotomies that permeate liberal analytical political philosophy. Such a project is inevitably driven by conflicting objectives. On the one hand, it must strive to be faithful to existing understandings as they are embedded in particular discursive traditions (in my case, the tradition of French republicanism). On the other hand, it must be made commensurable with other languages, notably that of Anglo-American liberalism. Whether these two concerns – intelligibility and integrity – can be balanced and reconciled is the central problem of cross-cultural theory.

Notes

Research for this project was funded by a Research Grant from the School of Humanities, King's College London, for which I am grateful. A version of this chapter was published in *Constellations. An International Journal of Critical and Democratic Theory*, Vol. 9 (2002). I am grateful to the editors and to Blackwells for permission to republish material for this article.

1 Two exceptions in English are: M. Levinson, 'Liberalism versus democracy? Schooling private citizens in the public square', *British Journal of Political Science*, 27 (1997) 333–60; and E. Galeotti, 'Citizenship and equality. The place for toleration', *Political Theory*, 21:4 (1993) 585–605.

2 See J. Baubérot, *Histoire de la laïcité française* (Paris: Presses Universitaires de France, 2000). For a historical overview in English, see K. Chadwick, 'Education in secular France: (Re)defining laïcité', *Modern and Contemporary France*, 5:1 (1997) 47–59.

3 This distinction, which is inspired by V. Bader ('Religious pluralism. Secularism or priority for democracy?', *Political Theory*, 27:5 (1999) 597–633, at p. 605), is in my view clearer than M. Barbier's distinction between 'separation', 'neutrality' and 'impartiality' in *La Laïcité* (Paris: L'Harmattan, 1995), pp. 84–8.

4 According to the famous phrase of Clermont-Tonnerre, cited in Pierre Rosanvallon, *Le Sacre du Citoyen. Histoire du suffrage universel en France* (Paris: Gallimard, 1992), p. 76.

5 J. Costa-Lascoux, 'La laïcité au défi du multiculturalisme', in Jean-Michel Lecomte and Jean-Pierre Sylvestre (eds), *Culture républicaine, citoyenneté et lien social* (Dijon: CNDP, 1997), pp. 213–25, p. 221.

6 See J. Zylberberg, 'Laïcité, connais pas: Allemagne, Canada, Etats-Unis, Royaume-Uni', *Pouvoirs*, 75 (1995), pp. 37–52. For a more sceptical evaluation of French 'exemplarity' (in the two senses of the term) see J. Baubérot, 'La laïcité française et l'Europe', *Philosophie Politique*, 4 (1991) 89–100.

7 See the good survey of Jean-Michel Lemoyne de Forges, 'Laïcité et liberté religieuse en France' in Joël-Benoît d'Onorio, *La liberté religieuse dans le monde. Analyse doctrinale et politique* (Paris: Editions Universitaires, 1991), pp. 149–70; the legal analyses of J. Robert, 'La notion juridique de laïcité et sa valeur constitutionnelle', in H. Bost (ed.), *Genèses et enjeux de la laïcité. Christiannismes et laïcité* (Paris: Labor et Fides, 1990), pp. 89–100; R. Drago, 'Laïcité, neutralité, liberté?', *Archives de Philosophie du Droit*, 38 (1993) 221–30; and F. Messner, 'Laïcité imaginée et laïcité juridique', *Débat*, 77 (1993) 88–94, which points to a gap between the strict 'ideological' interpretation of the separation of state and religion and the widespread practice of public subsidies to religious associations.

8 S. Pierré-Caps, 'Les "nouveaux cultes" et le droit public', *Revue de droit public*, 4 (1990) 1073–119.

9 For interpretations of the Separation Law as a 'tolerant' law, see J. Robert, 'La notion juridique de la laïcité et sa valeur constitutionnelle', pp. 89–100; J. Baubérot, *Vers un nouveau pacte laïque?* (Paris: Seuil, 1990); *La morale laïque contre l'ordre moral* (Paris: Seuil, 1997); J. Boussinesq, *La laïcité française. Mémento juridique* (Paris: Seuil, 1994), pp. 47–56.

10 Most of the conflicts over *laïcité* – which broadly defined the battle-lines between left and right in France – concerned the state funding of private (religious) schools. The traditional *laïque* battle-cry about education is: 'state funds for state schools, private funds for private schools'.

11 See J. Rivero, 'La notion juridique de laïcité', *Chronique du Recueil Dalloz*, 31 (1940) 137–40.

12 J. Ferry, 'Lettre aux instituteurs' (27 November 1883), *Pouvoirs*, 75 (1995) 109–16, at p. 111. For a legal analysis of neutrality in schools, see A. Thiriot, 'Le principe de neutralité et l'enseignement', *Savoir – Education – Formation*, 3 (1993) 403–23.

13 For a comparative perspective, see F. Champion, 'Entre laïcisation et sécularisation. Des rapports Eglise-Etat dans l'Europe communautaire', *Le Débat* 77 (1993) 46–63.

14 M. Barbier, *La laïcité* (Paris: L'Harmattan, 1995), p. 30.

15 M. Gauchet, *La religion dans la démocratie. Parcours de la laicité* (Paris: Gallimard, 1998).

16 P. Hayat, *La laïcité et les pouvoirs. Pour une critique de la raison laïque* (Paris: Kimé, 1998), p.130.

17 Y. Deloye, *Ecole et citoyenneté. L'individualisme républicain de Jules Ferry à Vichy* (Paris: Presses de la Fondation Nationale des Sciences Politiques, 1994).

18 C. Nicolet, *L'idée républicaine en France (1789–1924). Essai d'histoire critique* (Paris: Gallimard, 1994), p. 483.

19 Cited in P. Macherey, 'Philosophies laïques', *Mots*, 27 (1991) 5–21, at p. 18.

20 *Ibid.*

21 Rosanvallon, *L'Etat en France* (Paris: Seuil, 1990), pp. 93–135.

22 Emile Durkheim, cited in Gauchet, *La religion dans la démocratie,* p. 50 n1.

23 Charles Renouvier, cited *ibid.*, p. 49.

24 For the developments that follow, I have (freely) drawn on A. Gutmann, 'Civic Education and Social Diversity', *Ethics*, 105 (1995) 557–79; V. Muñoz-Dardé, 'Condorcet, Liberal Education and Ethical Pluralism', unpublished manuscript (on file with the author); and M. Levinson, *The Demands of Liberal Education* (Oxford: Oxford University Press, 1999).

25 G. Coq, *Laïcité et république. Le lien nécessaire* (Paris: Edition du Félin, 1995), p. 156.

26 Nicolet, *L'Idée républicaine en France*, p. 503. See also C. Kintzler, 'Aux fondements de la laïcité scolaire. Essai de décomposition raisonnée du concept de laïcité', *Les Temps Modernes*, 527 (1990) 82–90.

27 C. Kintzler, *La République en questions* (Paris: Minerve 1996), pp. 78–81, p. 85; 'Aux fondements de la laïcité scolaire', pp. 88–90.

28 Kintzler, *La République en questions*, pp. 18, 88, and 109. See also R. Debray, 'La laïcité: une exception française', in Bost, *Genèses et enjeux de la laïcité*, pp. 199–208; and in Charles Coutel (ed.), *La République et l'école. Une anthologie* (Paris: Presses Pocket, 1991), J. Muglioni, 'Philosophie, école, même combat?' pp. 74–80 and Jean-Louis Poirier, 'Troisième République', pp. 65–71; and A. Prost, 'La République et l'école', *Projet*, 213 (1988), pp. 85–95. For a critique of this conception of schools, see F. Lorcerie, 'L'école pourrait être un laboratoire de civilité' in *Hommes et Migrations*, pp. 1129–30 (February–March 1990), pp. 41–2.

29 A. Vivien, *Les Sectes en France. Expression de la liberté morale ou facteurs de*

manipulation? Rapport au Premier Ministre (Paris: Documentation Francaise, 1983), esp. pp. 25ff., pp. 111ff. Significantly too, in a 1992 ruling, the Council of State ruled that no breach of state neutrality or freedom of religion was involved in the government's decision to subsidise an anti-Church of Scientology association, in light of the risks posed by the sect, 'notably for young people'. See R. Drago, 'Laïcité, neutralité, liberté?', *Archives de Philosophie du Droit* 38 (1993) 221–30. The broadly tolerant treatment of sects by French law is well-documented in Stéphane Pierré-Caps, 'Les "nouveaux cultes" et le droit public', *Revue de droit public*, 4 (1990) 1073–119.

30 It was widely held that teachers should avoid displaying symbols of religious allegiances, but this was justified by a neutrality-based argument (*laïcité* A), not by an autonomy-related one (*laïcité* B). For a discussion, see Thiriot, 'Le principe de neutralité et l'enseignement'.

31 On Condorcet, see C. Kintzler, *Condorcet. L'instruction publique et la naissance du citoyen* (Paris: Minerve, 1984).

32 José Bory, 'D'une conception tolérante de la laïcité à la reconnaissance d'un droit d'ingérence des Etats', *Administration*, 177 (1997) 82–90.

33 Condorcet, *Premier mémoire sur l'instruction publique* (extract) in Coutel, *La République et l'Ecole. Une anthologie*, p. 176.

34 E. Morin, 'Le nouveau combat de la laïcité', *Le Débat*, 58 (1990) 40–1. See also, for a reading of *laïcité* inspired by Habermas's discourse ethics, P. Hayat, *La laïcité et les pouvoirs. Pour une critique de la raison laïque* (Paris: Kimé, 1998), Chapter 4.

35 Jean-Pierre Sylvestre, 'Les fondements de la conception laïque du lien social', *Raison Présente*, 122 (1997) 79–96, at p. 91.

36 Sylvestre, *ibid.*, p. 91.

37 E. Weber, *Peasants into Frenchmen* (Stanford, CA: Stanford University Press, 1976); Ernest Gellner, *Nations and Nationalism* (Ithaca, NY: Cornell University Press, 1983).

38 See, for example, Jean-Louis Willaime, 'La religion civile à la française et ses métamorphoses', *Social Compass*, 40:4 (1993) 571–80; J. Roman, 'La laïcité comme religion civile', *Esprit*, 175 (1991) 108–15.

39 On this point see J. Baubérot, 'Aux fondements de la laïcité scolaire. Réponse à Catherine Kintzler', *Les Temps Modernes*, Jan.–Feb. (1991) 163–71.

40 See J. Carbonnier, 'La culture française: une culture "catholique" laïcisée?', *Parole et Société*, 34 (1993) 173–87; Jean-Louis Willaime, 'La religion civile à la française et ses métamorphoses'.

41 Levinson, 'Liberalism versus democracy?', p. 353.

42 *Ibid.*

43 For a critical approach to the terms of this debate, see E. Balibar, 'Faut-il qu'une laïcité soit ouverte ou fermée?', *Mots*, 27 (June 1991) 73–9.

44 W. B. Gallie, 'Essentially contested concepts', *Proceedings of the Aristotelian Society*, 56 (1955–56) 167–98.

45 M. Freeden, *Ideologies and Political Theory. A Conceptual Approach* (Oxford: Oxford University Press, 1996), Chapter 2.

46 M. Gauchet, 'L'école à l'école d'elle-même. Contraintes et contradictions de l'individualisme démocratique', *Le Débat*, 36 (1985) 55–78.

47 R. Rémond, 'La laïcité n'est plus ce qu'elle était', *Etudes*, 360:4 (1984) 439–48; J. Baubérot, *Vers un nouveau pacte laïque?*; M. Gauchet, *La religion dans la*

démocratie; Françoise Lorcerie, 'Dissonance normative. A propos de la crise de la laïcité en France', *Printemps*, 2 (1996) 7–20; Jean-Louis Schlegel, 'Laïcité et religion dans la société française d'aujourd'hui', in Catherine Wihtol de Wenden (ed.), *La citoyenneté* (Paris: Fondation Diderot, 1988), pp. 295–306. For an extensive survey of the recent debates on *laïcité*, see P. Ognier, 'Ancienne ou nouvelle laïcité? Après dix ans de débats', *Esprit*, 194 (1993) 202–21.

10
Toleration of religious discrimination in employment

Stuart White

Introduction: toleration and equal opportunity

Two ideas feature prominently in contemporary accounts of the just society. One is the idea of toleration and the related idea of religious freedom. A second is the idea of equal opportunity and, derived from this, the idea that the state should protect its members from discrimination in relation to jobs and other important goods such as education. This chapter explores an apparent tension between these two commitments. In order to advance their goals, religious associations sometimes want to discriminate in employment decisions on grounds that are typically prohibited under anti-discrimination laws. They may wish to discriminate in favour of those with their own religious views or those with certain life styles, or on grounds of gender, sexual orientation, or even race. How should the state respond to this apparent conflict between religious toleration and equal opportunity? To what extent should the state permit religious associations to discriminate in employment? Recent policy developments, such as the British government's promotion of faith-based schooling and the European Union's recent framework directive on equal opportunity in employment, have increased the urgency of this question.

In this chapter, I explore the question in three stages. Firstly, I outline the key 'civil interests' that I take to be at stake in thinking about the issue of employment discrimination. I explain why a concern for these civil interests might plausibly be thought to support a general prohibition of religiously-motivated employment discrimination and, at the same time, some kind of exemption from anti-discrimination law for religious associations. This sets the scene for the rest of my discussion, in which I explore whether it is possible to craft an exemption that protects what is likely to be of most importance to the religious believer but at the same time secures the other civil interests at stake. I argue that the freedom of religious associations to discriminate in employment should be limited by two principles. The first principle, explored in the second section of the chapter, is that the discrimination should be on religion-relevant grounds. On the face of it, this may seem an innocuous enough. As we shall see, however, there is substantial controversy as to what kind of religion-relevant grounds the state should admit as permissible grounds for employment discrimination. The second principle, explored in the third section, is that discrimination should apply only to a restricted range of jobs that have, as I put it, a sufficiently central relationship to the religious activities of the association. I discuss the tricky question of how this principle might be operationalised, and I reject the view that the centrality principle is by itself a sufficient limitation on the freedom of religious associations to discriminate in employment. The concluding section of the chapter enters a final caveat to my account of the permissible grounds of employment discrimination by religious associations.[1]

The civil interests at stake

My discussion of the problem proceeds from a certain liberal conception of political legitimacy. The exercise of state power over individuals is legitimate, I think, when it is exercised in order to ensure the equitable protection of civil interests. Civil interests (a term I borrow from John Locke's *Letter Concerning Toleration*)[2] are interests that are at once basic and common to all citizens, notwithstanding their different conceptions of the good life. State power should be exercised for the sake of protecting these shared basic interests, rather than for the sake of promoting a given conception of the good life. Turning to the issue of religiously-motivated employment discrimination that is our specific concern in this chapter, at least three main interests seem to be at stake.

(1) *Opportunity*. Citizens have a fundamental civil interest in fair access to income, wealth, and jobs. In the case of jobs, I shall understand fair access in meritocratic terms, i.e., as requiring equal consideration for given employment on the basis of suitable, job-relevant qualifications. If someone is ranked lower in job selection than another on grounds other than those to do with genuine occupational qualification, then this civil interest is violated.

(2) *Civic virtue*. Citizens share an interest in seeing that other citizens share the specifically civic virtues necessary for the healthy functioning of a just society. These virtues centrally include the virtues of toleration of, and respect for, those of different religious (or irreligious) points of view. Social institutions and practices that militate against the cultivation of these virtues jeopardise this civil interest, and are suspect for this reason.

(3) *Religious liberty*. This encompasses two distinct interests that we will do well to separate. The first is what we might call the citizen's expressive interest. This is her interest in living in authentic accordance with her religious (or irreligious) beliefs, i.e., in living her life as an expression of the

said beliefs.[3] The second is what we might call the citizen's deliberative interest.[4] This is her interest in having the opportunity to endorse her religious beliefs on the basis of informed reflection or deliberation. The correct answer to the question, 'What is the good life?', is hard to see and, since nobody is obviously an infallible judge of the matter, each individual ought to be able to make her own informed judgement about where the truth of the matter lies. In thinking about religious liberty, then, we need to give attention not only to the freedoms that serve expressive interests, but also to those that serve deliberative interests. Sometimes a concern for A's expressive interest may conflict with a concern for B's deliberative interest, and I take it that, in such cases, deliberative interests should be given priority: A should not have the right to substitute her judgement on fundamental questions about the value and meaning of life for that of B (even if A is B's parent).

The expressive dimension of religious liberty may also conflict, of course, with other important civil interests. In some cases, our concern for other civil interests will properly trump the concern for this aspect of religious liberty. But at the same time I do think that the concern for the free exercise of religion, for the expressive dimension of religious liberty, is (or can be) a matter of legitimate intrinsic concern, and that we should factor this concern into our construction of a theory of justice. We should not think of religious freedom simply as a residual freedom to act as we like for the sake of religion within the bounds of laws that serve the public interest, but as something that should enter into our conception of what the public interest truly is.

Now, given a concern for the civil interests just described, it is not hard to make a good case for a general prohibition on religiously-motivated employment discrimination. For in a society where such discrimination is permitted, and widely practised, there would be serious injury to all three of these key background civil interests. Religiously-motivated employment discrimination by a prejudiced majority, such as that historically practised against Roman Catholics in the shipyards of Northern Ireland, might well violate the opportunity interest of those in religious minorities, by denying members of such minorities jobs for which they are no less, or even more, qualified than majority competitors. Secondly, workplaces constitute important social spaces in which lessons in tolerance and respect for those of different religions are learned. Permitting religiously-motivated employment discrimination therefore risks the informal education in civic virtues that workplaces otherwise provide.[5] Thirdly, permitting religiously-motivated employment discrimination might endanger the interests connected with religious liberty. Looked at from the perspective of the employer, this may sound odd: after all, if such discrimination is permitted, the employer is more free to shape the workplace in accordance with her religion. But of course we must consider the interests of the employee, or prospective employee, as well as the employer. If employment is conditioned on conformity to a given religion, then, depending on the character of the labour market and the background system of social rights, this threatens to compromise the expressive and deliberative interests of the employee. Individuals who desperately need employment might find themselves pressured to pretend to beliefs they do not have, or to perform actions (for example, bowing to an icon) that contradict their own beliefs. At the very least, their free deliberation about religious matters might be distorted as they seek to adapt their views to those of the employer.

At least some of these considerations motivated the US Congress to outlaw religiously-motivated employment discrimination as part of the 1964 Civil Rights Act. Title VII of this act prohibits employers from discriminating with respect to hiring, discharging, compensation, terms, conditions, or privileges of employment on account of race, colour, religion, sex, and national origin. However, for our purposes it also noteworthy that the Congress incorporated into the law an exemption for religious associations. In its original form, Section 702 of Title VII stipulated that: 'This subchapter [the Title VII prohibition on discrimination in employment described above] shall not apply . . . to a religious corporation, association, educational institution or society with respect to the employment of individuals of a particular religion to perform work connected with the carrying on by such corporation . . . of its religious activities.'[6]

What might motivate such an exemption? In terms of the framework presented here, the concern is presumably with the expressive interests of the religious. The freedom to give expression to one's religious beliefs in one's life typically requires the freedom to associate with like-minded others in expressive activities, and, in the process of associating, to employ people with the right qualities to guide and support the expressive activities of the association. If people lacking the right qualities are somehow imposed on the association, then its activities will cease to be expressive of its members' beliefs. As Brian Barry puts it: 'If you believe that the sacraments have efficacy only if administered by a man, you can scarcely regard the sex of the person administering them as irrelevant.'[7] For this reason, it might be thought that religious associations should be given some power to discriminate in employment in favour of those with what their members regard as the right qualities; and that, to this end, religious associations should be given some degree of exemption from general anti-discrimination laws as these apply to employment. The putative right to discriminate is grounded in a concern for the expressive dimension of religious liberty.

However, we cannot stop the discussion here. We have already acknowledged how religiously-motivated employment discrimination can jeopardise important civil interests. This prompts the question I shall address in the next two sections: Can we frame a right to employment discrimination for religious associations that (a) secures the core expressive interests of the believer, but (b) does not seriously threaten other key civil interests/the key civil interests of other citizens?

The relevance principle

The simplest way to protect the believer's expressive interest would be to give religious associations a blanket exemption from anti-discrimination laws in employment. Some argued for this in the Congressional debate surrounding Title VII of the 1964 Civil Rights Act.[8] But this is surely too permissive. Under a blanket exemption of the proposed kind, religious associations would not have to give any reason for a given act or pattern of discrimination. But if the rationale for giving religious associations a right to discriminate in employment is that this is necessary to protect the integrity of their religious activities, then, in principle, they should be free to discriminate only on grounds that are relevant to this task. In short, they should be free to discriminate only on what we may term *religion-relevant grounds*. We may refer to this simply as the relevance principle.

First and foremost, religion-relevant grounds include *religious belief*. In at least one type of case – appointments to the clergy – nobody disputes the legitimacy of conditioning employment on belief. Nobody seriously questions the right of, say, the Methodist Church to condition employment as a minister on being a Methodist. Controversy does begin to arise, however, once we extend the range of personal characteristics that are taken to be religion-relevant grounds for discrimination, and once we move beyond the clergy to consider other types of employment connected with religious associations. I will examine the second issue, which concerns the range of jobs to which the right of discrimination may apply, in the next section. For the remainder of this section I will focus on the question of what other personal characteristics, in addition to religious belief, might reasonably be seen as providing adequate, religion-relevant grounds for discrimination, assuming, for the moment, that we are considering appointments, like those to the clergy, that are uncontroversially integral to the religious activities of the association.

It seems fairly uncontroversial to include life style and behaviour amongst the grounds that can count as religion-relevant reasons for employment discrimination. If one is prospectively employed to propagate a given Church's creed, then it seems reasonable that the Church can take into account the compatibility of one's life style with this creed in deciding whether to hire one. Things get a lot more controversial, however, when we move on to consider whether certain ascriptive characteristics, such as race, gender, and sexual orientation, should be regarded as admissible religion-relevant grounds for employment discrimination. This is where the conflict with liberal norms becomes evident and the right to discriminate more worrying. The Roman Catholic Church, for example, will currently not consider a female applicant for the priesthood. Should religious associations have the freedom to discriminate in employment on the basis of characteristics such as these if and when their respective religions identify these characteristics as relevant to the performance of certain duties?

One response to this question holds that the right to discriminate on the basis of such characteristics is already entailed by the apparently uncontroversial right to discriminate (at least in the case of appointments to the priesthood and the like) in favour of those who hold the association's beliefs. If, as in the case of the Roman Catholic Church, it is a part of a given Church's established belief system that only men can be priests, then a woman who demands access to the priesthood apparently reveals herself to have unorthodox beliefs; and so, the argument runs, her exclusion from the priesthood is already entailed by the uncontroversial right to restrict the priesthood to orthodox believers.

However, in many religious communities there is some degree of contestation about belief, and, relatedly, about the relative significance of various beliefs in qualifying one to remain a member of the community in good faith. For example, many Roman Catholics, including many who oppose the ordination of women, do not think that the Church's view about women and the priesthood is a matter of fundamental Church doctrine. They thus have no trouble with the idea that a given person might dissent from the currently authoritative view on this issue and still quite meaningfully be a faithful Roman Catholic. In such a case, it is far from obvious that the right to restrict the priesthood to orthodox believers carries with it, automatically, as a definitional matter, the right to exclude those who dissent from the currently authoritative view about the ordination of women, including, of necessity, women who wish to be priests. Pushing this point a little further, consider how things would stand if a Church, like the Roman Catholic Church, did try to defend its exclusion of a woman from the priesthood in the suggested way. Would the Church also fire or refuse to employ as priests men who hold the dissenting view? (There are, after all, many priests in the Roman Catholic Church at present who do hold the dissenting view.)[9] If the Church does not refuse men entry to the priesthood on these grounds, this indicates that, in the case of male applicants to the priesthood, the Church does not regard a person's holding the dissenting view as sufficient grounds for disqualifying him from the priestly office. So if it then invokes possession of this view as grounds for disqualification in the case of women who wish to be priests, the Church is straightforwardly engaged in gender-based discrimination. It would be holding women, quite arbitrarily, to a different standard of belief than men.

It is by no means clear, then, that the right to discriminate in favour of orthodox believers directly entails the right to discriminate on grounds of gender, even where the authoritative view within the religious association in question is that women cannot hold certain positions.

Moreover, even if the right to discriminate on grounds of gender were directly entailed by the right to discriminate in favour of orthodox believers, the critic might simply argue that in this case the right to discriminate on the basis of belief should be compromised in the interests of securing gender equality. What initially seems an innocuous basis for discrimination is, it might be said, quite unacceptable to the extent that, for example, it sanctions women's exclusion from the priesthood.

The argument that the state should not permit religious associations to practice sexual discrimination in employment – even in relation to the clergy – is made by the legal scholar Jane Rutherford.[10] Rutherford points out that women in conservative religious groups increasingly perceive a terrible choice between exclusion from the priesthood and the exile involved in leaving their original religious community. Moreover, the fear of confronting such a choice might inhibit women believers from exploring their own beliefs.[11] In the terms of the argument here developed, Rutherford holds that giving religious associations the right to discriminate in employment on the basis of gender (or race), including the case of appointments to the clergy, objectionably burdens the expressive and deliberative interests of those people whose employment options are closed down by the resulting sexual (or racial) discrimination. Religious associations should not be free, she thus concludes, to treat gender (or race) as religion-relevant grounds for employment discrimination.[12]

On the other hand, according to Martha Nussbaum, 'it seems illiberal to hold that practices internal to the conduct of [a] religious body . . . [such as] the choice of priests' should be subject to this kind of regulation by the state.[13] Nussbaum does not say a great deal in support of this claim, but I suspect that she is right to view such regulation as inappropriate. A first point to make in response to Rutherford's position is that the demand to be a priest cannot be divorced from the demand that others acknowledge one's admissibility as a priest in the context of their religious community. However, it does not seem reasonable, as a general matter, to expect others to acknowledge this. What would Rutherford say, for example, in the case of a man demanding the right to undertake priestly functions in a 'Goddess religion' that ordinarily restricts these functions to women? Should the state compel women members of this religious group to admit maverick, but perfectly sincere, men as priests? It hardly seems fair to let such men, no matter how sincere they may be, impose themselves on the religious life of another group of citizens in this way.

But, it might be said, the women worshippers of the 'Goddess' do not manifest patriarchal prejudice when they demand the right to exclude men from their priesthood – indeed, they may trying to create a space in which women can recover from patriarchy – and this is the crucial difference between them and religious groups that wish to exclude women from the priesthood. The state should not pander to sexist prejudice, and since women's exclusion from the clergy necessarily reflects sexist prejudice, the state should not indulge religious groups that wish to practise such exclusion. It may, however, permit women-centred religious groups that exclude men from the priesthood because such groups may serve to help society recover from its legacy of patriarchy. The problem with this argument, however, is that it is in fact quite wrong – and quite prejudiced – to assume that the desire for an all-male priesthood manifests sexist prejudice. Such a view rests on a rather uninformed, simplistic appreciation of what may be going on in citizens' religious lives.

Consider the case of James, a 'theologically liberal Odinist'. James believes that there is a divine force in the universe and that we ought to try to live in ways that embody the qualities of this force. James believes that this divine force is represented symbolically in different ways in different religious traditions. There is, he thinks, no single representation that captures perfectly the essence of the divine force, but some representations are better for some people, given their situation and needs. Thus, he can quite understand why some women (or, indeed, men) find it imperative to imagine the divine force using feminine imagery, and why, accordingly, they would wish to restrict priestly functions within their religious groups to women. From time to time, he finds it helpful to participate in the rituals of such groups. But James has recently read Robert Bly's *Iron John*, and now believes that for him, and for some other people, it is better, at least for a period, to work primarily in a religious tradition that pictures the divine force largely in male terms. Specifically, he wishes to participate in a neo-Odinist group that pictures the divine force using figures from Norse mythology, and in which priestly functions are carried out by men. Perhaps James suffers from timidity, and he feels that he will overcome this, and so live a life more worthy of the divine force, by participating in a religious tradition that gives emphasis to the virtues of 'manly courage'. Other people may wish to focus on cultivating other qualities of the divine; or they may find other representations effective in cultivating the quality he is currently most interested in; and so, in James's view, they may find that other religious groups, with other representations of the divine, are more appropriate to them. But for him, as things stand, and for the time being, this form of neo-Odinism is, in his view, the appropriate group to join and participate in.[14]

Now, so described, James surely cannot be considered a sexist. His desire to worship in a religious community in which priestly functions are restricted to men does not reflect a view that women are inferior to, or less close to God than, men. It reflects a judgement as to what kind of symbolic framework is likely to be most effective in advancing the ethical project that he sees as central to his life, and there is nothing intrinsically sexist about this project in itself.[15] Now to say that the state should not permit religious groups to restrict priestly functions to men is to deny people like James the freedom to form and join religious groups that they judge most effective to advancing wholly non-sexist, and, otherwise, intrinsically decent, even admirable, personal projects. Perhaps there is some indirect consequence of allowing such groups that is so bad, in terms of the background civil interests, as to justify restricting the apparently unobjectionable freedom of James to form and join such groups. But what now seems wholly implausible is the claim that the state is justified in denying James this freedom on the grounds that all-male priesthoods are intrinsically sexist and (therefore) objectionable. With cases like that of James in mind, I am inclined to agree with the basic spirit of what Martha Nussbaum says when she writes that 'The choices of adult citizens to remain in a religious body that refuses to hire women as priests should . . . be respected as a part of what we agree to respect when we acknowledge that our society contains a plurality of reasonable comprehensive conceptions of the good.'[16]

Nothing I have said is meant to deny the reality of the agonising choices that many women in traditional religious communities face today as a result of their exclusion from the priesthood. But I would contend that this 'fact of agonising choice' cannot be a decisive objection to the practice of exclusion, for the simple reason that no coherent regime of religious liberty can protect people from this kind of choice. The decision to belong to a given religious community necessarily carries with it an acceptance of some immediate restrictions on the beliefs one has and acts from. If, on continued reflection, one's beliefs evolve, one cannot claim the right to remain a full member of this community, expecting it to accommodate one's new beliefs as one would like. Such an idea verges on incoherence: unless all believers change their beliefs in exactly the same way, at the same time, a right of the suggested kind could not be generalised to all members of a given religious community without generating claims for accommodation that contradict each other. The individual's expressive interest is protected by her having the freedom to exit from a faith community when her beliefs evolve away from the mainstream of the community and to join with like-minded others in new associations; not, as Rutherford implies, in having the freedom to avoid exiting, and to insist on accommodation when this happens.

The centrality principle

I tentatively conclude, then, that religious associations should be free to discriminate in employment on religion-relevant grounds, where these grounds include belief, life style and behaviour, and even ascriptive characteristics such as gender and race where there is an authoritative view within a given religious association that such characteristics are in some way relevant to the performance of certain ecclesiastical duties.[17]

By itself, however, the relevance principle does not place anything like a sufficient limit on the freedom of religious associations to discriminate in employment. To see why it is insufficient, consider another court case from the US, the notorious case of *Corporation of the Presiding Bishop of the Church of Latter Day Saints v. Amos*.[18] In the *Amos* case, a janitor, Arthur Mayson, who had been employed for sixteen years at a Mormon-run non-profit gymnasium open to the general public, was fired for not complying with the eligibility test for attendance at Mormon temples. He sued the Mormon Church for unfair dismissal, and won the case in the district court, only to have the district court decision overturned by the Supreme Court.[19] *Amos* is a clear case of discrimination on religion-relevant grounds as defined above: Mayson was fired because his life style was not compatible with Mormon beliefs. And yet it seems important that Mayson was, after all, a janitor, not a priest or a minister. Moreover, he was a janitor not in a church, but in a gym; and in a gym that wasn't even exclusive to Mormon users. Though an employee of the Mormon Church, the nature of his employment was clearly very remote from the activities that are central to the religious life of the Mormon Church, and the employment of non-believers and the like in positions so distant from these activities hardly represents a credible threat to the expressive interests of individual Mormons. No individual Mormon is going to find her ability to live in authentic accordance with Mormon precepts vitiated because a public gymnasium owned by her Church employs a janitor who has, outside working hours, a somewhat racy life style.

At the same time, granting religious associations a right to employment discrimination across the full range of jobs they control could well pose a serious threat to the background civil interests described above: opportunity, civic virtue, and religious liberty (the expressive and deliberative interests of actual and prospective employees). As Nancy Rosenblum and Brian Barry both point out, the Supreme Court's decision in *Amos* displayed an extreme preoccupation with possible threats to the liberty of religious associations, but no concern at all with the threats to the religious freedom of individuals like Mason who stand vulnerable in the face of the economic power of such associations.[20] The threat to background civil interests may not be that great where religious associations control access to a relatively small proportion of a society's employment. But the economic power, and control over employment, wielded by religious associations can actually be quite considerable. Sticking with the Mormons, for example, Nancy Rosenblum points out that: 'Among its commercial assets, the Mormon Church owns the top beef ranch in the world, the largest producer of nuts in America, the country's fourteenth-largest radio chain, and the Beneficial Life Insurance Company, with assets of $1.6 billion.'[21] Proposals in the USA and Britain for 'faith-based' social policy, using public subsidies to extend the role of Churches in the provision of social welfare, raise similar anxieties about the potential for religiously-motivated employment discrimination that violates important civil interests. In view of this threat, it seems appropriate to limit quite sharply the range of employment within which religious associations may be permitted to discriminate. The challenge we then face, of course, is how to define this limit. Focusing on what seems amiss in the *Amos* case, we might say that the right to discriminate may apply only to jobs that have a sufficiently central relationship to the religious activities of a religious association. We may refer to this as the centrality principle.[22]

As I have just stated it, however, the centrality principle is too abstract to be of much use. Clearly, we need to say more about how the state is to judge whether jobs have 'a sufficiently central relationship to the religious activities of a religious association' and about the sort of things it should look for in making such a judgement. So far as I can see, there are two basic approaches we might take here, neither of which is free of difficulty.

A first approach might be described as objectivist, because it involves constructing a public definition of what can count as the core, religious activity of a religious association, and then using this definition as an objective standard by which to assess any given association's claims that specific jobs should be covered by the right to discriminate. The approach might be developed along the following lines. First, we try to define a category of activity that is essentially religious: activity the meaning and purpose of which is necessarily religious, so that to speak of engaging in such activity outside a context of religious meaning and purpose is nonsensical. Participation in a ritual of worship, for example, is an activity that is essentially religious.[23] Other practices that arguably fall within the category of the essentially religious include: evangelism (bearing witness to religious ideas, spreading the 'good news'); spiritual guidance (advising fellow believers on how to live in accordance their religious beliefs); and religious education (teaching the faith, involving a combination of evangelism and guidance). These activities are at the core of our understanding of what a religious association does. Obviously, not all activities are essentially religious. One might, for example, seek to make a profit for its own sake, not because one thinks that doing so is the best way to serve the Lord; one might give to a charity out of brute sympathy for the victims of some disaster or injustice, not because of any religious belief. However, we can perhaps define a second category of mission activity. A practice is mission activity, as I here use the term, if the practice is not essentially religious, but if, for those engaged in it, it has a primary meaning and purpose that is religious. For example, providing hot food on a cold winter's night for the homeless might be a form of mission activity for members of a given religious group.

We might now say: the right to employment discrimination held by religious associations ought to extend to jobs that are integral to the essentially religious activity of the association. Appointments to the clergy most obviously fall into this category. But other kinds of employment, for example, as a church organist, also plausibly fall into this category. In this sphere of employment, concern for the expressive interest of the believer grounds a very strong presumption in favour of permitting employment discrimination. Beyond this publicly-defined sphere of essentially religious activity, as we move into the realm of what I have termed mission activity, some freedom to discriminate, on religion-relevant grounds, may be permissible. But the presumption in favour of this freedom in this area is weaker, and may well be outweighed by a concern to prevent religious associations exercising too much control over a given type of employment (for example, in the health-care and education sectors).

The objection to this method of implementing the centrality principle is that the attempt to construct a public definition of protected, essentially religious activity will probably conflict with the self-understandings of some religious groups. A given Church might well regard aspects of its mission activity, in the sense defined above, as no less an important expression of its beliefs than activities, such as worship, that the state defines as essentially religious. Indeed, the very distinction between worship and, say, commercial activity, is a distinction that some religious groups will not accept: on some religious views, making a profit – for the Lord – is itself a form of worship. So some religious groups stand to be much more heavily burdened by this approach, by the distinctions it draws, than others.

An alternative approach, which seems to avoid this objection, is subjectivist. In this approach, the kind of work that counts as central to the religious activity of a given religious association depends simply on what activities its members view as such. If the right of their Church to discriminate in relation to a given job is disputed, then the state requires the Church to show that its members generally regard the activity with which the job is concerned as central to the Church's religious activities.[24] However, while this approach would be more neutral in its impact on different religious groups, it would presumably result in religious associations' having freedom to discriminate over a somewhat wider range of jobs. In effect, it would extend this freedom to include broad swathes of jobs that concern what I referred to above as mission activity. But as I have just noted, such an extension carries the risk of greater injury to background civil interests. If we are to balance these civil interests fairly against the expressive interests of believers, we may find it necessary to develop some standard, or standards, against which we can assess the degree of priority we should give to believers' expressive interests. This, however, points us directly back in the objectivist direction, in which public criteria of centrality are articulated and then used as an external standard against which to judge specific groups' demands for discrimination. I suspect, then, that some non-neutrality of impact between religious groups is the price we have to pay to ensure the fairest overall treatment of the various civil interests at stake.

Some commentators, such as Bruce Bagni, argue that *all* the state need and should do in this area is condition the right to discriminate on some version of the centrality principle.[25] Bagni believes that we can define a 'spiritual epicentre' to the activity of religious associations (along objectivist lines), and that religious associations should then be given complete immunity from anti-discrimination laws as regards employment that has 'epicentral attributes'. Outside the epicentre, these laws should apply. This accords with the position adopted by US courts in disputes concerning appointments to the clergy. For example, in the case of *Simpson v. Wells Lamont Corporation*,[26] an individual claimed he had been fired from his position as minister in a church in part because of the colour of his wife. The local court refused to hear his case, arguing that appointments to the ministry are properly the concern of the relevant church alone: 'who will preach from the pulpit, and who will occupy the church parsonage', the court claimed, is a concern beyond the proper remit of a civil (as opposed to an ecclesiastical) court.

Jane Rutherford is critical of this practice, and I think she is right to be so. Rutherford cites the case of Darreyl M. Young, who, despite 'glowing reports' on her work, was sacked from her job as a minister with the United Methodist Church. Young claimed she was the victim of sexual and racial discrimination. As Rutherford puts it: 'If Young had worked for any other employer, the government would have assured her an opportunity to present her case of sex and race discrimination to a federal court. However, the district court dismissed the case on the basis of the Religion Clauses of the First Amendment before Young even had a chance to present the facts.'[27] It is hard to see why employees of religious associations, even those working in what Bagni would call the 'spiritual epicentre' of these associations, ought to be left so vulnerable to the arbitrary exercise of institutional power. On the one hand, I do not see how it would significantly burden the expressive interest of association members to insist that their association explain, in a court of law or relevant employment tribunal, the religious grounds for a disputed employment decision, even where the decision relates to epicentral employment.[28] On the other hand, the vulnerability that stems from exposure to unaccountable power could well threaten employees' expressive (and also, perhaps, deliberative) interests. Even if the employee is never actually victimised by such power, her freedom is reduced by the position of dependency and vulnerability this creates.[29] Those so dependent might readily become wrapped up in the game of pandering to those who hold arbitrary power over them, and this might easily encourage a superficial, inauthentic engagement with higher matters of the spirit.

Conclusion and caveat

For this reason, at least, I think the centrality principle should be combined with the relevance principle. Religious associations should be free to discriminate in employment, therefore, only on religion-relevant grounds, and only for jobs that have a sufficiently central relationship to their religious activities. I have argued that the relevance principle should be understood to admit gender and other ascriptive characteristics as permissible grounds for discrimination. I have sketched two ways in which the centrality principle might be operationalised, and I have argued that we probably strike the best, fairest balance between the various civil interests at stake if the state judges claims to centrality by reference to a public, external standard such as, perhaps, a public definition of 'essentially religious' employment.

In closing I would like to enter a final caveat concerning my defence of the right of religious groups to treat characteristics like gender as religion-relevant grounds for discrimination in appointments to the priesthood. One further objection to this practice, not considered above, appeals to the civil interest in civic virtue. In a just society, a key element of civic virtue is the disposition to respect other citizens, *qua* citizens, as equals: the disposition to wish to see them enjoy equal civil and political rights and economic opportunity. And it might be objected that exclusion from the priesthood sends a powerful symbolic message of women's supposed inferiority that undermines equal respect for women in the wider political community.[30] Now, were this the case, and were it also the case that there is no other effective way of undoing the harm in question, then I accept that the freedom of religious groups to exclude women from the priesthood would need to be reconsidered. Nevertheless, I think we should treat this sort of argument with great caution. It is all too easy to speculate that a given prac-tice has undesirable wider effects on our public culture. Before we proceed to take away the freedom of citizens to engage in any such practice, however, we should have sound evidence that the alleged effects are genuine. Moreover, we have seen above that there is nothing intrinsically sexist about a desire to form and/or join a religious group with a clergy exclusive to one gender. In some cases, this desire may be tied to perfectly decent, even admirable, personal projects. Consequently, even if we did have sound evidence that exclusion of women from the clergy of religious groups is harming women's standing in the wider political community, we would need to balance this harm against the harm we would do, in prohibiting such groups, to non-sexist men (and perhaps women) innocently seeking to form and join groups of this kind. As in other cases of disputed toleration, where similar harms are alleged, such as the dispute over pornography, a concern to protect intrinsically legitimate and valuable personal freedoms should incline us to look first to alternative remedies for the alleged harms, before we legislate to remove the freedoms.[31]

Notes

I would like to thank Chris Bertram, Selina Chen, Jurgen DeWispelaere, Peter Edge, Cecile Fabre, Diana Gardner, Paul Kelly, Steven Lukes, David Miller, Tariq Modood, Julian Rivers, Nancy Rosenblum, Gijs van Donselaar, and Katherine Wedell for comments on earlier versions of this chapter and/or on the topic it concerns.
  1 I should perhaps note that while my focus will be on religious associations, this does not reflect a judgement that the issue I discuss pertains only to religious associations. Parallel issues arise, I think, in the case of political associations, such as political parties, and I do not mean to imply that they should not have equivalent or analogous freedoms.
  2 See J. Locke, 'A letter concerning toleration', trans W. Popple, in D. Wootton (ed.), *Locke's Political Writings* (Harmondsworth: Penguin, 1993 [1689]), pp. 390–436. I do not claim that my use of the term, or my approach to the central question of this chapter, are such as Locke would approve of.

3 I take the term from J. Cohen, 'Freedom of expression', in D. Heyd, *Toleration: An Elusive Virtue* (Princeton, NJ: Princeton University Press, 1996), pp. 173–225, at pp. 185–7, though I should add that Cohen uses the term strictly to refer to the citizen's interest in articulating viewpoints and the like, whereas I am using the term in a way that encompasses a broader range of activities that can be said to be expressive of a given conception of the good. See also R. Dworkin, *Sovereign Virtue: The Theory and Practice of Equality* (Cambridge, MA: Harvard University Press, 2000), pp. 270–4.

4 Again, see Cohen, 'Freedom of expression', at p. 188.

5 See N. Rosenblum, '*Amos*: religious autonomy and the moral uses of pluralism', in N. Rosenblum (ed.), *Obligations of Citizenship and the Demands of Faith: Religious Accommodation in Pluralist Democracies* (Princeton, NJ: Princeton University Press, 2000), pp. 165–95, at p. 166.

6 Congress amended the exemption in 1972, deleting the word 'religious' in the final clause. In addition to the exemption carved out in Congressional legislation, US courts have repeatedly ruled that, under the free exercise clause of the First Amendment, religious associations have a more or less unlimited right to discriminate in relation to the employment of clergy.

7 B. Barry, *Culture and Equality* (Oxford: Polity, 2000), p. 174.

8 As one Senator Ervin put it: 'For the life of me, I cannot comprehend why the EEOC [Equal Employment Opportunity Commission] and why those who are championing this cause [anti-discrimination] are so greedy for power that they want to lay the political hands of Caesar on the employment practices of churches of God' (cited in Rosenblum, '*Amos*', p. 170).

9 See, for example, the 'Radical Catholic' website at: www.bway.net/~halsall/radcath.html

10 See J. Rutherford, 'Equality as the primary constitutional value: the case for applying employment discrimination laws to religion', *Cornell Law Review*, 81 (1996) 1049–128.

11 Rutherford, *ibid.*, p. 1085.

12 Rutherford would allow Churches to pay damages to women who are excluded from the priesthood instead of admitting women to the priesthood. But the financial implications of this could obviously have the same effect as a direct insistence to admit women.

13 M. Nussbaum, 'A plea for difficulty', in S. M. Okin *et al.*, *Is Multiculturalism Bad for Women?* (Princeton, NJ: Princeton University Press, 1999), pp. 105–14, at p. 114.

14 I confess that this example is based somewhat on my own speculative imaginings as to what contemporary Odinists believe and do. Nothing of substance in my argument actually hangs on James's desired religious group being specifically 'Odinist', and I apologise to any contemporary Odinists who feel this example misrepresents their religion. I am confident, however, that this hypothetical example is perfectly realistic in its essentials.

15 The project is to live in accordance with the qualities of the divine force, and James does not think this force is ultimately male or female, or that the totality of its qualities are in some sense more male than female.

16 Nussbaum, 'Plea for difficulty', p. 114. This conclusion also seems consistent with what John Rawls says about the relationship between 'principles of political justice' and associational life: '. . . liberal principles of political justice do not require ecclesiastical governance to be democratic . . . *nor need the benefits*

attached to a church's hierarchy of offices satisfy a specified distributive prin-ciple ... the principles of political justice do not apply to the internal life of the church, nor is it desirable, or consistent with liberty of conscience of freedom of association, that they should' (italics added). See J. Rawls, 'The idea of public reason revisited', in J. Rawls, *The Law of Peoples* (Cambridge, MA: Harvard University Press, 1999), pp. 129–80, at p. 158.

17 I have explicitly considered only the case of sexual discrimination for the priest-hood, but I believe similar considerations to those advanced above would also allow for racial discrimination where this has a basis in the religious associa-tion's belief system.

18 *Corporation of the Presiding Bishop of the Church of Latter Day Saints v. Amos* (483 U.S. 327 [1987]).

19 The Supreme Court did not determine that religious associations have a right to discriminate of this kind guaranteed by the US constitution (as part of the right of 'free exercise' of religion guaranteed under the First Amendment). The right to discriminate is based on the exemption to anti-discrimination laws that Congress granted (specifically, the Section 702 exemption to Title VII of the 1964 Civil Rights Act, as amended by Congress in 1972), and the Supreme Court held that this Congressionally crafted exemption was not unconstitutional.

20 See Rosenblum, '*Amos*', pp. 183–7, and Barry, *Culture and Equality*, p. 167.

21 See Rosenblum, '*Amos*', p. 186.

22 The European Union's recent anti-discrimination framework directive seems to be groping at such a principle when it says that discrimination on grounds of religion by religious associations is admitted specifically 'for the particular occupational activities within those organizations which are directly and essentially related to religion or belief', and where 'the nature of these acti-vities or the context in which they are carried out' are such that 'a person's reli-gion or belief constitute a genuine occupational requirement.' See Article 4, *Council Directive establishing a general framework for equal treatment in em-ployment and occupation (presented by the Commission pursuant to Article 250 (2) of the EC-Treaty)*, available at:
http://europa.eu.int/eur-lex/en/com/dat/2000/en_500PC0652.html.

23 Perhaps, it would be more exact to say that an essentially religious activity is one the context of which necessarily includes the religious. For a given worshipper, the activity of worship could have other meanings and purposes, to do for example with friendship and social life. But if someone attends rituals of worship only for these non-religious reasons, I would question whether what they are doing is in fact worship.

24 This version of the centrality principle is suggested by Nancy Rosenblum in her discussion of the Supreme Court's arguments in *Amos*. See '*Amos*', pp. 174–6.

25 See B. Bagni, 'Discrimination in the name of the Lord: a critical evaluation of discrimination by religious organizations', *Columbia Law Review*, 79 (1979) 1514–49.

26 *Simpson v. Wells Lamont Corporation* (494 F2d 490 (5th Cir. 1974)). See Bagni, 'Discrimination', p. 1535; Rosenblum, '*Amos*', p. 169.

27 Rutherford, 'Equality', pp. 1056–7.

28 Or to explain legitimate, non-religious grounds for a decision, for instance neglect of duties. It might be said that we should not insist on bringing Church

employees into state tribunals if we are satisfied that the Church itself has sufficiently fair internal appeals processes. But could we be sure these processes would be sufficiently fair and impartial? Note that even if a state tribunal finds against a Church in such a case, this need not entail Church members being lumbered with a cleric they do not want. The Church can be required to pay compensation instead.

29 See P. Pettit, *Republicanism: A Theory of Freedom and Government* (Oxford: Oxford University Press, 1997); and Q. Skinner, *Liberty Before Liberalism* (Cambridge: Cambridge University Press, 1998).

30 This point also features in Rutherford's argument against permitting sexual discrimination in employment, including appointments to the priesthood. See Rutherford, 'Equality', pp. 1087–9.

31 See Cohen, 'Freedom of expression', especially pp. 198–9.

11

Education to toleration: some philosophical obstacles and their resolution

David Heyd

Toleration as a perceptual shift of perspectives

Moral education has played a central role in all major ethical systems of thought from Aristotle to Kant, from the Torah to socialist ideology. Providing the young with *moral* education is particularly tricky, since moral judgement, and even more so moral behaviour, does not come naturally to human beings. The incorporation of moral values and norms requires a distinctive effort and often calls for overcoming natural inclinations and inborn tendencies. The main business of moral education in its traditional form has been the transmission of a set of principles of conduct, forms of judgement, beliefs and sensibilities deemed by the older generation appropriate, even necessary, for its successors. However, with the rise of liberal culture, moral education has become suspect, and its main tenets are often seen now as incompatible with the overall normative scepticism characteristic of this culture. The very right to educate, particularly in the realm of values, has become the object of critical examination. What qualifies parents or the state to decide the values and moral preferences of children and youth? Once moral objectivism or absolutism is abandoned, the grounds for the paternalistic inculcation of moral principles become shaky.

It is therefore typical of contemporary liberal attitude, both on the family level and that of schooling, to reject the traditional, 'rich' pattern of moral education. First-order virtues, principles, character traits and values are only cautiously suggested to the child or adolescent, usually as options in a wide repertoire of partly competing values and principles. The traditional commitment to such first-order moral values is characteristically replaced by the dominant effort to promote *second*-order values, most conspicuously autonomy, critical thinking, respect and tolerance. Moral training is accordingly seen primarily in terms of the capacity to make meaningful choices in one's life (self-critical exercise of autonomy), on the one hand, and the ability to live side by side with people who have different, often incompatible, values and life styles from our own (respect and tolerance), on the other. Beyond the implementation of the fundamental norms of social behaviour, the principal goal of moral education in liberal society is thus the creation of conditions for dealing with the absence of common standards and a shared commitment to the good in society.

To our liberal sensibility implanting the value of autonomy and tolerance seems to be a more minimal and hence an easier task than creating an all-round moral personality. However, there are particular difficulties, both conceptual and practical, in liberal education, and there is a strong analogy between the difficulties involved in teaching people to be autonomous and bringing them up on the idea of tolerance. The present chapter will focus on the problems of education to toleration. Its aim is primarily philosophical, that is, to expose the elusive nature of the very idea of toleration and its implications in education and to discuss some psychological and practical obstacles in educating the young to adopt a tolerant attitude to others.

The fundamental theoretical difficulty I am thinking of is associated with the well-known 'paradox of toleration'. Strictly speaking, tolerance is the attitude of restraint in responding to morally wrong beliefs and practices. Furthermore, as some philosophers insist, the 'nuclear' concept of tolerance is applicable only in situations in which the beliefs and practices are held as really, that is objectively, wrong, not only subjectively resisted or detested by the tolerant subject.[1] Put bluntly, the principle of tolerance calls upon us to tolerate the intolerable. Tolerant forbearance from a negative response stands in direct conflict with the judgement that the tolerated belief or practice is morally repugnant, obnoxious or wrong. How can we justify the abstention from acting against moral wrongs? And when we come to the sphere of education, how can we hope to raise a child to become a person committed to moral values, yet at the same time willing to tolerate their infringement?

One way to avoid the paradox of toleration is to relax the stringent conditions in the definition of the concept itself. Thus, toleration would characterise restraint in our response to beliefs and practices that we hold to be legitimate even though contrary to our own views. Such a concept of tolerance is typical of value pluralism: we refrain from persecuting other religions, from hindering the life plans that look to us wasteful and silly, or from trying to convince people that their aesthetic tastes are cheap, since we recognise them as legitimate even if wrong in our eyes or lacking in value. Pluralism has many versions: there is moral pluralism of the kind Isaiah Berlin (probably on the basis of J. S. Mill's view) has eloquently advocated; there is religious pluralism of the type developed in Locke's famous *Letters on Toleration*, according to which even if there is religious truth it cannot be established with certainty, let alone enforced on those who do not accept it; there is the pluralism of tastes and preferences that belongs to the aesthetic and personal realm to which our moral values are conflated. But what is common to all these versions is that the toleration they call for is always justified by some form of denial or weakening of the objective moral wrongness of the tolerated belief or conduct. Educating people to realise the plurality of values and preferences and teaching them to respond in a gentle manner to differences is certainly of much value; but it does not directly address the core of the paradox of toleration.[2] The difficult cases of toleration relate to beliefs and values that we know to be morally and objectively false or even dangerous. The inculcation of a pluralist view calls for the development of equanimity or even indifference in our response to other views and life styles, or at least of a detached curiosity. Toleration, on the other hand, is necessarily concerned with suffering; it has a price; toleration can never arise out of apathy.

Another way to relax the conditions of toleration is by focusing on its pragmatic nature. Tolerance, according to this approach, is primarily a political virtue. It brings peace and secures social co-existence in a society that is split in its moral and religious conceptions. Much of the early history of toleration in the sixteenth and seventeenth centuries appealed to this concept of toleration as compromise. We are willing to put aside our commitment to our moral beliefs, not because we think there are other legitimate options, but because we know there is no other way to maintain social stability. The call for mutual toleration between orthodox and secular Jews in Israel is typically guided by this idea of mutual concession rather than by that of mutual recognition.[3] And again, there is nothing wrong in such a political principle of pragmatic reconciliation. However, it again does not capture the core idea of toleration. Furthermore, as an educational ideal, compromise misses an important dimension in our relation to those who are seriously different from us, since by its nature it is guided by *ad hoc* considerations of relative power and by circumstantial social goals that justify the concessions involved in every compromise. The principle of toleration we are trying to articulate is a typically principled attitude, a virtue that is not based on epistemological or pragmatic considerations that are by definition contingent.[4]

I therefore suggest focusing on toleration as a principled forbearance from a negative interference in beliefs and actions that are thought of as (objectively) morally objectionable. Tolerated phenomena lie between that which should never be tolerated (violence or cruelty) and that which should not be objected to in the first place (racial differences or sexual inclinations). My own suggestion as to how to conceptualise and justify toleration might be called perceptual.[5] According to this view, toleration involves a perceptual shift in the way we look at a situation. Roughly speaking, we can either turn our attention to the belief or act in question and judge them on their merit, that is impersonally; or, alternatively, we can focus on the subject of the belief or the agent of the action and judge *them* as holding the belief or acting on their values, that is to say personally. I would like to claim that the two perspectives of judgement are separate, irreducible and often mutually exclusive. The perceptual shift from one perspective to the other may be compared to the *Gestalt* switch of the rabbit–duck type.

One can choose to see either a rabbit or a duck, but never both at once. One is usually inclined to see the one, but can train oneself or make an effort to see the other. Neither image is more valid or true than the other. Furthermore, as in a Gestalt shift, there is no direct balancing of reasons of the two kinds that makes one perspective superior to the other – only a general, second-order reason to switch from one point of view to the other.

Now, toleration means the shift from the impersonal perspective to the personal. Rather than judging the beliefs or actions in themselves, the tolerant party is considering the subject or agent behind them, the way the beliefs were formed, the manner in which they cohere together in a system of beliefs or constitute a life plan of an individual. According to this personal analysis, both the subject and the object of toleration must be human beings. Consequently, the state (at least in the modern, impersonal conception) cannot be said (strictly speaking) to be tolerant. It can be just and neutral, but it does not suffer or restrain itself from acting on what it deems right and just. Similarly, we tolerate people but not actions and opinions (despite ordinary parlance).

It is thus natural that most (though by no means all) accounts of toleration as a principled attitude refer to autonomy and respect as the ultimate grounds for tolerant restraint:[6] these are in the terms I am suggesting the justification for the intentional abandonment of the judgemental perspective of beliefs and actions as such. Unlike the rabbit–duck case, the two competing perspectives are not symmetrical. At least in some circumstances, there are good moral reasons for adopting the personal view. Many philosophers appeal to personal autonomy as the ultimate basis for the superiority of the personal to the impersonal perspective. Another view, which has received only little attention in the literature on toleration, is viewing it as supererogatory.[7] But in any case, the common underlying reason for switching to the personal point of view is that beyond our interest in truth and goodness in the abstract, we are often more interested in the way these are achieved and sustained by actual human beings. The validity of beliefs and values may be judged independently of their subjects, but their value for us is dependent on the way they cohere in a particular system of beliefs, the process by which they were acquired, the degree to which their subjects are committed to them. These are issues, to which much of the literature on toleration is devoted, but which lie beyond the scope of the present chapter. Our concern here is educational.

By separating two incompatible perspectives, the perceptual model suggested here may solve the conceptual paradox of toleration. There is no contradiction between judging an action as wrong and yet appreciating or respecting its agent (and of course no contradiction between loathing a person and yet at the same time judging one of his actions as right and just). But this does not diminish the difficulties in training people to acquire the ability to make the right shift in the right circumstances. For instance, we know that, in the realm of science, the impersonal perspective is the correct one, and that judging scientific statements about the world in terms of the history of their formation in the subject holding them or in terms of the way they fit with other beliefs of that subject is a fallacy (as, for instance, in the case of *ad hominem* arguments). Similarly, court judges are usually called to judge the case brought before them on its merits, that is, in impersonal terms; their job is exactly to decide whether an action was right or wrong, legal or illegal. However, psychologists are usually expected to adopt the personal point of view, to turn their attention away (even when it takes a special effort) from the inclination to judge the substantive worth of a person's behaviour. Similarly, in the moral sphere, forgiveness is a typical example in which we turn a blind eye to the insulting or offensive act itself and focus on the character of the agent, the previous friendly relations with her and her repentance for the wrong act.[8] Toleration belongs to this category of actions, in which the personal autonomy and the respect for the individual forming a meaningful life for herself are the grounds for the shift of attention from the judgemental, impersonal perspective to the personal.

It should, however, be noted that the ability to keep agent separate from deeds may come under particular strain when a good deal of the agent's actions are wrong or some of her actions are extremely repugnant. For the identity of agents is to a large extent dependent on their actions. Thus, we may forgive or tolerate a friend's misbehaviour as long as there remains enough in her character and record to justify the friendship. But once the behaviour reflects a major change in personality (for example, the person becoming a racist, a child abuser, etc.), it is no more the 'same' person with whom we had a relationship of friendship. This is exactly where the separability of agent from action becomes impossible and we refer to the wrong action as 'unforgivable' or 'intolerable'.

The difficulties in inculcating toleration in children

Children find such a separation of the personal from the impersonal difficult. On the one hand, they tend to view individual persons as constituted by their particular actions and beliefs; on the other hand, they judge the validity of beliefs and actions in terms of their attitude towards the individual holding them. Thus, children are even more prone than adults to *ad hominem* arguments or to arguments from authority. Accordingly, they are less capable both of impersonal objective judgement and of forgiveness and tolerance. This double deficiency defines the challenge of moral education in general and education to toleration in particular. Moral education aims to instil three capacities: first, the capacity to make normative judgements about beliefs and practices *in abstracto*; secondly, the capacity to relate to moral agents independently of their particular views or conduct; and thirdly, the capacity to distinguish between the contexts in which each of these perspectives should be adopted. Much of the literature on moral edu-

cation deals with the development of the moral judgement of the child –
that is to say, with the first perspective. Children gradually learn to detach
the evaluation of states of affairs (typically, distributions) from the natural
first-person bias. By that they internalise the idea of justice and fairness (in
a way that is analogous, as Piaget has taught us, to the acquisition of symmetrical thinking in scientific matters, which is equally 'impersonal'). The
inculcation of the second, 'personal' perspective is discussed much less.
How do we educate people to become forgiving, respectful and tolerant?
While the self-regarding second-order value of autonomy is easy for the
child to adopt owing to its egocentric nature, the ability to see the other as
the subject of such autonomy takes more cognitive and emotional effort.
It calls for an attitude that is potentially incompatible both with the child's
first-order beliefs of what is right and wrong and with her self-centred
interests.

The widespread strategy of turning the offended child's attention to the
intention or the motive of the offender is a step in the direction of the separation of person from action. 'He did not mean what he said', or 'he only
wanted to help you' are surely effective means of training the child to see
beyond the wrongness of the action itself. However, this is still not implanting the virtue of toleration. For these are cases that are conceptually more
similar to understanding, excusing, and condoning. These are attitudes that
call for a change in one's judgement of the action itself in the light of a
broader view of its circumstances (most ethical theories consider the intention or motive of the action as at least partly relevant to its moral status).
Tolerance, in the nuclear sense I am trying to examine here, implies a more
radical separation. It requires the complete abandonment of the judgemental perspective, turning a blind eye to a wrong that cannot be mitigated,
condoned or excused, but must simply be put aside in favour of an assessment of the individual who happens sincerely to believe otherwise. Tolerance is usually costly: as its etymology intimates, it involves 'suffering'.[9]

How does this analysis of the education to toleration work on the political plane, that which transcends responses on the individual level? Struc-
turally, political toleration is associated with the same tension between the
commitment of people to their own cultural heritage and identity and their
recognition of the legitimacy, even the inherent value, of other cultures.
Susan Mendus, following Bernard Williams, argues that toleration in a
multicultural society is based neither on the idea of the autonomy of other
groups to form their own culture (since the value of autonomy is itself controversial), nor on some notion of cultural relativism. The very comparison
between *our* culture and that of others is not the issue. At most the understanding and 'recognition' of other cultures may serve as a source for understanding the limits of justification of our own culture.[10] I wish to argue that
the tension between loyalty to cultural identity and commitment to democratic citizenship, highlighted by Mendus, is analogous to that between my
own concept of truth and value and my respect for other people. Political

toleration thus requires of the child the same feat of abstraction or separation of two incomparable points of view, that is to say, the adoption of a second-order reason for switching from the substantive identification with my group's values to the political recognition of the idea of equal citizenship, group autonomy, or irreducible plurality of ways of life that can never claim to have ultimate justification as the best or the superior.

A serious problem in the education to tolerance is that the educational relationship itself is often intolerant in its very nature. Even in liberal education based on the ideal of respect for the child, the educator's role is not a model of toleration. This model has to be imported from other contexts to which the child is exposed. We tolerate other people whose views and practices we find objectionable because we respect their autonomy – that is their capacity and right to make choices and live by them. However, with our children, or pupils, our principal aim is to create this capacity, to form an autonomous personality, and this involves the exercise of paternalistic authority. Exactly because we care so much and feel responsible for their future we do not tolerate the wrong beliefs and conduct of our children or students. An extreme, limiting case, which explains why tolerance is not the attitude we show to the people particularly close to us, is our attitude to ourselves: the reason we cannot be said to tolerate ourselves, is that the separation of action from agent, belief from subject, cannot be reflexively applied. We simply cannot view ourselves as distinct from what we do. The intimate proximity of personhood to its particular manifestation in action and belief is most conspicuous in first-person contexts. But it is also typical of the way young children view others. However, though the idea of forgiving or tolerating oneself is at most metaphorical, forgiving and tolerating others is a great virtue on which we try to bring up the young.

So even if the conceptual analysis of toleration I am suggesting here resolves the paradox of toleration, the psychological obstacles to creating a tolerant inclination in both children and adults are serious. In the same way as the personal and impersonal perspectives are mutually exclusive, so are the judgemental and the tolerant frames of mind or propensities. Even though moral pluralism or scepticism is not equivalent to toleration, as we have argued, they psychologically fit a tolerant attitude, or at least are of no hindrance to such an attitude. But there is a way in which even liberal education aims at the creation of individuals who are strongly committed to some of their beliefs and norms, who are convinced of the superiority of those values that constitute their fundamental life projects. As modern liberals like Joseph Raz have shown, the exercise of autonomy presupposes that the options for choice are genuinely valuable or good.[11] In other words, the goal of moral education consists primarily of the creation of a distinct moral profile. But the deeper the commitment of a person to a set of norms, the more dogmatic she will tend to become and the less tolerant to competing points of view. There is a point in both the accusations of liberals and those of religious fundamentalists: the one group is psychologically inclined to dogmatic and intolerant attitudes; the other to scepticism, pluralism, and indifference. But of course there is no symmetry between the two: non-liberal systems of values can do without the principle of toleration; they advocate the principle of compromise in its stead, and they do so without compromising in a deep sense their commitment to their normative principles. Yet liberals must incorporate a principled, second-order virtue of toleration, which is a more difficult task, since it conflicts with their first-order moral convictions.

Toleration versus other second-order responses

Education to toleration is just one part in the general teaching of second-order moral principles, such as punishment, forgiveness, and compromise, that is to say the correct response to the violation of first-order principles or norms. However, just punishment is itself part of the system of justice and hence can be taught fairly easily (although there is always the need to overcome the natural tendency to vindictive over-punishment, as Locke has taught us). Compromise is incompatible with a commitment to the right solution, but every child naturally adopts it, because reality forces upon everybody the realisation of the limits of one's power as well as the risk of ongoing rivalry and conflict. Furthermore, sheer fatigue from conflict and war may lead to that change of attitude that is associated with compromise in the first stage and toleration in the second. This was the historical case in the aftermath of the bloodshed of the wars of religion in the early modern period,[12] but can also explain the development of the capacity to tolerate in children.

Toleration is, however, trickier than compromise, since it requires the development of a sense of an independent value – that of respect for others. Education to toleration consists in the formation of a capacity to see beliefs and actions not in the light of some impersonally validating criteria but as parts in a coherent whole, constituting a moral personality or character and being the consequence of a sincere attempt to achieve meaning and truth. It takes moral imagination, the ability to see the other from her point of view. And unlike the development of the sense of justice, or the realisation of the inevitability of compromise, which are universal and independent of any specific moral view, toleration is a 'local', culture-dependent value, which can be given meaning only within a liberal morality. There is nothing in the nature of society or human nature as such which makes toleration necessary.

It should be noted that less restrictive analyses of toleration, such as Peter Gardner's, view it as an attitude that does not necessarily involve dislike or disapproval by the tolerator. Toleration, according to these accounts, means more openness, less certainty about one's beliefs, the willingness to deliberate and change one's opinions. People can be tolerant towards practices and beliefs that they themselves neither disapprove of nor dislike, but that *others* would be likely to disapprove of or dislike.[13] Consequently, education to toleration requires the development of open-mindedness, critical scepticism, the power of deliberation, and the willingness to change one's attitude. This concept of toleration eschews the difficulty of the more restrictive concept, according to which toleration means the commitment to a particular opinion that excludes the tolerated one. Education to toleration, in this case, does not imply supporting children's biases and prejudices.[14]

Gardner's conception of toleration definitely accords with everyday usage of the term. However, it does not capture the most difficult and demanding contexts in which toleration is called for (and considered as intrinsically valuable). It tends to blur the boundaries between tolerance, on the one hand, and open-mindedness, critical scepticism and moderate judgement, on the other. It does not do justice to the suffering of the tolerator, the price of restraint and the effort involved in it. And although it considers tolerance and respect as compatible, it does not distinguish between the tolerance and respect shown to the person and the disapproval and lack of respect for the belief or practice as such.

In 1998, the Israeli Ministry of Education officially declared the school year as that of 'the right to self-respect and the duty to respect'. The aim was surely political, and the basic idea was to ease the social and ideological tensions following the trauma of Rabin's assassination. But I believe that there was something philosophically correct in the juxtaposition of the right to self-respect (or to be respected) and the duty to respect others. Ultimately, the source of our awareness of the intrinsic value of other people's lives and personalities grows out of our sense of the infinite (immeasurable) value of our life to ourselves! This is not only in line with the Kantian heritage in ethical theory but also the basic clue as to the educational means for promoting a tolerant perception of moral differences. Even if I am convinced that you are morally wrong in the way you are leading your life, I can perceive the independent value of your personality analogically to the intrinsic value that I ascribe to my own life. For I basically value my own life and autonomy irrespective of the particular views I hold or even the actions that I take.

A similar projection of self-centred values to the way we view others occurs in the education to autonomous choice. The separation of the personal from the impersonal is manifest in teaching the young that the way in which beliefs and values are adopted is of no less importance than their truth or validity. The educator's intellectual effort in the inculcation of critical thinking and autonomous choice often constitutes a conscious tempering of the pursuit of truth as such. Children and adults are called to experiment with ideas even at the risk of error, since the experiment itself is regarded as having an intrinsic value. Now, it is relatively easy for the subject herself to recognise the value of such authenticity, free choice, or critical reflection. But symmetrical thinking leads to the ascription of the same value to others. This is one of the main routes to toleration: patience with other people's mistakes, the moderation of the judgemental attitude, or the capacity 'to deliberate with equanimity'.[15]

And yet the transition from the duty to respect others to the ideal of toleration is neither necessary nor morally neutral. Non-liberals can consistently adopt the norm of respect and at the same time interpret it as fully consistent with or even requiring of an intolerant interference in the lives of those who happen to be wrong in their beliefs and values. Sincere paternalistic concern for the welfare of heretics motivates many forms of religious intolerance. Only in the liberal understanding of respect does a principled restraint, toleration, follow from the principle of respect. This is a notion of respect that is constituted by the ultimate value of the subject's free choice and the relevance of the manner in which the beliefs are formed in the subject. Therefore, education to toleration is possible, but only within a general liberal framework. And even within that framework it is far from easy, since it involves a schizophrenic, two-level view of the nature of moral judgement, and the versatile capacity to switch from the one to the other and to do so in the right circumstances.

Our philosophical analysis of the concept of toleration has demonstrated that the concept is elusive. The pure concept turns out to have little concrete application, since the space between what should not be opposed to begin with and what should not be tolerated is very narrow. Thus, we learn that in most uses of the concept of tolerance what we really mean is either compromise, or recognition of plurality, or even indifference. The notion of tolerance is not only conceptually evasive; it is historically and psychologically intermediary in nature, merely a stage between intolerant opposition and positive recognition. This conclusion is of a significant educational import, since as a matter of fact we are justified in hoping that by the promotion of the capacity to compromise, which we showed to be an easier task, we gradually learn to tolerate others; and that by acquiring a tolerant disposition, we progressively move towards full recognition of at least some of the opinions and practices of other people. Thus, through the general capacity to separate subjects from their actions, human beings can learn first to compromise, then to tolerate, and finally to fully respect and accept other individuals.[16]

Notes

1 For a powerful and convincing defence of this strong sense of tolerance, see J. Horton, 'Toleration as a virtue', in D. Heyd (ed.), *Toleration: An Elusive Virtue* (Princeton, NJ: Princeton University Press, 1996), pp. 28–43.

2 See Rainer Forst's contribution to this volume.

3 This particular case can also serve to illustrate a very interesting model of convergence of two different modes of concession: the liberal secular sector shows tolerance (in the principled sense) towards the orthodox, while the orthodox –

lacking a principled value of tolerance – are willing to 'tolerate' the secular for their own theological reasons (such as the common ancestry and Jewish identity). This convergence is obviously contingent and hence not very stable, but it may prove to be of much pragmatic social and political value.

4 For a sophisticated justification of toleration in utilitarian terms, see D. Lewis, 'Mill and Milquetoast', *Australasian Journal of Philosophy*, 67 (1989) 152–71. Lewis rejects Mill's account of toleration in terms of its overall utility from an impersonal (neutral) point of view, but he believes that the parties to a conflict may be led to tolerate each other by considerations of the personal risks and benefits involved in pursuing intolerant behaviour. Lewis's approach might be relevant to education, but his concept of toleration is closer to that of pragmatic compromise than to a principled notion of toleration along Mill's line.

5 David Heyd, 'Introduction', in Heyd (ed.), *Toleration*, pp. 10–17.

6 M. Lorberbaum has convincingly shown that respect for the integrity of another individual does not necessarily mean the recognition of autonomy as a fundamental value. In the Jewish tradition the idea of tolerance is associated with the willingness to accept certain kinds of errors in moral judgement, those that have 'grounds'. Lorberbaum's analysis leaves room for a 'non-liberal' concept of toleration, which even if deviating from the strict sense that we are (somewhat artificially) ascribing to the concept in this chapter, is both widespread and of educational significance: M. Lorberbaum, 'Learning from mistakes: resources of tolerance in the Jewish tradition', *Journal of Philosophy of Education*, 29 (1995) 273–84.

7 See G. Newey, 'Against thin-property reductivism: toleration as supererogatory', *Journal of Value Inquiry*, 31 (1997) 231–49. H. Ben-baji and D. Heyd, 'The charitable perspective: forgiveness and toleration as supererogatory', *Canadian Journal of Philosophy*, 31 (2001) 567–86.

8 For a strong argument for the separation of agent and act in the analysis of forgiveness, see T. Govier, 'Forgiveness and the unforgivable', *American Philosophical Quarterly*, 36 (1999) 59–75.

9 Contemporary educational conceptions of tolerance often emphasise the ability to put up with difference. But it should be noted that tolerance requires more than the sheer civilised management of public disputes. It involves both the ability to listen seriously to the other (taking her point of view) during the discussion and tolerance of the remaining disagreements at the end of the discussion. See V. Waksman, 'What we talk about when we talk about tolerance', *Thinking*, 13 (1998) 46–9.

10 S. Mendus, 'Toleration and recognition: education in a multicultural society', *Journal of Philosophy of Education*, 29 (1995) 191–201.

11 J. Raz, 'Autonomy, toleration and the harm principle', in S. Mendus (ed.), *Justifying Toleration* (Cambridge: Cambridge University Press, 1988), pp. 155–75.

12 R. H. Dees, 'Trust and the rationality of toleration', *Nous*, 32 (1998) 82–98. Dees correctly points out that toleration requires more than a 'conversion', and that for its long-term maintenance toleration must be thought of as a value and not just a compromise. Toleration can be achieved only on the basis of trust, which is a fragile achievement.

13 P. Gardner, 'Tolerance and education', in J. Horton (ed.), *Liberalism, Multiculturalism and Toleration* (New York: St. Martin's Press, 1993), p. 87. Gardner distinguishes between dispositional and deliberative tolerance, the former being

a character trait (which does not imply disapproval), the latter being a judge-mental conclusion (which presupposes disapproval).

14 *Ibid.*, p. 98.

15 L. Burwood and R. Wyeth, 'Should schools promote toleration?', *Journal of Moral Education*, 27 (1998) 465–73.

16 For a similar conclusion, though not based on the same analysis of toleration, see G. Haydon, *Teaching About Values* (London: Cassell, 1997), pp. 56–9, pp. 127–9. Haydon argues that only on the basis of a pragmatic approach to tol-eration can we hope to show that toleration is not another, sectarian (liberal) value and educate non-liberals too on the ideal of mutual restraint.

Index